Work/Life City Limits

Work/Life City Limits

Comparative Household Perspectives

Helen Jarvis
University of Newcastle, UK

First published 2005 by
PALGRAVE MACMILLAN
Houndmills, Basingstoke, Hampshire RG21 6XS and
175 Fifth Avenue, New York, N. Y. 10010
Companies and representatives throughout the world

PALGRAVE MACMILLAN is the global academic imprint of the Palgrave Macmillan division of St. Martin's Press, LLC and of Palgrave Macmillan Ltd. Macmillan® is a registered trademark in the United States, United Kingdom and other countries. Palgrave is a registered trademark in the European Union and other countries.

ISBN-13: 978–1–4039–1496–5   hardback
ISBN-10: 1–4039–1496–6   hardback

This book is printed on paper suitable for recycling and made from fully managed and sustained forest sources.

A catalogue record for this book is available from the British Library.

Library of Congress Cataloging-in-Publication Data
Jarvis, Helen, 1965–
    Work/life city limits : comparative household perspectives / Helen Jarvis.
      p. cm.
    Includes bibliographical references and index.
    ISBN 1–4039–1496–6 (cloth)
    1. Work and family–Cross-cultural studies. 2. Urban anthropology–Cross-cultural studies. I. Title.

HD4904.25.J37 2005
331.25–dc22   2005047529

10 9 8 7 6 5 4 3 2 1
14 13 12 11 10 09 08 07 06 05

Printed and bound in Great Britain by
Antony Rowe Ltd, Chippenham and Eastbourne

To my daughter Miriam

Contents

List of Figures, Photos, Tables and Boxes

List of Figures

Photographs in chapter headings (all source: Helen Jarvis)

Photographs in text (all source: Helen Jarvis)

List of Tables

List of Boxes

Acknowledgements

The author and publishers would like to thank Carfax for permission to reproduce short excerpts from a paper originally published in Housing Studies and Sage for permission to reproduce elements of a paper originally published in Time and Society.

I wish to acknowledge funding provided by ESRC award no. R000271085 as well as small grants awarded by HSBC Holdings (distributed by the RGS-IBG) and the University of Newcastle. I also wish to extend my appreciation to Jennifer Nelson at Palgrave and to Shirley Tan for technical assistance in the production process.

There are a number of people I wish to acknowledge who commented on draft versions of this book or selected chapters. Diane Perrons diligently read through a full first draft, as did Tony Champion, both making constructive suggestions and offering welcome encouragement. Simon Duncan provided incisive comments on selected chapters at a crucial juncture. Any errors and omissions are my own. I would like to thank Andy Pratt, as mentor and friend, for collaboration on the subject of work/life and live-work in San Francisco; also Linda McDowell and Anne Green for encouragement with respect to formative working papers. I would also like to acknowledge friends and colleagues at the University of Newcastle who have contributed technical advice, ideas, and support, in particular; to Seraphim Alvanides (for help with census data), Ann Rooke (for the maps), George Kania (IT), Jane Wheelock, Alastair Bonnett, Nick Henry and Jean Hillier; also Angela Brady (then a University of Northumbria student on work placement) for helping to compile a news archive. As a visiting scholar at the University of Washington I benefited from a stimulating intellectual environment. Thanks in particular to Kim England and Suzanne Withers. Also as a visiting scholar at UC Berkeley I was warmly welcomed by the co-directors of what was then the Centre for the Study of Working Families, Arlie Russell-Hochschild and Barrie Thorne, and enjoyed discussing the new urbanism with Marta Guttman, now at City College New York. I would also like to acknowledge enthusiastic exchanges with Chuck Darrah and Jim Freeman of the Silicon Valley Cultures Project at San Jose State University. I am greatly indebted to family and friends who provided me with shelter and local knowledge in the field: Jeannette Henderson, my one-time landlady, friend and source of background articles on

Seattle; my sister Kathryn on Bainbridge Island; Paulette Zamora who introduced me to struggling artists in Oakland; Kathryn and Eric Lesh in Portland (now Seattle); Ferhan and Erik Pagano in London; and Stuart Johnston in Edinburgh. I am truly grateful to my parents, Denis and Janet Jarvis, for providing me with a welcome retreat in Corvallis as well as unstinting support and a great deal of practical assistance.

It is only fitting in a book about work/life reconciliation that I acknowledge the people who have enabled me to keep working. It is not possible to mention by name the day-nursery staff plus friends and neighbours who together make up the patchwork of my daughter's childcare, but especial thanks must go to Duika Burges Watson for helping me to solve the perennial challenge of attending evening seminars and overnight business trips.

Finally, I owe a particular debt of gratitude to the household members interviewed in London, Edinburgh, San Francisco, Seattle and Portland, who must remain anonymous, without whose personal testimonies this book would be far less rich.

1
The Personal *is* Political

A day in the life

Slowing down: a day out with the kids in London

Riding the Washington State Ferry one evening rush hour, I overheard a conversation between a man and a woman (lets call him Bob and her Jean), both in their late 30s. They were acquainted through travelling the same ferry each day between jobs in downtown Seattle and homes on Bainbridge Island. Jean asked Bob about his new job. Bob was enthusiastic but uncertain of the future. Having switched firm four times in as many years he typified the new breed of 'portfolio-worker'[1]: what he gained in experience of new people and projects he lost in

1

time and energy spent securing the next contract. Bob asked Jean about her commute, wondering how she managed to get her daughters to day-care and kindergarten and still make the 8 am ferry. Jean acknowledged she continually watched the clock and feared something inevitably failing in this fragile arrangement. She had to manage her domestic and professional lives as if no conflict existed between them. With mobile phone and Filofax in hand,[2] she variously struck deals and kept track of family members – from her car, on the ferry and from duplicate offices at home and downtown. Her routine typified the complex integration of 'work' and 'life' popularly described as a 'balancing act'.

Watching Bob, Jean and a crowd of smartly dressed commuters position themselves with expert knowledge at the quickest point of exit; I wondered how this stretched out, stressful existence could be reconciled with a quality of life clearly prized but little enjoyed on the island. With this thought in mind, I made my way through the pedestrian tunnel and out to the parking lot vista greeting visitors to the small town of Winslow. It was 1995 and I was over from London touring parts of the US West Coast. Earlier I had visited friends in San Francisco where I used to live as a student. I had driven through neighbouring Silicon Valley where my parents first emigrated from Britain in 1981 (before bidding a retreat to Oregon in the 1990s for a less pressure-cooked retirement). I had been shocked to witness the pace of new development in the Bay Area, with traffic in a permanent state of gridlock. Now I hoped to squeeze in the briefest of visits with my sister Kathryn who lived with her husband and two young children on the island, a popular suburb for working parents who commuted to Seattle by ferry.

It had been difficult to find a time when Kathryn would be home. Her marathon schedule was the stuff of legend. Friends did not believe me when I told them she camped out in the lab where she worked three nights a week. This practice began when she was lured away from an established downtown biotechnology firm with the prospect of potentially lucrative stock options. Steep commercial rents and lack of suitable laboratory space forced the new firm to set up business in Bothell, a small sub-division north of Kenmore (one of the case study areas featured in this book). Faced with more than three hours commuting by ferry and car each day, Kathryn negotiated an unorthodox four-day week – leaving home very early each Monday morning, not to return again until Thursday evening.

Kathryn had been sleeping in the office (in the shower room, in the sick bay, wherever she could find a suitably dark and quiet corner) for nearly a year by the time I caught up with her. It was not ideal. Her husband complained because he had to fit his full-time local government job (and the driving around it entailed) between trips to and from day-care. He also had to supervise the evening meal and bedtime routine. Kathryn spent each Friday preparing meals to freeze for the coming week. She left a lot of lists. The kids were stoic; while Kathryn was not allowed to make long distance calls from the office she arranged for her husband to phone her at fixed times, morning and night, so she could chat to them about their day. The janitors complained that Kathryn presented an obstacle to efficient cleaning. Working for a minimum wage, the only way they could earn a living was to work all hours of the night at a furious pace to move on quickly to the next job. Added to the pressure of working long hours for low pay the janitors also faced a long commute. Two good salaries were the passport to secure even modest housing in the vicinity of the new high-tech businesses. Restricted by low wages to more affordable but peripheral housing south of Seattle, the janitors had to travel for over an hour each day in a van pool. The boss too had started to complain because, as the company began to prosper, he thought the sleeping bag image was bad for business.[3]

It is tempting to regard this sort of spatially fragmented lifestyle and a culture of long working hours as being peculiar to the USA, especially world-class cities and affluent professionals. Yet this trend is far more pervasive than suggested by this one illustration. While problems of urban sprawl and social exclusion are endemic in the USA, a growing mismatch between where people live, work, go shopping and send their children to school is increasingly apparent across the entire English speaking advanced world (the UK, Australia, New Zealand and Canada) (Giuliano and Narayan 2003; Timmermans et al. 2002; Cervero and Wu 1998; Kasarda and Ting 1993). This is evident in widespread concern for the social and environmental costs of congestion, pollution, childhood obesity, and road safety. At the same time the Continental European tradition of generous holidays and shorter working hours appears to be under threat. The French Prime Minister has made it known he wants to abandon the hard won 35 hour week and instead allow businesses to arrange their own working time arrangements up to the European Union 48 hour limit (Fagnani and Letablier 2004).

Similarly, the German government proposes a reduction in the number of statutory public holidays to help improve its competitiveness abroad. It is debateable whether European universal welfare systems are in the process of being dismantled or if they are simply being reformed in the wake of global competition (Taylor-Gooby 2001; 2001a). Rather than engage with this question of European policy transformation (see instead Taylor-Gooby 2004) this book highlights what might be considered the 'worst case scenario' – where the USA has a very poor record for poverty reduction, income equality, environmental protection and social integration (Goodin et al. 1999).

Two similar extremes?

Different versions of capitalism are practised across the world. Will Hutton (1996) identifies separate European, American and Japanese types, while Adair Turner (2001) differentiates between a European and an American (more particularly US) model. Comparisons are typically drawn between the weak welfare state and long work hours of the USA and strong welfare and short hours of most European states (Hayden 1999: 172). Viewed this way the USA symbolises the 'laggard' model of welfare development (Kudrle and Marmor 1984: 81) while the UK is the European anomaly. On domestic affairs the UK government claims to be 'neither European nor American' but instead promotes 'flexibility too often neglected in Europe combined with fairness too often neglected in America' (Brown 2003). The UK and USA have shared a common ideology with respect to economic liberalism and a 'rolling back' of state control ever since Margaret Thatcher famously declared in 1987 there was 'no such thing as society – just individuals and families'. Both seek to reduce public spending through an emphasis on self-help and self-reliance: 'care in the community' (by unpaid wives and mothers) is the euphemism applied to this approach in the UK (Himmelweit 1995; for the home as the locus of long-term care in Canada see England 2000). In many cases these measures appear to endorse the traditional family (Brenner 1993, cited in Somerville 2000: 137). This pattern of inequality contrasts with social democratic welfare regimes which emphasise collective responsibility (in the performance of care and by redistributing the costs of care work) and the promotion of more democratic gender relations. This point is taken up again in the next chapter.

A shift toward economic liberalism certainly describes the extreme cases of the USA and UK better than it does Continental Europe at the present time. But concern must be raised that a dominant set of economic values (competitiveness, entrepreneurialism, flexibility, unequal affluence over general sufficiency) are crowding out alternative systems of governance. Peck and Tickell suggest this hegemony in the way they identify a 'rolling-back' of state bureaucracy in the 1980s followed by a 'rolling out' of neo-liberalism across the globe throughout the 1990s (Peck and Tickell 2002). Arguably the micro-social implications of this process are less well understood than the macro-economic patterns (to review the literature calling for fine-grained urban feminist analysis see Bondi and Rose 2003).

It is with the aim of better understanding this threat to collective responsibility and social democratic values that two similarly extreme cases of market orientation are selected for close scrutiny in this book. Associated with this is a second aim to critically examine the extent to which middle class working families in market-oriented societies would prefer, and are able, to resist the treadmill of working long hours, parenting intensively and consuming voraciously. A third aim is to highlight 'differences between the British and American pursuit of market-oriented policies' (Jacobs 1992: 43) by focusing on specific urban contexts. Together these aims require a research approach which looks beyond headline differences in policy and aggregate working hours data to reveal the hidden realm – elsewhere dubbed 'the secret life' – of individual preference formation and household decision-making (Jarvis et al. 2001). Before telescoping down to this fine-grained household analysis in Chapters Three and Four, it is first necessary to understand the global processes of restructuring which have altered the way cities and families function today.

Three spheres of restructuring

Over the past 30 years the profile of the urban economy has changed strikingly across the developed world. Most scholars date this from the first OPEC oil crisis in 1973 when a quadrupling of petroleum prices precipitated global economic downturn. Dismantling protective trade barriers exposed deficiencies of underinvestment and lack of training in established manufacturing and heavy industries (Sayer and Walker 1992). This process of restructuring saw good skilled manual jobs lost to increased automation, mass unemployment, and new international divisions of labour – including the transfer of labour intensive production by multinationals to low cost less developed countries (Logan and Swanstrom 1990: 7; Wallace 1990: 152). Firms in North America and North Western Europe responded to this crisis by seeking competitive advantage in high-value, high-tech sectors (Atkinson and Meager 1986; Gallie et al. 1998). States responded by replacing Keynesian job-creation initiatives, and support of welfare provision, with monetarism reinforced by a neo-liberal mode of social regulation (Pacione 1997: 3; Jessop 2002). Accelerating this highly uneven flow of capital accumulation was the expansion and differentiation of consumer expectations, particularly relating to labour-saving domestic appliances, novel electronic gadgets and the personal computer.

This shift from manufacturing to the production of ideas and provision of services had a marked spatial impact within, as well as between, competing nations. Whereas the 'old' economy prospered alongside the nineteenth century industrial city, this 'new economy' increasingly favoured more cosmopolitan post-industrial cities and metropolitan regions. Some areas recovered from de-industrialisation far more successfully than others in part because they could boast superior social, cultural and environmental assets (Lever 2002). It is by this subtle measure of attractiveness to skilled workers and venture capital that, by virtue of their competitiveness, some cities are 'successful' while others remain moribund (Begg 2002). Yet the five 'successful' cities featured in this book (introduced in the next chapter) tell another story. Behind the veneer of competitiveness there are profound signs of stress. Evidence that success is double edged is witnessed in the frustration and discomfort of unreliable and crowded public transit, traffic in a state of gridlock, workers commuting long distance to reach a home they can afford or a school they are prepared to send their children to.

To understand this paradox it is important to make connections between three discrete spheres of restructuring. First is the sphere of employment. This governs both the distribution and quality of jobs and the supply of labour by gender, race and class. Second is the sphere of gender relations. This is of crucial significance because, from a household perspective, gender, identity and power effectively mediate aspects of decision-making and behaviour central to daily life. Third is the sphere of housing and urban structure. This concerns the location of homes in relation to jobs and how people co-ordinate journeys to work with routine circulation and pressure to be available to businesses operating 24/7 (24 hours a day, seven days a week). A great deal has been written about the transformations which have occurred in these spheres *individually* but little about the way they overlap through the mutual constitution of social, economic and environmental structures of constraint. This is because debates concerning the future of cities and urban 'liveability' typically occur in isolation from those concerning work/life balance. It is therefore worth rehearsing each of these transformations in turn so as to assemble all three together within a single volume, as a first step towards a more integrated analysis in the following chapters.

Flexible labour

One of the most significant transformations over the last half-century has been growth of women's employment. This, together with more varied household types associated with delayed marriage, longer life expectancy and the advent of birth control, combines powerfully with a fundamental shift in the global economy. The decline of heavy industry and manufacturing brought with it a permanent loss of skilled blue-collar jobs previously paying large numbers of men a family wage. Jobs gained in the service sector, though numerically significant, have provided no straightforward replacement for those lost. In the UK, for instance, the shift from manufacturing to service sector job concentration contributed to a drop in full-time employment from 21 million in 1952 to 19 million in 1995 (Hakim 1996: 74). Moreover, most new jobs in the growing service-producing sector today require skills that are socially constructed as 'feminine' and attract low wages and non-standard working hours. Others in the knowledge and ideas based 'new economy' also break with traditional terms of full-time, permanent employment. Workers are expected to cultivate transferable skills as protean or 'portfolio' workers. A combination of increased job insecurity and exposure to economic risk motivates the majority of couples to believe that both partners have to work if living standards are to be maintained (Somerville 2000: 6). In the 1950s more than 70 per cent of American families maintained a 'traditional' structure whereby economically inactive wives stood by breadwinning husbands. By 1980 this figure had fallen to 15 per cent (Rowbotham 1997: 455).

Not only has the economic base changed, so too has the human resource base shaping labour market supply. Advanced economies are commonly experiencing a shrinking working age population relative to elderly and other non-working populations (Evans 1992: 132). Nancy Folbre (2001: 102) points out that while in 1930 the proportion of the US population over age 65 represented 5.4 per cent, in 1990 this had risen to 12.5 per cent and is projected to constitute 20 per cent by the year 2050. In order to maintain national productivity, governments depend increasingly on the continuing (uninterrupted) participation of 'prime-age' women in paid employment and thus rising numbers of dual income and multi-job households (Levy and Michel 1991). This demographic reality combines with the neo-liberal state in the assumption of a 'universal worker' model[4] (Lewis 2002). Somerville (2000: 231) points to the impact this has had on middle class families in particular where, until relatively recently, a male breadwinner earning a family wage coupled with a full-time homemaker signified high social status.

One consequence of restructuring is the apparent concentration of income, power and status in the hands of a college-educated, often-times 'creative', or entrepreneurial, middle class, while at the same time reducing opportunities for poorly educated or otherwise disad-vantaged minority groups (Brooks 2000; Florida 2002). Another is the rising number of two worker and multi-job households. Yet the nature of uneven labour market development in both countries is such that employment combinations include underemployment (low wage); overemployment (extension of working hours whether to generate a living wage or to demonstrate commitment to a particular career); and precarious employment (periodic unemployment, reduced hours, job-hopping) (Atkinson 1987). Together these characteristics of restructur-ing contribute both to overall growth in the number of dual-earning households as well as growing *diversity of experience* within this sub-population. Another explanation originates in uneven housing market development and pressure on workers to be increasingly geographically mobile. These features are discussed in more detail in Chapter Five. As a consequence of growing house price divergence between dynamic and moribund urban areas, for instance, most first-time buyers and those trading small apartments for family homes require significantly more than one income to secure the necessary finance. Downs (1989) observes that young families without two earners appear to be falling behind in their efforts to achieve upward mobility in the USA. In Britain, the Low Pay Unit calculates that there would be one million more households living in poverty, if both partners were not working (LPU 1994). Some scholars see a distinct polarisation of advantaged and excluded labour market extremes while others point to the supe-rior purchasing power of an expanded professional consumer class (for more on this debate see Sassen 1991; Hamnett 1994; Butler and Robson 2003). Whatever the local pattern, income inequality is made worse by the concentration of employment characteristics in symmetrical household structures. Because most couples are from the same occupa-tional class, the population is increasingly divided between 'resource rich' dual career households, 'multiple job' low-income households and 'employment deprived' no earner households (McRae 1986; Jarvis 1997). Will Hutton describes this pattern in terms of a '30-30-40 society' (Hutton 1995).[5] The implications of growing inequality are discussed in more detail in Chapter Five.

Gender dynamics

Women in the UK and the USA have entered the labour market in growing numbers but the impact of this restructuring has been uneven, incomplete and contradictory (Dex and Shaw 1986). Women are popularly observed to experience 'role strain' carrying a 'dual burden' of paid employment and unpaid domestic and caring work. Outside the home women frequently work alongside other women in jobs which look remarkably like those of caring, domestic and emotion work performed unpaid at home. This describes a horizontal segregation of jobs and occupations constructed either as 'women's work' or 'mother friendly' (Glover 2002). Vertically too, women are concentrated in jobs outside the boardroom (Schwartz 1994). This points to the way jobs are not gender neutral but instead culturally constructed as appropriate for either men, or women, and the gender identities of both jobs and workers are negotiable and contestable. Work and the performances of workers are 'constituted and maintained by sets of social practices that embody socially sanctioned but variable characteristics of masculinity and femininity' (McDowell 1999: 135; Nicholson 1990; Stichter and Parpart 1988). Bridget Pfau-Effinger (1993; 1998) adopts this approach to explain the transmission of gender norms through moral negotiations in relation to overlapping public and private spheres: home, work, family, neighbourhood, and community engagement. She emphasises cultural (geographical) variation by scrutinising what constitutes the normatively sanctioned 'best' or 'right' course of action in a given situation. This recognises that people build moral identities and reputations (as the 'good enough' mother, the loyal worker or supportive spouse) on the basis of particular competencies and resources (Lawler 2000; Gardiner 1997). It suggests too that 'the limits on women's everyday activities are structured by what society expects women to be, and therefore to do' (Standing 1999: 16). People negotiate these identities and reputations in relation to others. Thus when relationships are changed, for example through divorce, people may respond by renegotiating their identity (Smart and Neale 1998).

Despite what Sheila Rowbotham (1997: 585) describes as women's 'long trek into (almost) equal citizenship in the public sphere', most men in the UK and USA 'continue to avoid the second shift' at home (Ehrenreich and Hochschild 2003: 9; Lewis 1992). Similarly, Nancy Folbre (2001: 17) observes that as a consequence of a 'liberal and highly individualistic form of feminism in the USA (...) even women who earn considerably more than their husbands seldom persuade their guys to put more hours into family work'. Consequently, the symmetrical family Young and Willmott (1973) predicted 30 years ago is far from democratic. Blair and Lichter (1991) found that American women in the early 90s performed three times as much domestic labour than American men. Better educated women appeared more able to control the allocation of domestic labour but their second shift was reduced more by the use of labour-saving technology and paid help than by increases in men's housework. Gershuny and Robinson (1988) found similar results for the UK. The feminisation of domestic labour appears to be etched deeply into the male-female dyad. Here the contrast is with same-sex couples with children where the research suggests that the practice and management of housework is far more democratic (Dunne 1998; 1997). There is some evidence in recent analysis of time-use diaries to suggest that men in dual earning couples are more willing than in the past to share in tasks like childcare and cooking and that differences which once existed between working class and middle class men are diminishing (Sullivan 2000). Nevertheless a wealth of literature on the subject suggests that change is slow and, overall, women have made far greater progress toward equal breadwinning than men have picked up their share of caring, cooking, cleaning and organising the household (Pilcher 2000; Kramer 2000).

This latter point concerning women's disproportionate burden of household *management* needs to be emphasised as it is an issue highlighted in the household narratives. It is with respect to everyday co-ordination (checking that family members are where they need to be, picked up when necessary, escorted to clubs and parties wearing the right outfit or carrying an appropriate gift for each event) that feminised social reproduction work is least visible and most undervalued. Ironically, just as women's time availability for this managerial work is shrinking, they face a growing range and rising standard of domestic and parenting expectations (see Galinsky and Friedman 1995).[6] As one interviewee wryly claimed, she is 'the conductor and the first violinist', orchestrating family personnel and events while working full-time, deprived of the luxury of losing herself in her paid work but instead always with one eye on the clock and a list of 'things to do' running through her head. This multi-tasking is stressful and largely incompatible with the sort of single-minded concentration demanded by most top jobs. The popular expectation that fathers are entitled to compartmentalise their lives in a way mothers are denied helps explain the persistent gender gap in wages. Women in the UK and USA earn 72–73 per cent of the wage rate of men, a gap which is only partially explained by differential investments in human capital (education, experience and hours worked) (England 1992; McDowell 1999: 126). Chapters Three and Four go on to examine the implications of flexible labour market policies from a household perspective as another way to highlight these gendered inequalities.

Urban split

Most textbooks identify broadly similar processes of urban change for all advanced economies. These chart a course of urbanisation, accompanied by suburbanisation and 'counterurbanisation', as well as more recent evidence of reurbanisation through gentrification and state sponsored inner city regeneration (Champion 1989; Johnson and Beale 1998). Urbanisation associated with industrialisation essentially represents the migration of people and jobs from rural areas and small towns to metropolitan areas. Yet planners and environmentalists in most advanced economies have for some time shared a common concern for the *loss* of population from cities (Champion et al. 1998) and the negative impact widespread decentralisation has on transport behaviour and the environment (Garreau 1991). The dominant shift through employment restructuring has been from central business districts to new industrial spaces creating auto-dependent suburban corridors, 'technopoles' and 'technoburbs' (Fishman 1987). At the same time, urban residents (particularly middle class families) have for half a century pursued a course of residential mobility and housing choice favouring suburban and non-metropolitan locations. This revealed preference is strongly associated with the quest for affordable detached family housing, especially at a life-stage of family formation (Germain and Rose 2000). In the USA it is popularly dubbed 'white flight' because white middle class parents in particular have long used geographical distance, and the purchase of a home in an environment populated by families of like race and class, to improve the chances their offspring have of attending 'good' schools and achieving a level of cultural capital denied to children growing up in minority population neighbourhoods experiencing 'blight' and 'decay' (see for instance Suarez 1999: 9–43). This splintering of jobs and homes away from traditionally compact urban areas exacerbates problems of auto-dependence, sprawl and pollution.

Running alongside this trend of decentralisation is another of limited reurbanisation. By this process selected cities act as magnets for a distinctly urban professional population where cultural cachet is attached to the renovation of run-down vintage properties in once

working class neighbourhoods. Neil Smith (2002) argues that the transfer of de-industrialised inner city areas to professional owner occupiers
is now 'thoroughly generalised' in the practices of urban regeneration.
Consequently it is less meaningful to apply the term gentrification,
which 'initially emerged as a sporadic, quaint and local anomaly in the
housing market (of 'global' cities)' to large-scale demolition and commercial redevelopment. This argument is developed in Chapter Four
with specific reference to a 'live-work' property type designed to
combine activities of living and working under one roof.

Arguably the changes that have occurred in recent decades in
employment, gender relations, and urban structure are mutually co-
constitutive. By way of example, the normalisation of the dual
earning household tends to reduce housing and labour market mobility while at the same time increasing routine transport circulation.
Couple households with both partners working full-time are less likely
to migrate between labour markets than the traditional male breadwinner structure. Co-earning women, particularly those in full-time
professional careers, better resist being the 'trailing spouse' in situations of migration for male spouse promotion (Jarvis 1999; Boyle et al.
1999). Alternatives to the wholly moving household include dual-
location living. This is used as a temporary or permanent strategy so
couples can live together while maintaining careers in different locations (Hardill 2002: 27). The more usual solution of course is for one
spouse or both to increase the length or complexity of their journey
to work.

Four conceptual themes

Working families across the advanced world face very similar
dilemma's in the way that they have to reconcile competing responsibilities at home, at work, towards family, friends and communities.
This is apparent in the universal resonance of the term work/life
reconciliation. While it enjoys widespread currency the work/life reconciliation debate is for the most part too narrowly confined. Largely
neglected is the existence of a material world: where people shop,
socialise, feel vulnerable; how they communicate with others and
move about and what prevents them from doing either as freely as
they would wish. Exceptions to this narrow view are local time use
initiatives such as '*i tempi della città*' in Modena (discussed further in
Chapter Seven). Nevertheless, while these make significant strides
in reducing temporal friction (between shift working and crèche

opening hours for instance) (Pillinger 2001) they pay little attention to unequal household resource distributions (time not being available to all in equal measure) and uneven development. Instead, time usually assumes the dominant frame of reference: the duration and timing of events and the ability to synchronise these with others. It is popularly identified with 'famine', 'squeeze' and accelerated use (Hochschild 1989; 1997; Schor 1992; Robinson and Godbey 1999; Gershuny and Sullivan 2001). Yet as this introductory chapter illustrates, time-use studies remain one-dimensional where they neglect important geographical considerations – such as *where* suitable (affordable) homes and nurseries and schools are relative to *actual* employment opportunities for two working parents, given limited resources of time, personnel, transport and finance.

This book addresses these gaps in understanding by fusing together two debates which are usually confined by disciplinary divisions to exclusive discourses and separate policy prescriptions. The aim is to initiate a conversation between urban studies (especially the new urbanism expanded upon in the following chapter) and social policy (notably working hours and childcare). Few attempts have been made to map reconciliation behaviour onto the land-use functions of the material city. Instead the trend has been for sociologists to focus on conditions and divisions of work, employment and public policy (see for instance Gornick and Meyers 2003; Beck 2000), while urban planners focus on settlement patterns, and the role of technology, emphasising mechanisms to achieve sustainable development and improve urban quality of life (see for instance Blower 1993; Marshall 2000; Thorns 2002). The problem with a discipline specific approach is it artificially separates aspects of human behaviour and withdraws this from its material setting: it depopulates the physical ecosystems (of scarce resources and waste sinks) which ultimately support human life. Neither debate takes sufficient account of the transcendent influences of rising consumer expectations and increased spatial mobility. These limitations are here addressed by an integrated approach to everyday life in dynamic cities. To make sense of the many multiple points of interconnection highlighted by this approach it is useful to draw on four conceptual themes: the material situation of everyday life, the practical limits to co-ordination (in terms of distances travelled, hours worked, risks taken, debt carried), time-space-matter, and rising neo-liberalism. Each theme represents a different 'cut' through the integrated nature of everyday life; a way of opening up to scrutiny the particular local contexts and co-ordination dilemmas explored in Chapters Three to Six.

Everyday life and the material city

One of the main themes of this book, explored in depth in Chapters Two and Three, is the material situation of everyday life in the city – not just 'the city' in a general sense but particular cities and neighbourhoods. Analysis at this scale highlights the frustrating obstacles we all experience in our daily life (traffic congestion, parking restrictions, schools closure, getting household appliances repaired). It also reveals the impact routine solutions to co-ordination have on environmental quality (such as pollution and added congestion caused by an increase in the number and length of car journeys to shop, school and work). Moreover, while we are witnessing signs of 'hyper-mobility' in travel behaviour (people moving about more frequently and over longer distances) (Adams 1999; Doyle and Nathan 2001), it is evident most people still live intensely local lives based on repeated (usually daily) movement between familiar 'stations' or intersections (home, office, supermarket and petrol/gas station en route to children's school) (Dyck 1990; Skinner 2003). This reminds us too that movement restrictions are more often experienced by women than men, especially those assuming the mantle of caring responsibilities (whether for young children, disabled or elderly relatives) (England 1993; Gilbert 1997; Aitken 2000; Camstra 1996).

All aspects of daily life function according to an infrastructure which can be enabling or constraining. Like that of the streets, tunnels and telephone cables we are familiar with in the built environment, this infrastructure has a material quality, but it also serves to convey local knowledge through institutional regimes and moral rationalities. A material context is evident in the distribution of fixed assets such as housing, schools, shops as well as transit stops and traffic bottlenecks. Institutional regimes encompass all manner of regulation from that functioning within the household to that of the state and the extent to which it regulates behaviour and subsidises private markets. Moral rationalities suggest the collectively realised (geographically uneven) cultural understanding of gender roles, preferences and expectations (Vincent et al. 2004). One group of women, for instance, might view motherhood and paid work as integral, while for another the priority is to be at home with their children regardless of foregone earnings or childcare costs. Thus cultural and moral rationalities explain why narrow assumptions of 'rational economic (man)' utility maximisation fail to explain variation in parenting values, working practices and consumption norms (Duncan and Edwards 1999: 273–276). None of these spheres function in isolation, nor is there a clear separation between the choices people make (whether to commute to a new job) and structures of constraint (such as housing costs and spouse employment). As Nancy Folbre (2001: 6) observes, 'choice is a funny thing, affected by both moral values and by social pressure's. This is why too much choice – or too little social co-ordination of choice – can lead to outcomes that can be just as problematic as having no choice at all'. It is interesting to witness in this regard that as people's lives get busier, filled with fast paced, long hours of paid work, the practice of consumption is growing more complex too. Affluent shoppers are faced with a widening and constantly changing product range. Choosing bread and orange juice in a US supermarket can be very labour intensive – with dozens of grain types, juice concentrations and textures, all with detailed descriptions of production methods and contents to be read and worried over.

With respect to such matters of human agency it has become a cliché to quote Harvard economist James Duesenberry's comment on Becker that 'economics is all about how people make choices; sociology is all about why people don't have any choices to make' (1960: 233). This claim reinforces the sense of opposition between those who assume a world of free agents and those who see agency reduced to, or determined by, external structures such as the state (or poverty). Recent theoretical development maintains that both polar conceptions are untenable. Lawson (1997) for instance views social structure (such as rules, positions and relations) as a precondition for intentional action and consequently attributes the existence of social structure to the continually reproduced, and always evolving, routines and practices of human actions. Social structures come about and endure, whether or not individuals have an awareness of this process (Lawson 1997: 168). Bridging the dualism of structural constraint and human agency has long been the endeavour of critical realists as well as those employing a framework of social theory known as structuration, which is largely attributed to British sociologist Anthony Giddens. The approach of structuration is useful to the aims of this book because it connects up social interaction and material context, taking us back to the intimate (and precarious) relationship between human society and the natural environment. Accordingly, behaviour is understood to be moderated through agent-structure interaction (by a 'duality of structure') and by this process is liable to generate unintended or unacknowledged outcome (Giddens 1984; Gregory and Urry 1985; Jarvis et al. 2001: 90). This duality governs the ongoing process and cycle of market performance as much as it does political systems and households – reproduced as 'structures of interaction, with change recognised not as (or not only as) an external happening, the result of an external or exogenous shock, but as an integral part of what the system in question is' (Lawson 1997: 171).

Practical limits to growth

This brings us to a second theme which connects concepts of urban social cohesion and environmental sustainability in Chapters Two and Six to highlight *practical limits to growth*. It is important to distance this discussion from the original publications bearing this title while at the same time reviving the critically important human-environment interface. Concerns associated with a broad anti-growth movement developed in strength 30 years ago, first (most controversially) in response to the so-called population 'explosion' and subsequently with respect to urban containment, environmental conservation and attempts to curb excessive consumption as part of a global restructuring of living standards. Of course it is important to remember that while drawing on the language of containment and capacity the city limits in the title of this book are largely illusory. Few of us live in cities with clearly defined boundaries or edges: medieval city walls or other physical, administrative or symbolic city limits have little relevance to the way cities function today. Nevertheless we all recognise very real parameters to our daily life whether the limitations we encounter are consciously declared or unconsciously felt. This is evident in terms of distances travelled, hours worked, risks taken, debt carried, favours asked and granted (for a sense of emotional 'limits' in this respect see Reay 2000). Limits are thus conceived here as the socially constructed outcome of everyday routines and practices which are negotiated, in turn, through the household collective. In this way they are intimately enmeshed in local contexts of urbanisation through the infrastructure of everyday life identified above. This book goes on to argue that there are, or in some cases *should be*, moral limits too, such as consumption based on sufficiency rather than status.

According to O'Riordan (1981) and more recently Pepper (1996), stakeholders value the environment and identify solutions to environmental problems along a continuum from extreme ecocentrism to extreme technocentrism (see also Dowie 1995). The extreme ecocentrist believes natural resources and the capacity of the earth to process waste are *strictly* limited. According to this paradigm nature is to be protected and preserved for its intrinsic value. A strict 'nature before society' position such as this was adopted by the earliest claims of the Club of Rome. Absolute ecological limits were predicted using computerised 'world model' simulations of the burden of projected population growth on finite resources (such as land, food, water, fossil fuels) and the earth's capacity to process waste (pollution) (Forrester 1971). Publication of the original Limits to Growth in 1972 triggered widespread hostility, not least because it questioned the sovereignty of economic growth as the hallmark of progress (Meadows et al. 1972). Critics argue that this model assumes that population growth corresponds with the US pattern of consumption which, in practice, far exceeds that found elsewhere. To many scholars the method and assumptions of such a closed physical system represents none other than 'Malthus with a computer' (Cole et al. 1973).

A less extreme form of ecocentrism is apparent in the understanding that an 'ecological footprint' of varying magnitude corresponds to settlement patterns and transport modes in terms of land-take, resource consumption and waste generation (Rees 1992). Rather than view all growth as contributing to irreversible environment overload this approach recognises that some economic development is more damaging than others. It is currently estimated, for example, that the average North American requires more than 12 hectares to support food, housing transportation and other consumer 'needs' (WWF 2000, see Chapter Two – Table 2.4 for international comparisons). As Beatley and Manning (1997: 8) point out, this lifestyle based on increasing consumption is supported in large part by appropriating the resources of less powerful, less developed regions of the world. Accordingly, one of the chief concerns of the environmental movement is to expose the hidden environmental cost of globalisation whereby consumers are encouraged to seek more and varied goods and resources as if distance and place of origin are of no consequence. To some analysts this means that 'any product purchased and consumed in Britain, say, carries an 'ecological rucksack' comprising the environmental externalities associated with (among other things) its journey to the point of consumption' (Thornley and Rydin 2002: 2; see also Swyngedouw and Kaika 2000: 568).

Gloomy predictions of dwindling non-renewable resources are readily quashed by the extreme technocentric paradigm. According to this view, limits exist only until sufficient demand (or scarcity) triggers the profit incentive (coupled with advances in technology) to deliver substitutes. An example of this would be development of solar power as a partial substitute for fossil fuels. For the extreme technocentrist, the best thing government can do for environmental protection is to liberate the market from costly regulation so as to give free rein to technical innovation. Of course, critics point out that any number of innovations improving fuel efficiency and emissions reduction for motorised transport can never tackle problems of traffic congestion, where it is the sheer volume of vehicles on the road which causes road traffic accidents and gridlock. As Anders Hayden (1999: 25) observes: 'More energy-efficient cars are now being designed and built, but with more cars on the road and more miles driven there is more – not less – energy consumption in transport'.

Following the 1992 Rio Earth Summit a moderate form of technocentrism emerged as the dominant ideology, as expressed in the language of 'sustainable economic development'. Arguably, while a pluralism of interests and value systems marks the course of modern environmentalism, technocentrism is bound to dominate government policy because it accepts the assumptions of neoliberalism: faith in a free market and belief that economic growth and environmental protection are not mutually exclusive. There are those for whom environmental protection still calls for a change in lifestyles and reduced rate of commodification (Leiss 1988; Harvey 1982). Others focus on the *social* limits to growth associated with alienation at work and deterioration in city living (Hirsch 1977; Bookchin 1991; Berger 1998). Arguably we need to view the city less instrumentally and instead shift the emphasis of planning and policy from a technical fix to a more holistic ambition based on wellbeing and quality of life (Landry 2000: 62).

Time-space-matter

A third concept explored in Chapters Three and Four focuses on time-space co-ordination. Whether everyday co-ordination involves long journeys or local interaction, knowledge of where, when and how activities and relations are to be conducted is essential. Associated with this are now ubiquitous tools of Information and Communications Technology (ICT). The proliferation and fantastic reduction in cost of ICT is such that today being 'at work' or 'the responsible parent' is never confined to one place or time but roles practised all the time and everywhere. This reflects the reality that, despite information and telecommunications 'saturation' (especially in 'silicon places'[7] such as those associated with the five featured cities), most of us spend much of each day orchestrating continual movement in relation to others. In the absence of teleporting we have to move our bodies and co-ordinate with those of others; this takes time and energy, and has to be factored in. Just because you can call the childminder and tell them that you are late doesn't remove the fact that you have to get there and pick up your child somehow. Workers have to anticipate what will slow them down and thwart their efforts to juggle home and work demands. Living this close to the constant threat of crisis is very stressful. The daily routine is practised to a fine art. Knowing local traffic conditions might mean if you get on the freeway at 7.25 you are at work in 20 minutes but waiting until 7.30 it takes you 40 minutes or more. There are continual pressures here to be on the move and always busy. The theoretical possibility for ICT and home-working to liberate working parents from the stress of dashing between fixed appointments appears to remain just that, theoretical.

This is not simply to make the plea that 'geography matters' in work-life balance research. Indeed, as Sayer (2000: 19) points out, the concrete (material world) is always already spatial so it is not necessary to 'add on space'. Any observations of socio-temporal organisation in urban daily life necessarily encompasses spatiality, even if this is then abstracted or alluded to in the form of distance and travel to simplify explanation. Nevertheless, to explain social and geographic variation in property values and the 'pace of life', the role of time, space, and situation specific social processes need to made explicit. Again, Sayer (2000) warns against the erroneous use of 'space' and 'time' as contentless abstractions (separately, or together). He argues instead for a concrete, situated analysis: space-time-matter. Thus, space (and time) are not considered important in a general or universal sense, but rather as a specific set of contingent relations (of timing and of spaced persons) that may, or may not, enable a causal process.

The beginning of a situated analysis is evident in pioneering time-geography research (see for instance Pred 1981; Parkes and Thrift 1980). Central to this approach, Törsten Hägerstrand (1982; 1976) identifies three constraints with respect to individual paths through time-space. The first of these, the capability constraint, concerns physical limits to movement including the inability to be in two places at once. Second, a coupling constraint describes situations which compel people to come together at certain times and locations such as for face-to-face service delivery, breakfast meetings, family celebrations, medical appointments and the like. Finally, Hägerstrand points to authority constraints associated with legal sanctions and regulations. The visual qualities of the time-space prism lend themselves particularly well to the aims of an integrated approach. By way of example, the type of logistical constraints encountered by one of the sample households are illustrated in the form of a time-space prism in Chapter Five (Figure 5.1). While these 'simple but fundamental' concepts have contributed greatly to social theory (Davies 2001: 133), application to questions of work/life balance and time-squeeze remains limited in practice (but see in the GeoJournal special issue Ellegård 1999; Vilhelmson 1999). This is largely because preoccupation is with time as a constant and finite resource where in practice the limits to its use are not so defined. Time is not equally available to all as a measure of the calendar or clock and space is not a gender-neutral, fearless dimension (Davies 2001; Bianchi and Robinson 1997; Friberg 1993).

Neoliberalism and local cultures of resistance

A fourth theme, developed in Chapters Four and Five, concerns the local transmission of global competition, labour market flexibility and neo-liberalism. Reference to the term neo-liberalism corresponds with a revival of classical belief in market liberalism (market orientation, competition and emphasis on free trade). In literature on the developing world the term is frequently used as shorthand for globalisation and programmes of structural adjustment. In this sense it conveys a rather different relationship between the state, market and family than is the case here where reference is variously made in the Anglo-American context to economic liberalism or economic rationalism and in the case of the United States 'advanced liberalism' (Rose 1996). A shift toward neo-liberalism is recognisable across the English speaking advanced world where governments have engaged in a 'rolling back' of state control of industry (such as with the privatisation of transport and utilities) and the introduction of 'quasi-markets' in public services (such as healthcare and education) (Marvin and Graham 1994) (see Chapter Two for international comparisons of private spending on healthcare). In this process, Zygmunt Bauman (1997: 5) identifies a subtle shift in popular understanding from welfare as something 'that is our right' to something 'we cannot afford'. Likewise Jordan et al. (1994: 42) note the emergence of 'a certain kind of moral order of individualism' which characterised UK social relations in the 1990s following 'a government programme of American-style economic liberalisation'. They argue that this cultivated both increased self-reliance as the state withdrew from collective concerns (such as income for retirement) and it afforded low priority to other commitments (such as to geographically distant parents) that once would have been viewed 'as morally important sources of self identity'.

This climate of individualism and competition endows private market initiatives with privileged status, assuming that markets are the most efficient mechanisms for achieving economic growth. The point to stress here is that the objective is headline growth rather than a fairer distribution. This shift is evident more subtly too in the development of techniques of auditing, accountancy and management that enable a 'market' for public services to be established independently of central control (Barry et al. 1996: 26). In this sense the shift is from government intervention in the market to an embodiment of the market in government, a feature which is important in the context of this book. This shift highlights the paradox whereby individuals and families are encouraged to take responsibility for their own welfare as 'enterprising' selves, through privatisation and individualism, while heavily constrained by the political, legal and institutional conditions constructed by government to 'free-up' these markets. Whereas the post-war settlement identified individuals and families as the object and target of governmental action (holding unconditional rights) today they constitute partners or accomplices of government and have 'no rights without responsibilities' (Giddens 1998: 65). The climate of governance cultivated is one based on opportunity (for entrepreneurialism), individual responsibility (to safeguard the family) and community (to reinforce and police notions of good citizenship). According to this view, there comes with individualism 'an extension of individual obligation (such as) to look actively for work' (Giddens 1998: 66).

By highlighting everyday household behaviour against a back-drop of state governance in cases of extreme market liberalism, this book recognises what feminists have argued since the 1970s – that the personal *is* political. Rather than being the preserve of party politics and structures of representation, the dynamics of power resides 'within the encounters that make up the everyday experience of individuals' (Rose 1996: 37). We see this in the way the family as an institution is being asked to assume increasing responsibility, as a matter of good citizenship, for organising private welfare, delivering universal wage labour and managing numerous 'problems of living' (Rose 1996: 37).

Summary and structure of this book

This introductory chapter has uncovered the personal realm of everyday life in a number of ways. The opening vignette illustrated the speeding up and dislocation of daily life in the Western world with reference to a personal narrative. This is an established technique in the field of work/life reconciliation research. Indeed, by employing the household as a lens and conducting in-depth interviews with working parents this book sits firm on the foundations of existing research and commentary. Exemplars include Elizabeth Bott's 'Ordinary Urban Families' (1957), Sandra Wallman's 'Eight London Households' (1984), Marianne Gullestad's 'Kitchen Table Society' (1984), Arlie Russell Hochschild's 'The Time Bind' (1997) and Margaret Nelson and Joan Smith's 'Working Hard and Making Do' (1999). Typically the focus is on detached families, particularly male-female balancing acts in dual career couples (Blood and Wolfe 1960; Morris 1990; Hardill 2002) or alternatively the moral rationalities of lone mothers (Duncan and Edwards 1999). This parallels a long tradition of interpreting household 'coping strategies' in the developing world context (Kabeer 1994; Creighton and Omari 1995; Chant and McIlwaine 1998; Momsem et al. 1999) and more recently making connections between first and third world issues in literature on globalisation and the transnational family (Ehrenreich and Hochschild 2003). The proliferation of 'work rich' dual earning households has been reported in national and regional studies in the UK (Singell and Lillydahl 1986; Brannen and Moss 1991; Snaith 1990; Green 1995; Hardill et al. 1997) as well as the USA (Hood 1983; Bielby and Bielby 1989; Hertz 1991). Comparisons have been made cross-nationally too, though research is limited to a review of the literature (Goldthorpe 1987; Lewis et al., 1992), or the application of large-scale secondary data (Crompton 1996; Frankel 1997; Rubery et al., 1998; O'Connor et al., 1999). Consequently a gap in knowledge exists with respect to household and city level variations in dual earning coping strategies.

This chapter introduced three spheres of restructuring and four conceptual themes as a framework within which to develop an integrated 'whole economy' approach to household behaviour. This refers to the total productive system comprising not just the partial economy represented by cash transactions or GDP but the non-monetised social co-operative informal economy and the (often taken for granted as 'free') natural resource base. Hazel Henderson (1990) represents this whole economy as a 'three-layer cake with icing' (see also Brandt 1995: 47). This framework reveals how private solutions to everyday logistical constraints are not confined to personal choice or the domestic sphere in which they appear to be made. On the one hand, individuals and households make choices and reach decisions in a political economic environment over which they have little control. A particular material context (of streets, houses, transit, shops and schools) can provide obstacles as well as solutions to the way a house-hold might respond to wider economic restructuring (firm closure, urban blight). On the other hand, private actions impact on the social fabric and wider environment. One way this book contributes to new knowledge, then, is by viewing household behaviour as both contingent upon and presiding over local environmental transformation. To understand the practical limits this 'being in place' imposes on daily routines, and the private and social costs these compromises incur, research has to be conducted at the interstices of social and environmental studies. This integrated analysis can usefully start from renewed interest in 'quality of life' considerations. This has seen usually discrete issues such as time-squeeze, work-related stress, the dominance of a consumer treadmill, fears over the loss of community and frustrations with a congested and degraded physical environment brought together in a single debate for the first time (see for instance Callahan and Heintz 2000: 7). Democrat Al Gore raised awareness of the poor quality of life in many US cities in his November 2000 failed presidential campaign. His most attentive audiences hailed from high-growth areas such as Silicon Valley where evidence of environmental degradation in the midst of economic success was stark. Indeed, the political weight behind this movement is evident in the roll-call of names associated with one particular Demos publication: Quality of Life 2000. Contributors include Juliet Schor, economist author of 'The Overworked American' (1992), Ellen Galinsky, president and co-founder of the non-profit organisation Families and Work institute, Robert Liberty, executive director of 1000 Friends of Oregon, a non-profit advocacy group supporting urban containment and integrated land use planning, Ray Oldenburg sociologist author of 'The Great Good Place' (1999) and the Communitarian Amitai Etzioni. This profile demonstrates how the quality of life agenda combines social democracy with environmentalism – values explicitly endorsed by this project. Of course it is easy to see the catch in this assemblage, by evidence around us of essentially elitist 'Not In My Back Yard' (NIMBY) middle class environmental action designed to protect property values. Nevertheless, putting cynicism to one side, important lessons can be usefully drawn from this movement.

In another sense too this introductory chapter reflects a personal politics in the way I periodically allow first-person authorship to animate the otherwise carefully controlled parameters of social science research. I believe it is important for the reader to know, for instance, that I have a personal connection with each of the five cities explored in this book. Inevitably I have also had to overcome my own constraints to balancing 'work' and 'life', especially parenthood. Writing this book has taken over large chunks of my time and energy. In many ways it represents the sort of creative project (with deadlines that can be moved only so many times) typical of the narratives of high-tech and creative industry workers featured in this book. The task of writing spilled over into any time of the day or night when my young daughter slept and I felt capable (with the aid of matchsticks and caffeine) to focus on the computer screen. While the lone parent is widely perceived as the antithesis of 'having it all', my own experience suggests a different reality. Not having to negotiate the terms of my working 'all hours' with a partner was a positive advantage at times. Of course this admission suggests why it might be that relationships falter under pressures of the kind of single-minded commitment to economic creative work many of us are being asked to make – in a political climate valuing productivity, self-reliance and entrepreneurship above all else.

Each of the following chapters explores a different dimension of the way people organise their working lives in post-industrial cities. This way of bracketing the evidence takes into account the contingent and situated nature, as well as the unintended social and environmental impact, of this balancing act. The aim is to view the future of work and the future of cities through the common lens of the household and the role this complex institution plays in mediating urban social and economic change. The following chapter introduces the research approach in relation to key scales of analysis: nations, cities and families. After first charting key international differences in the support given to families and the way cities are laid out it establishes the basis on which specific axes of comparison are made in subsequent chapters (UK-USA; five successful cities, 100 working families). Chapter Three introduces the sample of households interviewed. It then elaborates the paradox of a strong economy in the extreme case of San Francisco. Chapters Four, Five and Six use detailed biographical analysis to explore three major themes of work/life reconciliation across the five cities: flexibility, equity and sustainability. The final chapter sums up the nature and scale of the problem and draws lessons from cross-national comparison as inspiration to re-invent the mixed economy as a moral economy based on collective responsibility.

If this book has one objective above all others it is to set in train new conversations across academic disciplines and government departments to ensure that 'work', 'life', cities and families no longer feature as discrete entities to be 'brought into line'. This is more than a simple plea for 'joined up thinking' (though this would in many cases merit a start). Instead it is a plea for greater public debate about core values. Belief that there are (or should be) moral limits to growth, where wealth accumulation is obscenely unequal across the globe, is not a retreat into some sort of bunker mentality. Quite the opposite, it is about showing greater humility in pursuit of the good life.[8]

2
Cities and Families

Research approach

> Families with kids are like little welfare states. They prioritise something other than their market earnings and the adult earners tax themselves heavily in terms of both money and time to fulfil obligations to their dependents (Folbre 2001: 202).

The household provides one of two essential sites in which to unravel connections between home, work, the city and daily life. The other is the web of networks locating the household geographically and culturally; to social and kin networks, resource provision, information, knowledge, and learning. It is in relation to this milieu that strategies of behaviour are reflexively constituted. Couples seek to make sense of everyday experience at a level which is perceived to be 'local', within social networks of 'sense-making, unravelling the complexities of colliding worlds; gender, generation, uncertainty and change' (Kvale 1996: 52–58; Dyck 1990: 462). These settings transmit 'mutual knowledge' whereby 'agents make sense of what others say and do' (Giddens 1987: 99). This duality of people-place relations establishes the rationale for building three scales of analysis into the comparative perspectives presented in this book. First is the micro-social household scale of everyday decisions and behaviour. Second is the often neglected meso-scale of the city and its environment; the natural attributes and morphology of the place combined with its historic pattern of transport development and growth politics. Third is the macro-economic paradigm of the state. While the main focus is on the household and its internal relations of gender, generation, identity and power, the enquiry is at all times conducted as a *situated analysis*. Consequently all three scales are built into the research approach.

Taking the household as the primary 'lens' through which to view contemporary restructuring builds on a broad consensus along the lines that the home (and its inhabitants) provides greater salience to individual life chance than the workplace (Hodgson 1988; Morris 1990; Allen and Hamnett 1991). This is because the individual worker is attached to a household institution and therefore rarely acts outside this context (Williams and Windebank 1995; Jarvis 1997: 523). It is within the household that individual and group interests are compromised and continuous adjustments are made to changing events through 'a multiplicity of often minor processes' (Foucault 1977: 138). This way the household should be viewed as neither a 'helpless victim' of changing economic situations or as the systematic master of a bounded domestic universe (Thrift 1995: 29–31). Consequently this book peers inside the 'black box' of household decision-making, understanding this as a site of conflict and negotiation (of gender roles, labour divisions, power relations and over the allocation of resources) (Sen 1990; Burgoyne 1990).

At all times the household research considers a specific sub-population of middle class (mainly white) two parent families. Working families which fit the criteria were selected in batches of twenty across five equivalent case studies: three dynamic cities of varying size and status on the US West Coast (San Francisco, Seattle and Portland); and two similarly buoyant high-status UK cities of contrasting size (London and Edinburgh). This chapter provides a brief outline of the research approach (further technical details are provided in Appendix A). Discussion then turns to the overall context of the household research, namely the 'successful city' and extreme market liberalism. An important debate within which to locate the study is that relating to an apparent renaissance in city living and urban cultural cachet. This is introduced in relation to an uneasy alliance between urbanism and environmentalism which is suggested in a popular 'new urbanism'. Finally, selection of the working families is considered together with the way they are represented in particular neighbourhood settings in the following chapters.

The research replicates a well established two-tier schema combining intensive in-depth analysis of household biographies and narrative vignettes with extensive secondary data in a complementary mixed method approach (Sayer 1992; Jarvis et al. 2001). This time-consuming approach allows active engagement with evidence of attitudes and preferences, decision-making and routine behaviour in real-life situations of practical (environmental) and moral (cultural) constraint. An essential stipulation is that data collection reflects an understanding of the 'whole economy' supporting everyday life. This takes account of not only production (paid work) but also social reproduction (unpaid caring, domestic and emotion work) and consumption (also a form of work as well as an expression of status). This mirrors the practical limits on choice, activity and movement experienced daily by particular working families in specific local urban contexts. The aim is to observe activities, schedules (and disruptions to these routines) in their material settings as well as to acknowledge situated processes of interpretation which give meaning to these activities and settings (Smith 1987; Boulin and Mückenberger 1999).

Secondary data from labour force surveys, census of population and urban planning archives provided the basis not only to make comparisons between national portraits of restructuring but also the means by which to identify suitable neighbourhoods within the five cities for in-depth research. For each metropolitan area, one central and one or more outer urban/suburban neighbourhood was selected, each representing wards/postal districts where 'family' and two-income households feature alongside relatively high levels of owner occupation. Differentiation between urban versus suburban neighbourhoods flowed from locally established property/real estate classification as well as land use density and proximity to the core business district. Selection was confirmed on the basis of local knowledge of the area from site visits. The aim was to identify 'ordinary' residential neighbourhoods sharing broadly similar (modest) middle class characteristics, avoiding such extremes as purpose-built 'yuppie' central city apartments as well as sprawling suburban 'monster' homes.

It was expected on the basis of existing survey data and from personal experience of living and working in each of these places that on close examination working families would be found to face quite different opportunities and constraints. We shall see that the results do indeed reveal cross-national differences, whereby historic legacies of spatial planning and cultural expectations contribute to a markedly different neo-liberal imprint *on the ground*. Illustrations of this are provided with respect to flexibility over time-use in Chapter Four, equity and unequal resource entitlements in Chapter Five and sustainability with respect to land use planning in Chapter Six. At the same time situated analysis exposes a number of transcendent influences based on a form of 'lifestyle politics'. In addition to well known variables relating

to family, career, partnering and parenting (Holloway 1998), the research found cross-cutting sources of identification associated with
consumption practices, civic engagement and environmental awareness. Consequently those households across the sample which shared
identifications in common, such as a priority to 'simplify' their daily
routines for family or environmental reasons, tended to reconcile
conflicts between home, work, family and neighbourhood in remarkably similar ways.

Successful cities

The successful city commands a dominant position in the high value
added sector and it manages to attract and retain a pool of internationally mobile skilled labour for this purpose. As well as good transport
and communications it draws on a critical mass of government,
research, venture capital and cultural facilities (Parkinson 2001: 79).
Viewed this way it is easy to see why moribund cities seek to emulate
this success through the regeneration of abandoned industrial sites and
promotion of a tourism and heritage industry. More particularly, it is
popular in the urban studies literature to define success specifically in
terms of creativity. This drives the search for those essential factors in
urban planning, architecture, governance and culture which serve to
incubate creative talent. In the widely cited book *The Rise of The
Creative Class*, for instance, Richard Florida (2002) argues that regional
competitive advantage in the USA charts a geography of innovation
and high-tech industry which maps onto the highest concentrations of
college educated creative and knowledge workers (243; see also Landry
2000; Begg 2002). As will be shown in Chapter Three, the clustering of
creative enterprise (new media, graphic design, film and advertising)
relies on a diverse pool of talented labour which in turn thrives on a
liberal politics, urban 'vitality' and cosmopolitan lifestyle. This is why
associations are frequently made between creativity and the openness
of an area to diversity, such as that measured by the Gay Index and
concentrations of same-sex partnerships (Florida 2002, 245; see Black
et al. 2000; and for the UK Duncan and Smith 2004).

The problem with viewing competitiveness in terms of this melting
pot 'beauty contest' is that the criteria for success neglects the hidden
costs of restructuring and growth in terms of social division and environmental stress. An obvious conundrum is that attractiveness rests
with an unstable mix of environmental quality and economic vitality
which typically function in opposition. Arguably, the capacity to

attract and retain a professional elite rests not only with the right real estate and a certain cultural cachet, but also the ability to find an affordable home, fulfil childcare and school preferences and to move around with ease and safety. It is in this respect that success is double edged. Concentrated growth puts pressure on land for development, raises the price of accessible real estate and chokes transport circulation in peak hours. It contributes to the perception that each household requires more than one good income to enter the housing market or maintain living standards.

The paradox is that in dynamic, affluent cities such as those examined in this book it is increasingly normal to find both parents in two-parent families employed for long hours, while it is difficult for this arrangement to survive the effort and emotional toll it takes to maintain daily life. In order to co-ordinate housing, childcare and schools together with the competing demands of their paid employment, parents frequently find themselves increasing the number of journeys and distance they travel each day. This contributes to a growing separation between daily activities identified in Chapter One as the jobs-housing mismatch (Jarvis et al. 2001: 5–10, 50). Yet these mundane private costs which prop up the postcard image rarely feature in the literature (see Perrons 2001 for costs with respect to gender inequality) because success is measured in terms of GDP alone. It is in order to highlight these private costs and internal contradictions that this book scrutinises the way families cope with daily life in these dynamic cities, questioning their 'liveability' in practice (Crookson et al. 1996). The results highlight the need to re-orient policy and debate to recognise the powerful influence of non-financial variables on wellbeing (social cohesion, a healthy environment, good and democratic access to urban amenities). This critique is framed by the influential 'new urbanism' which has emerged out of an uneasy alliance between urbanism and environmentalism.

Urbanism meets environmentalism

In recent years otherwise antithetical groups of architects, planners, environmentalists, property developers and elected officials have rallied, as if in unison, behind the benefits of a quintessentially urban vision of the future. Unsurprisingly this counter-intuitive alliance is uneasy at best. That it exists at all is the enduring legacy of two landmark books, both published in the 1960s. In the first book, *The Death and Life of Great American Cities*, published in 1961, New York Times journalist Jane Jacobs invoked a searing critique of modernist urban functionalism. She lamented the wasteful use of land and limited opportunities for social interaction typical of modern auto-dependent development. She argued that 'cars don't represent progress anymore' as Le Corbusier claimed they did in the 1920s, when he referred to streets as factories for producing traffic and modern industrial production as the paradigm for urban life (Ley 1996: 225). Instead Jacobs celebrated the cultural and economic diversity of successful 'traditional' urban neighbourhoods such as New York's Upper east side (not for nothing is Greenwich named a village) and San Francisco's North Beach – Telegraph Hill (Jacobs 1961: 149). She advocated a 'finely textured urban environment of social diversity and mixed land use, paying attention to the particular opportunity provided by ethnic neighbourhoods, artistic quarters and heritage buildings' (Ley 1996: 231).

Forty years on it is difficult to find a new housing scheme or planning brief which does not imitate the physical attributes she espoused: sidewalks with trees and street furniture, on-street parking and walkable networks of mixed-use varied building designs. Of course the values of good neighbourhood design pre-date the twentieth century. Images of homes communally arranged around a village green and streets furnished to human scale are typically European in origin and historically associated with the official Utopia's of nineteenth century model settlements.[1] Similarly Arcadian visions of ideal village congregations have resurfaced in notions of 'liveability' and 'quality of life' (see for instance Oldenburg 1999) breathing fresh life into the long romance Americans in particular have had with their neighbourhoods – as the building blocks of community pride and household lifestyle choices (Kaplan 1999: 28).

A second landmark book, *Silent Spring*, was published by former US Bureau of Fisheries natural historian Rachel Carson in 1963. It set out in meticulous detail how the pesticide DDT entered the food chain and accumulated in the fatty tissues of animals (and ultimately humans) causing cancer and genetic damage.[2] Publication of this slim volume aroused such public outrage that use of DDT was ultimately banned by then US President John F. Kennedy's Science Advisory Committee (Lear 1998). Of relevance here is not the detail of Carson's attack on the chemical industry but the lasting impact this confrontation had on civil society. It showed how a member of the public (who was courageous and well informed but otherwise lacking authority) could transform commercial practice by harnessing mass media publicity together with consumer boycotts, petitions and protests.

Publicity surrounding *Silent Spring* raised awareness of the intimate relationship between human activity (such as settlement patterns and transport behaviour) and environmental despoilation. By shifting public attitude towards natural history conservation and landscape stewardship it effectively launched the modern environmental movement. On the one hand this spawned a number of large and powerful environment movement organisations (EMOs), many such as Friends of the Earth UK and the US Sierra Club with local chapters campaigning on a wide range of national and international environmental issues (Rootes et al. 2001: 10). On the other hand it also saw the proliferation of issue-oriented groups typically organised around middle class 'nimby-style' neighbourhood campaigns. In recent years attention has shifted away from pure conservation to focus more on localised transport related urban environmental issues such that direct environmental action is today strongest in heavily populated urban areas where a particular quality of life (clean air, green public space) is perceived to be under threat (Rootes et al. 2001: 40).

A legacy of these two seminal texts is the illusion of common ground in the parallel promotion of urbanism and environmentalism. Cities are today seen as part of the answer to environmental problems rather than their cause (Beatley 2000: 22). The problem with this joint assembly is that a common cause can mean all things to all people. Nicholas Schoon (2001: 220) makes this point when he observes that 'Jacobs' followers comprise a broad church and sing from a variety of hymn sheets'. While *The Death and Life* is required reading for students of urban planning everywhere, it would be wrong to suggest it is transforming the way towns and cities accommodate growth. Consumer preference still rests with new detached single-family dwellings located on the edge of major conurbations, close to, but not part of, the vitality offered by the big city. Others move to regenerated inner cities for aesthetic reasons rather than to rationalise or 'simplify' busy, hyper-mobile routines (see Chapter Three).

Despite widespread consensus that cities play a pivotal role, there is less agreement as to how in the future they can be more socially and environmentally sustainable. On the one hand there are those who identify problems of social exclusion and urban sprawl with too little or the wrong sort of planning. From this the solution is identified as a matter of improved urban design: a technical fix. We see evidence of this in the neo-traditional architectural movement in the USA, where historically planning responsibilities have been abdicated to the private sector using legal instructions to homeowners to ensure aesthetic standards (Beatley 2000: 66; Marshall 2000: 21; Dear 2000). On the other hand there are those who believe too much 'top-down' interference from the state undermines grass roots initiatives to cultivate close-knit communities disposed to soft modes of transport such as walking or cycling. An extreme example of the self-sufficient eco-village is Christiania in the centre of Copenhagen, once a military camp which was taken over by squatters in the 1960s[3] (Rudlin and Falk 1999: 148). Paradoxically, both top-down and grass-roots visions promote the attractiveness of traditional mixed-use high-density neighbourhoods (MUHDs or more popularly 'urban villages') as a way of containing urban growth and curbing excessive reliance on private motorised transport. Indeed, belief that compact urban living can deliver a more sustainable city firmly underscores both the UK Urban Task Force (1999) report *Towards an Urban Renaissance* and the US Department of Housing and Urban Development (2000) report on *The State of the Cities*. This way liveability is defined as: 'the ability to walk to the corner shop for a quart of milk' (HUD 2000: 75), or, put another way, it is measured by the 'popsicle test': whether a child can safely walk to a nearby store to buy an ice-lolly (Bartlett 2003). These documents mark a turning point in the language of planning in the UK and USA as we shall see in comparisons between these two planning systems below (see also Chapter Six). They reflect the dominant influence in the UK of the urban village movement and in the USA of the Congress of New Urbanism. One consequence of this influence has been the widespread adoption by municipal authorities across the English speaking advanced world of cosmetic design solutions to serious environmental problems.

The UK urban village movement

Ever since Ferdinand Tönnies (1887) famously identified in modern urbanisation a transition from *Gemeinschaft* (community) to *Gesellschaft* (association), ambivalence towards the city has reflected alienation and self-interest (Bauman 1998: 14, Clark 1982: 79). Indeed we see the re-emergence of such claims today in Robert Putnam's (2000) bestseller *Bowling Alone* and Richard Sennett's influential (1998) *Fall of Public Man*. Nevertheless for urban sociologist Herbert Gans (1962) there was nothing inevitable about urban disaffection. Writing at the same time as Jacobs he employed the concept of the 'urban village' to describe the supportive social networks he found among members of close-knit ethnic communities in European inner cities which he believed could be cultivated through good governance and good design. These same principles characterise the UK urban village movement, first under the auspices of community architecture and later through the work of the UK Urban Village Forum, and they crop up repeatedly in the government urban renaissance discourse. Notwithstanding strong anti-urban sentiments in the UK, where aspirations for a rural (or semi-rural suburban) lifestyle are widespread (ODPM 1999: 4–6), public support galvanised around the now famous speech Prince Charles made in 1984 to the staunchly modernist Royal Institute of British Architects (RIBA). In it he highlighted the virtues of 'traditional scales' and 'vernacular design' (www.princes-foundation.org). This marked a turning point in plans for urban regeneration.

Prince Charles went on to commission the noted architect and town planner Leon Krier to design the first official UK urban village, Poundbury, on part of his Duchy of Cornwall estate (Schoon 2001: 231–2). Begun in 1993, this development will eventually accommodate some 2,400 homes, along with shops, light industry, schools and community facilities, clustered in tight rows around narrow winding streets. The size of the eventual settlement is determined as a 'ped-shed' – an area it would take no more than ten minutes to walk across. This is one of a series of principles laid down by the Urban Village Forum for creating mixed use urban developments on a sustainable scale (Aldous 1992; Urban Village Forum 1988). The intention in designing a 'walkable' settlement size is to reinvent the street as a place for doorstep conversation, free from the noise and pollution of motorised transport.

Reaction to Poundbury suggests it is loved and loathed in equal measure. Critics declare the scheme is neither urban nor environmentally sustainable. While cars are banished from sight they are no less relied upon by residents than in the average edge of town subdivision (Thompson-Fawcett 2003). The village is too small to be self-sufficient with respect to jobs and services and it functions instead as a satellite community to the Dorset market town of Dorchester. More recently, the Urban Village Forum has shifted attention to the revitalisation of existing run-down towns and city centres. This is illustrated in the list of new schemes adopting urban village status: Hulme and Ancoats in Manchester; Crown Street in Glasgow; West Silvertown and the flag-ship Millennium Village development at Greenwich in the east-end of London (Urban Village Forum 2003). This emphasis on infill and refill brownfield development reflects growing collaboration with Government departments engaged in planning for housing, notably the Office of the Deputy Prime

Minister (ODPM). This partnership also signals a twist in the convoluted tale of policy development by the fact that in 2003 John Prescott (deputy prime minister) visited a flagship development of the US Congress of New Urbanism. The strict codes of design he saw in Seaside so impressed him that he told his hosts he wanted to import this vision (which of course parodies the nineteenth century English garden city movement) *back* to the UK (Hetherington 2003).

The US Congress of New Urbanism

A group of US architects coined the term new urbanism in the 1980s protesting 'the placelessness of modern suburbs' (Congress of the New Urbanism 1999: 1; Katz 1994). Publication of a formal charter secured the movement's official status, ambitiously setting out physical design solutions to a whole host of urban ills (Talen 1999). This design manifesto persuasively reinvented the fine-grained neo-traditionalism of Jane Jacobs (1961) and Kevin Lynch (1960), tripping through the scales of region, metropolis, neighbourhood, corridor, block, street and building, to address 'the restoration of existing urban centres within coherent regions (and) the reconfiguration of sprawling suburbs into communities of real neighbourhoods and diverse districts' (Congress of the New Urbanism 1999: v). Most observers retain an impression of new urbanism inspired by the early Congress of New Urbanism (CNU) new town projects. Seaside was the first neo-traditional town founded by Andres Duany and partner Elizabeth Plater-Zyberk, two of the best known CNU proponents. Constructed in North West Florida in the 1980s, Seaside bears all the CNU hallmark features: front porches, picket fences and statuesque houses. From the outset it attracted harsh criticism because it functions as a resort rather than a 'real town': it is said to demonstrate the same artificial self-containment as the average college campus (Marshall 2000: 36). There is here none of the messy bustle of competing time-pressured activities: such 'pristine, kitschy, pseudo-communities' are 'worlds apart from the everyday disorders of life' (Sennett 2000: 70; Thorns 2002: 225).

From these origins the movement has been dogged by association with a Disney-like pastiche imitation of small town America, an image reinforced by the role played by the Disney Corporation in the construction of the new town of Celebration. Alex Marshall (2000) examines this project in detail in his book *How Cities Work*. Wanting to capitalise on the financial success of Disney World in Florida, the Disney Corporation identified land at the intersection of two highways for which they sought zoning and development rights for new housing built around a downtown school, town-hall and main-street shopping. This they achieved in the early 1990s, outmanoeuvring local environmental protestors by agreeing in exchange to create a wildlife conservation area on another site. By effectively creating a new town out of an exit ramp, Celebration exists for the purpose that: 'a Disney employee (can) drive right down U.S. 192 to work, while an Orlando businessman (can) hop on I-4, which leads the roughly twenty miles to downtown Orlando' (Marshall 2000: 5). Marshall criticises CNU architects for promoting a superficial change in style which does nothing to rethink the mechanisms of urban growth. In Celebration, for instance, homes are grouped in tight blocks of tree-lined streets, attractively emulating the eighteenth or nineteenth century town, yet each house retains a two-car garage to suit the needs of a thoroughly contemporary, convenience-based lifestyle (Marshall 2000: 25).

The ambiguity of new urbanism as a widespread movement is made no less confusing by the fact that Marshall (2000), while scathing of CNU projects, admits to being a new urbanist himself. He contrasts the cosmetic exercise of CNU with the principles of new urbanism underpinning Smart Growth. This is defined by the American Urban Land Institute (1996) as incorporating both sustainability and neo-traditional arguments (Thorns 2002: 224). Rather than being architect-led, Smart Growth is articulated through a broad coalition of interests which look to the strengthening of strategic planning initiatives, such as urban growth boundaries (much like Green Belt regulation in the UK) to contain development and encourage efficient use of urban transit systems. By contrast CNU proponents generally resist the idea of urban growth boundaries: most of the several hundred CNU projects designed or under construction in the USA today are 'on the fringes of the metropolitan area, adding to, not subtracting from, the problems of sprawl' (Marshall 2000: 37). Moreover, the CNU has itself split along the lines of environmental awareness in recent years. This is described in terms of a latent schism between the original East-Coast faction and a breakaway West-Coast group emerging out of the environment movement. The East-Coast CNU proponents typically construct exclusive 'common interest' self-contained purpose-built small-towns on greenfield sites (Duany and Plater-Zyberk 1991). In contrast, West-coast CNU architect-planners such as Seattle based Douglas Kelbaugh and California based Peter Calthorpe, advocate the development of sustainable transit-oriented-development (TOD) within existing urban areas (Calthorpe 1993).

Critique of the new urbanism

A characteristic shared by the new urbanism in its broadest definition is an assumption of spatial determinism. Graham and Marvin (2001: 415) argue that this takes 'a narrow view of the relationship between built form, infrastructure, mobility and the time-spaces of urban life'. Neglected is an attempt to understand (and influence) household decisions linking residential location, housing choice, household structure and travel behaviour. Neither does new urbanism confront the issue of social justice (Thorns 2002: 225) instead it inadvertently fuels 'the secessionary tendencies of socio-economically affluent groups' (Graham and Marvin 2001: 415). This is illustrated in the case of one family interviewed in San Francisco who subsequently moved to Davis, a CNU new town, to solve the problems they had reconciling home, work and family life. The ease with which they found they could go about daily life in Davis, managing with one car rather than two and reducing their combined working hours, had very little to do with the connected cul-de-sac development form, or indeed its impressive bicycle system. Instead it had far more to do with access to affordable detached housing and good state schools. Chapter Seven returns to this particular household biography.

What is worrying about the rise of the new urbanism is the way spatial determinism and the principles of neo-traditional design have entered the mainstream planning repertoire. For instance the UK Government's 1998 policy statement on housing explicitly endorses the urban village concept, promising to locate as much as 70 per cent of new housing within the footprint of existing settlements. Likewise the Congress of the New Urbanism (CNU) was well placed to offer its 'expertise and vision' to the US Department of Housing and Urban Development (HUD) when urban revitalisation became a priority during the Clinton Administration (Weiss 2000). The close adoption of CNU principles in national programmes and local development strategies is evident in the publication New American Neighbourhoods: Building Homeownership Zones to Revitalise Our Nation's Communities (US HUD 1996). Neither are such initiatives limited to the Anglo-American context. Arguably, planning assumptions based on the new urbanism are rolling out across the advanced world. The result is that radical challenges to the pursuit of growth and uneven development are being side-stepped by environmental claims which are frequently based in rhetoric rather than conviction. While property developers routinely emphasise proximity to museums, galleries and high-class restaurants as a way of selling downtown executive apartments: having

Photo 2.1   The city on your doorstep – London

'the city on your doorstep' (see Photo 2.1), environmentalists insist that promoting such proximity is about encouraging a car-free lifestyle.

In short, new urbanism is counter-productive to the environmental cause because it peddles the myth that 'cosmetic solutions' such as the application of front porches, cobbled paving and tree planting schemes, the eradication of 'snout houses'[4] and installation of street furniture, combat urban sprawl simply by improving the appearance of the inner cities, drawing people back into a contained area (Marshall 2000: 35; Beatley 2000: 21; Thorns 2002: 205). According to Bridget Franklin and Malcolm Tait (2002), while so-called urban villages have been springing up all across the UK in recent years, the idea that urban villages create sustainable environments is more imagined than real (Biddulph et al. 2001). In most cases the urban village label is used to get planning permission, as a marketing device to sell houses in urban areas, rather than as a commitment to providing a radical alternative to the auto-dependent housing estate. This point is reinforced in Chapter Six in relation to evidence of household travel behaviour.

Five city postcards

By any conventional measure, all five of the cities featured in this book are 'successful'. They escaped the worst effects of depopulation and deindustrialisation by cultivating high-value knowledge and service economies. At the same time the way that growth is being managed in these areas highlights the dominant influence of the new urbanism. As subjects of comparative research the five cities share many common characteristics but they also offer important variation in status, cosmopolitanism and official response to growth. San Francisco, Seattle and Portland provide examples of 'world', 'national' and 'regional' cities respectively, all sharing a common bioregional 'wilderness' culture which is under threat from pressures of migration and sprawl. London (a 'world' city) and Edinburgh (a 'national' city of similar size to Portland) are both financial and political capitals. A clear 'rank order' exists in terms of size and global recognition from the scale map in Figure 2.1 as well as the demographic data presented in Table 2.1. Figure 2.1 identifies the scale of the built up area associated with each population base. This gives some indication of the function of natural containment as well as living densities associated with historical growth management. For example, Portland adopted legislation to contain urban growth for environmental reasons in the 1960s and has a more sophisticated system of planning compared with Seattle and San Francisco.

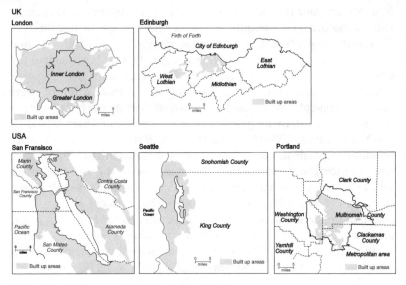

Figure 2.1   Scale map of the five featured cities

Table 2.1 shows that Portland and Edinburgh are smaller and whiter, with Portland accommodating more families with children than Seattle which is inhabited at lower densities by a greater proportion of single person households. Dual earner childless couples are over represented in Edinburgh, while London and San Francisco are more ethnically diverse and densely populated. These demographic trends suggest the return to city living is not catering for a general or balanced population. Indeed, Hall and Pfeiffer (2000: 96) suggest that families with children are the new urban minority (see also Logan et al. 2001). This is the case in San Francisco and Seattle in particular where the population is so tilted in favour of young childless professionals in their late 20s and 30s that children under 18 make up just 16 per cent of the population in the City of San Francisco and 20 per cent of the urban population of Seattle (see also Brookings Institution 2003: 5). This compares with the national average of 32.8 per cent (US Census Bureau 2000). Likewise just 18 per cent of the city of Edinburgh population are 0–17 years old compared with 24 per cent in the surrounding Lothian region (regional data includes the city of Edinburgh and this explains the lower average shown). The high cost of living in these cities is also suggested by relatively low rates of owner occupation. While on average 65 per cent of the US housing stock is owner occupied, in the

Table 2.1 Comparative demographic profiles of the five featured cities

	London		Edinburgh		San Francisco		Seattle		Portland	
	Inner	Greater[1]	City	Lothian[1]	City	Metro[5]	City	Metro	City	Metro
Size (million)	2.77	7.17	0.45	0.75	0.8	7.0	0.9	3.5	0.65	2.2
% non-white	34	29	3	2	46	36	25	16	17	12
% pop. 0–17 years old	22	23	18	24	16	26	21	27	25	28
% families	47[2]	59	54	59	45	65	51	65	56	66
% 'nuclear' families[3]	13	18	16	23	–	–	–	–	–	–
% women in employment[4]	55	57	55	57	61	60	64	62	63	61
Household Employment Structure[2] (UK universe = all *parents* aged 16–74 with Dependent Children in Couple families; US universe = all *'couple'* households with children)										
% No earners	18	11	6	6	14	12	11			
% One earner	38	35	25.5	25	26	28	31			
% Two earners	44	54	68.5	69	60	60	58			

Notes:

[1] Greater includes Inner London and Lothian includes city of Edinburgh.

[2] 28.3 per cent of Inner London households are single persons of working age, compared with 17.7 per cent of Outer London households. As a consequence, a smaller proportion of Inner London households comprise families.

[3] Couple households with dependent children where this includes all mixed backgrounds (including mixed with white) and both married and cohabiting couple households.

[4] Women in employment as a percentage of all females 16–74.

[5] Metro data is for the related Consolidated Metropolitan Statistical Area (CMSA).

Sources:

(UK data) 2001 Census; Key Statistics and Standard Tables. Census output is Crown copyright and is reproduced with the permission of the controller of HMSO and the Queen's Printer for Scotland.

(USA data) Census 2000 Gateway and US HUD State of the Cities Data system (SOCDS).

city of Portland this tenure represented 53 per cent in 1990, down from 57 per cent in 1970. In the city of Seattle just 49 per cent of the housing stock is owner occupied, down from 54.2 per cent in 1970. While the city of San Francisco witnessed slight growth in the rate of owner occupation over the same period, just 35 per cent of households owned their own home in 1990 (US Census Bureau 1990). (See also Table 2.4 below for international comparisons.) Similarly the national average rate of home ownership in the UK is 69 per cent yet in Inner London just 39.7 per cent of all households own their own home (either outright, with a mortgage, or through shared ownership) (National Statistics Online 2001).[5] By contrast, 68.6 per cent of city of Edinburgh households are owner occupiers. This relatively high rate, close to the national average, reflects an occupational profile skewed toward the professions and a high proportion of couple families with both parents working. Table 2.1 also provides some indication of cross-national differences in headline inequality with a much higher propor-tion of families with children in the three US cities having no parents in paid employment. In short, the successful city appears to be a hostile environment for dependent populations such as children and the elderly as well as those living on a limited income.

The five cities are introduced as a series of 'postcards' in Boxes 2.1–2.5 below. Each contemporary portrait briefly identifies the characteristics which make them popular and dynamic places for professional migrants as well as those which suggest that success is double edged. Each postcard physically locates the study neighbourhoods in which the interviewee families are drawn (see Figures 2.2–2.6).

Box 2.1   Moving to London Time

London is the largest UK city with an inner urban core accommodating 2.8 million inhabitants at relatively high density and a total metropolitan (Greater London) population of 7.2 million projected to reach 8.1 million by 2016. As well as housing the seat of political power at Westminster it also serves as the UK capital of culture and information production (Fainstein and Harloe 1992: 2, 6; for a historical overview see Hall 1976; Hebbert 1998). Yet London has the dubious honour of being the most congested, expensive and divided of European cities (Parkinson 2001: 78). For years now, three topics have dominated middle class conversation: traffic congestion, house price inflation and the shortage of nannies, cleaners, teachers, nurses and con-struction workers. Service sector employment is polarised around two extremes: well-paid professions are overrepresented as are low-status (typically feminised) personal services. Moreover, a ready supply of economic migrants feed a heavily exploited, unregulated, shadow economy (Anderson 1993; Gregson and Lowe 1994). The city conforms neither to the auto-dependence

Box 2.1   Moving to London Time – *continued*

of the US city nor the public transit and soft mode (walking and cycling) orientation of Continental European cities. Transport costs (in time, stress and cash terms) are extraordinarily high, with travel by London underground costing double the equivalent journey on the Paris Metro (Clark and Muir 2004).

Containment of the metropolitan area is managed by way of land designated as Green Belt in the late 1950s restricting development at the outer limits. But the spatial economy of London is largely inseparable from that of the South East region and in this respect housing and labour markets have no regard for administrative boundaries. City workers commuting in from outlying areas further distort the magnitude of the London economy by exporting the true measure of the price paid for its productivity. Inner London labour markets tend to import white collar workers from outer suburban settlements while many Inner London residents, especially those taking up retail, catering and unskilled jobs; often have to travel long distance to suburban labour markets such as those concentrated around airport facilities (Jarvis et al. 2001: 49). Ensuring affordable housing for key workers and reducing the push toward long distance commuting pose significant challenges. There is high profile evidence of urban neighbourhoods transformed through 'gentrification', attracting a middle class elite back to the inner city where many of them work (Butler and Robson 2003). Yet the daily commute for the majority of workers reflects a significant mismatch between where people choose or can afford to live and where they find jobs to suit their skills.

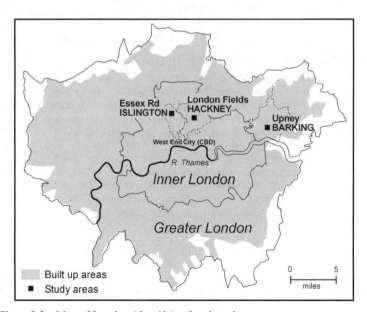

Figure 2.2   Map of London identifying local study areas

Box 2.1   Moving to London Time – *continued*

In Figure 2.2 Greater London is identified as the built up area contained by the M25 motorway. This map also identifies three neighbourhoods which are the sites of in-depth household research in the remaining chapters. The first is situated in Islington which is centrally located to the north of the central business district. This is a partially gentrified previously run-down inner city area which includes large swathes of socially deprived social rented housing. Hackney to the North East limits of Inner London accommodates an ad-hoc jumble of residential, commercial and industrial activities (Ackroyd 2001: 686). It represents a buffer zone between Islington 'yuppification' to the West and working-class struggles to the East. It is an area being transformed by a concentration of 'new media' in the form of dot-com start-ups and desk top publishing enterprises. At the same time it remains poorly served by public transit (Butler 1997). Despite regular lobbying it has never gained essential connection to the London Underground system. Barking lies on the eastern fringes of Outer London. Until recently access to well paid skilled manual jobs for men at the nearby Dagenham Ford motor works reinforced the image of this as a conservative area featuring strong kin networks and the normalisation of 'traditional' gender roles (Willmott and Young 1957; O'Brien and Jones 1996; Duncan 1991: 103). But in 2002 the last car rolled off the assembly lines. While new jobs growth and housing demand continues to focus on the West (with nearly two thirds of jobs and half of the population growth concentrated in just six boroughs), planners intend to build new 'urban villages' nearby in the 'East Thames Gateway'.

Box 2.2   Edinburgh: all that glitters is not gold

The capital of Scotland is a fraction of the size of London. It has a core population of 0.45 million extending to 0.75 million within the otherwise largely rural Lothian region. Edinburgh's famously compact, mixed use, high density form offers the ideal test site in which to pose the question whether this spatial arrangement makes it easier for busy working families to juggle home, work and family in environmentally benign ways. Car ownership rates are lower here among middle class residents than for equivalent households in similarly sized, lower density urban structures. The city's compact form is maintained by a heavily enforced Green Belt, first determined in 1956 (Mazza and Rydin 1997: 50). This, coupled with tight restrictions on development in the historic core has pushed new economic growth into a corridor of suburban science parks dubbed 'silicon glen', centred on the new town of Livingston to the west (Mazza and Rydin 1997: 50) between the traditionally competing cities of Edinburgh and Glasgow (Haug 1986: 106).

Edinburgh has always been professionally top heavy with the Kirk (church), the law, the Scottish civil service, medicine and architecture all centred here (Rowan 1990: 39). The resident workforce is highly educated

Box 2.2   Edinburgh: all that glitters is not gold – *continued*

and professional in profile with 40 per cent of adults holding degree level qualifications compared with an average of 27 per cent for Scotland as a whole (Scottish Executive 2001). Service sector industries account for 86 per cent of all jobs. At one level this reflects long established strength of the public, financial and business service sectors which together contribute 60 per cent of all city jobs. At another level, low paid, routine, retail and tourism employment account for one in four jobs (there are one million visitors to the Castle each year alone, Winterbottam 1990: 71). These figures dwarf the relative contribution of the highly regarded Scottish Electronics Industry (SEI), which attracts significant inward investment, constitutes half of all manufacturing, but contributes just five per cent of local labour market opportunities (Turok 1993: 403; Scottish Executive 1999).

Much has been made of Edinburgh's gentrification but this is not a recent phenomenon (Bondi and Christie 2000). A long established taste for central city living has led to comparisons being made with continental European cities. Of all UK cities, Edinburgh is the most like Continental Europe in terms of its long tradition of tenement living, where 'living over the shop' (LOTS) in the inner city is considered bourgeois rather than low-status (Petherick 1999) (see Photo 2.2). While the city always benefited from being Scotland's capital city, the 1999 addition of the newly devolved Scottish Parliament stimulated renewed property market activity in the 'boom' period 1996–1999 (Bondi et al. 2000). Since this time the global downturn in the electronics industry, responsible for major job losses at Motorola and Mitsubishi in May 2001, has stemmed the rise in house price inflation somewhat but first time buyers on median incomes still struggle to enter owner occupation.

Edinburgh is sometimes dubbed 'the Athens of the North' in view of its rich collection of historic buildings and monuments. Like contemporary Athens, it too today faces growing transportation problems. In practice it functions poorly in terms of containment. Having large numbers of people living centrally at high density does not necessarily mean those same people live, work, shop and socialise 'locally' as suggested by land-use arrangement (Mittler 1999). While the city 'imports' one in four of its workers from outside the area, one in ten Edinburgh residents travel to jobs outside the area (ONS 1991a; see also City of Edinburgh 2003). The nature of this mismatch is more than a simple numbers game. For some affluent workers the city is a dormitory, lifestyle settlement. For others it is a site of low-wage hospitality employment in which it is prohibitively expensive to secure accommodation convenient to places of work.

Figure 2.3 identifies the city of Edinburgh as being contained to the north and east by the Firth of Forth and to the south and west by the A720 city by-pass (which coincides with the Green Belt outer limits to permitted development). Also identified on this map are the study neighbourhoods. Newington is centrally located, compact, housing a middle-to-high income population. It is characterised by generously proportioned Georgian terrace houses with street parking and access to shops along Nicholson and Clerk streets. Leith is situated on the Waters of Leith to the east. It is inner urban, compact, housing a low-to-middle income population. After the 1980 decision to build a new Scottish

Box 2.2   Edinburgh: all that glitters is not gold – *continued*

Photo 2.2   Living over the shop – Edinburgh

Box 2.2   Edinburgh: all that glitters is not gold – *continued*

Office building at Victoria Dock, bringing around 1200 employees into a previously abandoned site, Leith experienced significant commercial regeneration (Edinburgh City Council 1998). While still 'affordable' (by New Town standards), renewed demand for this previously working class residential neighbourhood has pushed up prices to meet those of other accessible central locations. Most of the interviewees in Leith live within five minutes walk of local shopping and are two miles from Princes Street, the putative city centre. Housing is made up of a mix of stone tenement blocks and maisonettes (for housing types specific to Edinburgh see Pipes 1998). Five miles from the city centre, Craigmount has a far more suburban feel to it. Housing is at a far lower density, characterised by 1930s single family detached villas with small gardens, accommodating low-to-middle income families.

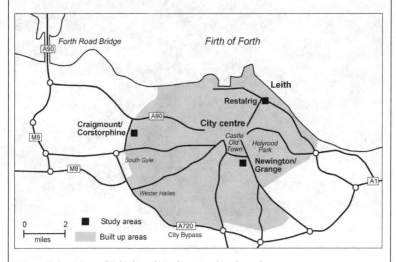

Figure 2.3   Map of Edinburgh indicating local study areas

Box 2.3   The lights go out on San Francisco's Golden Gate

San Francisco's postcard image is iconoclastic and will always draw admiration (see Photo 2.3). It is popularly viewed as the most European of US cities, with a relaxed, vibrant, compact character, widely admired by residents and visitors alike (Hartman 1984). Artists, musicians and liberal-arts graduates typically embrace the co-mingling of ethnic cultures characteristic of the inner city area, providing a distinctly 'bourgeois urbanism' skewed toward young, educated adults (Walker 1995: 33). Development of the city itself has been physically contained by oceans, bays and steep hills. Yet satellite images show how San Francisco sits at the top of a megalopolis, or 'metroplex',

Box 2.3   The lights go out on San Francisco's Golden Gate – *continued*

stretching north-south through Silicon Valley to San Jose within which it is hard to know where each city ends and the suburbs begin (Villaraigosa 2000). Today the private and commercial costs of congestion rank among the highest in the US (California Government Datamart 2000) and the city has one of the most expensive housing markets in the world. The recent downturn in commercial real estate has done little to reduce residential demand, especially for the scarce commodity of the single family home. The profile of household employment reflects this high cost of living with 60 per cent of families comprising two or more wage earners.

Photo 2.3   San Francisco's famous 'little boxes on the hillside'

In the Bay Area, 'good jobs' are defined by the 'new economy' where real wage increases far outstrip those in financial services, commanding salaries 50 per cent higher than the Bay Area average and public sector pay has fallen still further behind (PG&E 1995: 7). To the extent that San Francisco neighbourhoods are most sought after by affluent new economy professionals, less advantaged workers 'either crowd into inner city apartments or flee to the far suburbs in the San Joaquin valley for affordable housing' (Walker 1996: 82). There has consequently been a widening separation of residential locations and work-sites across the region which contributes to sprawl, traffic congestion, pollution, energy consuming 'wasteful journeys' and social division (Cervero 1986, 1996; Cervero and Wu 1995; Fulton 2000: 4). San Francisco consequently imports 46 per cent of its workers, principally those in public sector, essential service and low wage occupations, while at the same time exporting 20 per cent of its employed residents to Peninsula firms. At the extreme, only 58 per cent of San Mateo and 60 per cent of Contra Costa employed residents work in their home county (California Government Datamart 2000).

Box 2.3   The lights go out on San Francisco's Golden Gate –
continued

While San Francisco prides itself in a history of local resistance to Los Angeles style development, leading the way in the 1955 Freeway Revolt, weak regional strategic planning and a state culture of non-intervention in market-led development has left the city vulnerable to rapid, high-profile growth (Walker 1998: 5). Today, soaring electricity rates and anxiety about the threat of rolling power outages add to long-standing urban irritations threatening the Bay Area quality of life. In June 2000 the world media watched in amazement as grocery store customers shopped by candlelight as bills were calculated with the aid of battery operated calculators (Borger and Teater 2003). Explanations for the crisis are complex, though in essence they stem from excess energy demand relative to supply (Solomon and Heiman 2001: 464). By an ironic inversion of the presumed role of sophisticated ICT, residents and businesses are invited to sign up to email 'energy forecasts' as a means of gaining early warning of anticipated blackouts in their neighbourhood.

Figure 2.4 identifies the neighbourhoods selected as the site of in-depth household research. These comprise: central Mission/South of Market (SoMa); outer urban Bernal Heights/Excelsior; and suburban East Bay/ Alameda. The latter lies outside the city limits but it represents one area of relatively affordable housing for San Francisco workers, notably those in blue collar and public sector jobs as well as artists and musicians. The SoMa area in contrast accommodates a high concentration of 'new media' creative workers at relatively high density and cost, while Bernal Heights is a working class neighbourhood witnessing upward mobility, featuring popular Victorian family homes at medium density.

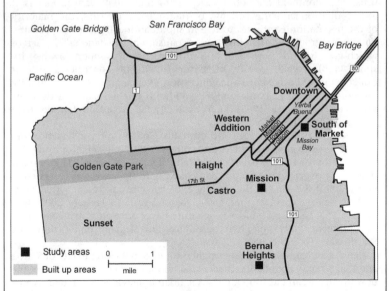

Figure 2.4   Map of San Francisco indicating local study areas

Box 2.4   The Seattle way

Seattle has an impressive setting with snow-capped mountains of the Cascade and Olympic ranges dominating the horizon to east and west. Physical containment explains the pronounced north-south axis and relative compactness of the 'downtown' area which has a core population of some 0.9 million people wedged between the Puget Sound and Lake Washington. Beyond this the Seattle-Tacoma-Bremerton Consolidated Metropolitan Statistical Area (CMSA) represents an uninterrupted region of low density development currently accommodating a population of 3.5 million, predicted to rise to 5 million by 2050 (Kelbaugh 1997: 16). King County encompasses the City of Seattle and is visibly divided north and south of the downtown core. The north is developed at a higher density and features the highest average house prices and greatest concentration of high-value service sector employment. The south features lower density, poorer quality housing and the legacy of traditional 'blue-collar' industries which have seen steady decline (Boeing, timber industries, the port of Tacoma, Seattle Airport and associated transport industries). Today the proportion of the population qualified to university degree stands at 40 per cent compared with an average of 27.2 per cent for Washington state overall) (US Census Bureau 2000). This youthful, educated profile drives a much vaunted 'can do' entrepreneurial culture which is credited for bringing niche products to market ranging from coffee-roasting to climbing gear. The early 1990s witnessed the celebrated 'dot com boom' whereby Seattle joined the ranks of city-regions with 'silicon status' (English-Lueck 2002: 20, 110).

Growth management systems were not established in the region until 1989 (DeGrove 1994: 238). While Seattle experienced a far less dramatic urban abandonment than other cities facing more significant problems of ethnic division and the collapse of traditional industries, the majority of the population continues to live in suburban locations at low density. Population growth consistently trails expansion of new land take, much of which goes towards new roads and infrastructure to support low density single family dwellings (City of Seattle 1997). This contributes to 'that unlikely mix of both sprawl and congestion' (Kelbaugh 1997: 26). The City promotes itself as 'a city for families' and holds a 'sustainable Seattle' as its vision (City of Seattle 1997: ix). Yet the city fails to attract families with young children (US HUD 2000).

Rapid growth has not been without pain. Coffee-shop conversation frequently turns to clogged bridges and congested highways. Epitomising this is the anti-growth bumper-sticker: 'Californians, go home!' The popular image of a rising tide of Californians moving to the area is exaggerated at best (Abbott 1994). Yet the problems of congestion are such that Greg Nickels was sworn in as the 51st Mayor of Seattle in January 2001 on a promise that he would build a 21st century transportation system. Noted for his optimistic 'Pollyanna pitch' he claims as his strategy 'doing things the Seattle way' (Fullerton 2001).

Figure 2.5 identifies the study neighbourhoods in relation to city of Seattle and King County boundaries. Greenwood is located immediately north of the downtown area and features modest Victorian homes at medium density in a

Box 2.4   The Seattle way – *continued*

mixed but upwardly mobile inner urban area. Kenmore sits at the northern tip
of Lake Washington, on the King County-Snohomish County border. Schools
in this low density suburb have a good reputation and this attracts a large
number of families with children to the area.

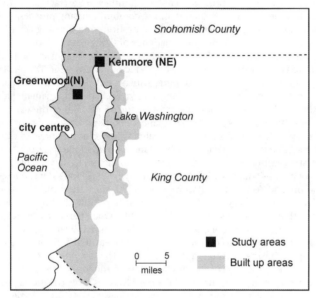

Figure 2.5   Map of Seattle indicating local study areas

Box 2.5   Portland: from timber to technology

Portland functions as the compact core to a polycentric metropolitan area
housing 2.2 million people. It has multiple nodes of employment, many coin-
ciding with transit intersections and corridors, surrounded by low density
housing and supported by neighbourhood shopping facilities. In terms of
urban structure, Portland most resembles the closely integrated arrangement
of housing, shops, schools and parks typically assumed to foster self-
contained, localised living (Newman 1999). Sprawl has been limited by the
adoption in 1973 of a strong Urban Growth Boundary, strengthened in 1998
to curtail outer-area growth (Newman 1999: 192). Yet despite the importance
attached to environmental planning, the car remains the dominant mode of
transport and pressures of population dispersal continue at the margins as in
other US cities (Hall and Pfeiffer 2000: 29; Marshall 2000: 106, 171–74).

   Pressures of growth stem from proximity to dynamic economies to the
north (Seattle) and south (San Francisco and the Bay Area). In-migration

Box 2.5   Portland: from timber to technology – *continued*

accounts for more than half of Oregon's population growth whereby one in
six residents have moved to Portland from another US state in the last five
years (US Census Bureau 2000; Dicken and Dicken 1982: 157; Allen 1987). Net
in-migration is associated with political determination to create and maintain
a 'liveable city'. Young professionals and families are attracted to this area
because it offers a particular quality of life combining rising prosperity with a
widely valued west-coast pattern of consumption, one drawing on access to
land, spatial mobility and private experience of the 'great outdoors'.

Following national trends, Oregon has seen a decline in manufacturing employment and a commensurate rise in service producing employment. The retail sector
alone accounts for 18 per cent of employment and three healthcare facilities
feature in the top ten largest Portland employers. The employment profile is
skewed toward the middle class professional and 28 per cent of the working age
population have a Bachelors degree or above. Portland trades on proximity to
California's world famous 'silicon valley' claiming that a 'silicon forest' of new business service development (Hamilton 1987) has risen up in the space of the former
timber based economy. Despite superficial transformation to silicon rank, Portland
has regional rather than 'world city' status (Harvey 1996). Indeed it is the sense of
community and 'feel' of a small town which Portlanders strive most passionately
to protect. Some feel they are being drawn unwittingly into the San Francisco Bay
Area growth phenomenon 600 miles to the south. One interviewee went so far as
to claim they were all 'part of California now' (Mr Parker 1999 interview).

Figure 2.6 identifies two neighbourhood study areas. The Fremont area is close
to the central business district in the north east. The second is in Garden Home
which is close to the edge of the city boundary to the south west. Both are situated within Multnomah County but Fremont features more traditional medium
density housing (with front porches off paved sidewalks). Garden Home by contrast is developed at far lower densities and roads and a popular consideration
for residents is the 'rural feel' of not having paved sidewalks.

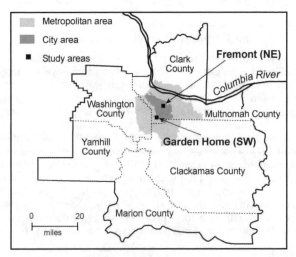

Figure 2.6   Map of Portland indicating local study areas

International comparisons

How particular nations compete in the global world economy is the subject of great interest, as are the local prospects for 'winners' and 'losers' among industrial sectors, firms, workers and families (Lever 2002: 11). This is why international comparative research is widely used to try to build up a picture 'both of patterns of difference and of broad directions of change' (Cochrane and Clarke 1993: 9). The problem is the choice of suitable variables. Existing attitudinal surveys, for instance, suggest any meaningful comparison of family earning and parenting arrangements must take full account of gender role and cultural variation. Likewise, it is stressed throughout this book that transport behaviour is at best partially determined by the system of land-use planning adopted. Yet most analysis focuses exclusively on fiscal policy, welfare provision and headline macro-economic indicators. This is true of comparative research both in urban studies and social policy, two discrete bodies of literature which are fused together here. It is usual in the work-life reconciliation literature, for instance, to differentiate between public policy regimes on the basis of the support they provide to families, such as a willingness to redistribute the costs of social reproduction or make direct provision for early years care and education. The best known typology identifies the UK and USA together at one end of the spectrum as 'liberal' welfare regimes (along with Canada, Australia and New Zealand). At the opposite end are the 'social democratic' regimes of which Sweden is archetypal (also Denmark, Norway and Finland) (Esping-Andersen 1990, 1996; Duncan 1995). Between these two extremes are 'conservative' (statist-corporatist) welfare regimes (typical for instance of France, Germany, Austria and Italy) in which the state is willing to regulate private market activity to achieve desired social goals, but tends to do so to safeguard traditional 'family values', assuming a male breadwinner and dependent female spouse (Lewis 1992: 165). This comparative approach is adopted by Janet Gornick and Marcia Meyers (2003: 6–7) as a means by which to shift policy debates in the United States beyond the belief that care-giving is a private concern and instead to demonstrate that better alternatives are practiced successfully abroad (see also O'Connor et al. 1999; Esping-Andersen 1999).

Similarly, it is usual in the urban studies literature to differentiate between discrete national transport and land use planning systems, contrasting unregulated North American 'sprawl' with tightly regulated 'compact' European cities. Timothy Beatley's (2000) book *Green Urbanism* is typical of this approach. It too seeks to influence planning policy in the United States by learning from European Cities. Clearly, by scrutinising state, city and household level distinctions *within* an ostensibly similar market-oriented extreme, this book deviates considerably from the convention of distinguishing between contrasting regime types. The reasons for this approach are two-fold. First, it is argued that broad-brush international comparisons tend to convey only a partial reality, one which overlooks within-type inconsistencies and change over time. One future scenario suggested in Chapter One, for instance, is that standards of competition set by extreme market liberalism threaten to undermine more democratic models of work-life reconciliation practised elsewhere. We see evidence of this in a common shift towards more elaborate household lifestyles (witnessed in trends of hyper-mobility, rising consumer expectation and debt, and the universal applications of new technology). More importantly, within-type analysis highlights the prospects for within-type 'winners' and 'losers' in relation to household and city level variations in cultural expectations and coping strategies. The limitations of broad-brush claims are suggested below with respect to headline indicators which look first at support for working families and then urban planning systems. Second, within-type analysis can serve to highlight the urgent need for public debate in the UK and the USA, where the future choice is to moderate, or accept the negative consequences of, extreme market orientation. As argued in Chapter One, the UK is neither European nor American in its outlook yet in recent years it has imported an increasing number of urban social policy ideas from the USA (Dolowitz 1998; Wollman 1992; Walker 1998). The Office of the Deputy Prime Minister (ODPM) launched a new Academy for Sustainable Communities in February 2005 which claims to have strong links with the US Congress of New Urbanism. This follows a high profile visit Deputy Prime Minister John Prescott made to Seaside in Florida, as noted in Chapter One. One way of pressing for the UK to import social democratic rather than transatlantic policy solutions is to highlight the negative consequences of extreme market liberalism for households and the environment in which they co-ordinate daily life.

Support for working families

Who would not be struck when considering the data presented in Table 2.2 by the 65 weeks (15 months) of paid leave parents in Sweden are entitled to share (at 80 per cent of earnings for 12 months) compared with the 12 weeks of *unpaid* family and medical leave parents in the USA *might* be entitled to use to care for a new born child if their work history and employer satisfy the eligibility criteria. It is easy to see why stark comparisons are drawn between the low taxation, weak social security of the USA and the high taxation, generous

Table 2.2 Parental leave and early childhood care compared by welfare regime type

	Parental and family leave entitlements	Early Childhood Education and Care (ECEC)	Family allowance	Child and family tax benefits
USA	'Liberal' welfare regime type No national maternity, paternity or parental leave policy. The Family and Medical Leave Act (FMLA) of 1993 provides employees in firms of more than 50 staff unpaid leave for 10–12 weeks to cover pregnancy and maternity. Individual states are starting to experiment with European style state-administered employee-funded paid leave. From July 1 2004 13 million California workers can now receive income replacement (55 per cent up to $728 a week) to care for an ill family member or a new baby.	No national system. Most children attend kindergarten at age 5 and begin primary school at age 6. Preschool ECEC is concentrated within the private for-profit and voluntary (church, non-profit) sectors. Where Federal funding is available it is targeted on low-income children and children with special needs.	None	A variety of tax benefits and credits; dependent care tax credit applies to childcare, refunding a proportion of expenditures up to a fixed limit per child.
UK	'Liberal' welfare regime type New framework from 2003 provides up to 52 weeks maternity leave (26 of which paid; payment varies by employer, from full pay to	From 1998 the National Childcare Strategy requires local authorities to provide a place for all 3–5 year olds for two-and-a-half hours daily. Special funding is allocated	Universal monthly Child Benefit up to age 18. New one-off 'Baby Bond'	A Child Tax Credit with Child care Tax Credit element introduced in 2003 replaces the previous Working Family Tax Credit. In addition

Table 2.2 Parental leave and early childhood care compared by welfare regime type – *continued*

	Parental and family leave entitlements	Early Childhood Education and Care (ECEC)	Family allowance	Child and family tax benefits
	£100 flat rate). Two weeks paid paternity leave (£100 flat rate). Further unpaid parental leave available contingent on length of service/age of child/notice to employer.	for disadvantaged areas through the Sure Start scheme. There is little or no public day-care provision and consequently most care for 1–3 year olds is private. Compulsory education begins the year a child turns 5.		employers can subscribe to a voucher scheme to allow employees to pay for a proportion of their childcare costs pre-tax.
Canada	'Liberal' welfare regime type As of 2001 maternity and parental benefit is provided by a system of Employment Insurance EI (Unemployment Insurance previously paid 55 per cent of wages for 15 weeks). The parental portion of the leave was extended from 25 to 50 weeks at the same 55 per cent of wages up to a maximum. The new parental leave has led to an increase in the number of fathers claiming a share of leave. EI also allows a six week compassionate leave benefit for the care of any close kin.	Universal free kindergarten only available from age 5–6. Pre-school ECEC is fragmented and in short supply. Parent fees are the major source of finance as well as province allocations targeted on special needs.	Income-tested national child benefit.	The Canada Child Tax Benefit is being increased and indexed to inflation but it applies only to low-income families.

Table 2.2 Parental leave and early childhood care compared by welfare regime type – *continued*

	Parental and family leave entitlements	Early Childhood Education and Care (ECEC)	Family allowance	Child and family tax benefits
Australia	'Liberal' welfare regime type Since 1994 Federal work-place relations legislation entitles parents to 52 weeks unpaid leave on a shared basis. Except for one week at the time of birth, each partner must take parental leave at different times. Within this provision, public sector employees receive 6–12 weeks paid maternity leave. Elsewhere access to paid maternity leave is at employer discretion (c. 42 per cent of permanent female employees in workplaces of 20+ employees receive paid maternity leave). A one-off maternity allowance linked to child immunization is paid for each child.	Compulsory schooling begins at 6 but 74 per cent of 5s are in pre-school or kindergarten. Limited state assistance for childcare and the private sector is very important. For pre-school children informal arrangements with relatives are common.	Baby Bonus per child for up to five years	Family Tax Benefit and limited income-related (not means tested) childcare fee relief. Rebates for all families with children in registered care may cover up to 30 per cent of weekly costs.
Germany	'State corporatist' (conservative) welfare regime type Paid, job-protected maternity leave for 14 weeks, paid for by Social Security and topped up	Germany has an explicit family policy, historically designed to support the traditional two-parent	Universal child Benefit for all children up to age 18+.	Tax credits are designed to redistribute the cost of child-rearing; specifically an income tax child

Table 2.2 Parental leave and early childhood care compared by welfare regime type – *continued*

	Parental and family leave entitlements	Early Childhood Education and Care (ECEC)	Family allowance	Child and family tax benefits
	by employer. No separate paternity leave but a two-year flat-rate, income-tested Parental Leave and a further three-year Job-Protected Leave as an extended benefit following childbirth. Although both parents are eligible for this, less than one percent of fathers take any part of this leave. Working adults in a two-worker family also have the right to remain at home up to ten days per year to care for an ill child under 12.	family with an 'at home' mother caring for the children. There is good publicly subsidized pre-school provision (90%) for the 3–5s but with half-day operation and very poor coverage (5%) for infants and toddlers or for children whose mothers work full time. Pre-school 3–5 care is viewed as the primary stage of education.		allowance and income tax care allowance.
France	16–26 weeks maternity leave at 80 per cent of earnings (up to a maximum). As of January 2002 14 days paid job-protected paternity leave (paid as a basic social security cash benefit). Parental or 'child rearing' leave follows on from maternity leave and is unpaid for the first child	A publicly funded preschool programme exists for all 2–6 year olds which is administered under the Ministry of Education. This is free for the standard school day (8.30–4.30) with 'wrap-around' services (lunchtimes and holidays etc.) paid for by a meanstested fee. Crèches provide care for children from three months to age and	Universal cash benefit for each child beginning with the second – up to age 19. The first child receives no benefit.	From 2004 a new universal allowance replaces five existing benefits (the parental childrearing allowance, the young child allowance, the nanny allowance and the family childminder grant) with a self-select 'stop work' supplement or a 'childcare supplement'. In addition there are childcare tax credits.

Table 2.2 Parental leave and early childhood care compared by welfare regime type – *continued*

	Parental and family leave entitlements	Early Childhood Education and Care (ECEC)	Family allowance	Child and family tax benefits
	paid for the second and subsequent child at a flat rate. Parents may take the leave at the same time or sequentially. Sick child Leave is provided for all working parents for up to five days a year and is fully paid.	two and charge means-tested fees. Low-income families pay nothing.		
Sweden	*'Social Democratic' regime type*			
	Swedish Parent Insurance is a universal social insurance benefit which provides 14 weeks of maternity leave and two weeks of paternity leave after childbirth followed by up to 18 months of parental leave of which at least two months must be taken by the father (so called daddy days) or lost. The first 13 months of leave is paid at 80 per cent of wages, another three months at a low flat rate	Swedish childcare comes under the remit of the Ministry of Education and Science. Group care is the norm and ECEC covers the normal work day and year, is publicly funded and available to all children under school age with working mothers or mothers who are full time students. Parents pay fees amounting to 1–3 per cent of family income. This covers about 17 per cent of operating costs. More than 90 per cent of children are in public or publicly funded childcare.	Universal cash allowance based on the presence and age of child.	Individual taxation based on a policy of gender equity means there are no special tax concessions for families.

Table 2.2 Parental leave and early childhood care compared by welfare regime type – *continued*

Parental and family leave entitlements	Early Childhood Education and Care (ECEC)	Family allowance	Child and family tax benefits
and the final months unpaid. The parental leave can be pro-rated or shared by mother and father. Working parents may take up to 60 days a year paid leave to care for an ill child under age 12 and as of 2002 each parent is entitled to five days a year for personal child needs (such as to visit a child's school).			

Sources: OECD (2002a) Country Profiles, http://www.oecd.org/; The Clearinghouse on International Developments in Child, Youth and Family Policies at Colombia University (2004), http://www.childpolicyintl.org/countries/; DTI Employment Relations – Work and Parents; http://www.dti.gov.uk/er/individual/workparents_features.htm.

welfare provision of Sweden. US employees pay less in taxes when compared to other states but they pay significantly more in private healthcare and for the opportunity costs of maternity and early years care and education. Swedish employees pay far more in taxes but as shown in Table 2.2 these are used to redistribute the costs of caring for children across society. This means that from the age of one year (before this children are cared for at home though paid parental leave) children are entitled to publicly funded day-care up to the age of six (the age when children in Sweden enter the school system) for which parents contribute fees amounting to 1–3 per cent of family income. By contrast parents in the UK who pay for private day-care after up to six months of paid maternity leave typically pay full fees amounting to some 30 per cent of family income. The social democratic countries recognise the need to offer practical help in the form of public child-care provision to enable every working age adult to remain in employment and this way contribute to the broad tax base necessary to finance universal welfare. For many commentators this represents the closest approximation to a dual-earner-dual-carer society (Gornick and Meyers 2003: 91) though it is questionable whether a truly symmetrical structure of shared earning and co-parenting exists anywhere in practice (Clement 2004: 47).

It is in this respect that welfare regimes are said to correspond with different gender arrangement types (Orloff 1993). For instance Rosemary Crompton (1998) locates individual states on a continuum of models on the basis of breadwinning and care-giving behaviour (see also Lewis 1992; Pateman 1989). Dual earning couples with children are more likely to constitute two full-time working parents in the USA than in the UK where part-time employment is the norm for mothers of young children (Evans 1992: 138). One explanation for this is that US state policy steers women toward full-time rather than part-time employment after childbirth because healthcare insurance is costly and generally only available to full-time workers (Scott and Duncombe 1992: 38). Cherlin (1988: 6) also explains that in the US 'the 'cost' of staying home has increased for mothers, in terms of foregone earnings'. This is especially true for college-educated middle class mothers able to claim tax relief for childcare expense. These women 'now face better employment opportunities and enjoy higher wages than in the past' (Cherlin 1988: 6). Arguably though, divisions of paid work, ways of protecting those who are unemployed and public support for working families all tell of a partial economy, one which neglects women's disproportionate contribution to unpaid domestic and caring work. Consequently while gender inequalities persist in the UK and USA (more so than in social democratic regimes) there are notable differences in opportunities for social mobility by race and class, as well as cultural variation in attitudes to family, welfare and work. Critics also point to the questionable assumption that a private reality (cultural tastes, preferences and behaviour) can be read off from systems of public policy. It is mechanistic to assume that the existence of a policy, such as encouraging paternity leave, will bring about a change in male employment behaviour (Glover 2002: 258).

Turning to the matter of working hours Table 2.3 shows that while the UK holds the record for providing workers with the least public holidays, US employees have *no* statutory annual leave entitlement. Provision for paid leave rests with individual employers and few private sector firms offer more than 10 days (rising to a maximum of 20 days after 10 years continuous service). Adair Turner (2001) argues that the big difference between US and European neo-liberalism is not productive efficiency but social choice. Put crudely, it is the choice to work through lunch and cut back on family vacations. Newspaper headlines heralding 'Burn-out Britain' would lead us to believe that Britons are skipping lunch more frequently than their European counterparts, despite European Union membership. Nevertheless the headline statistics presented in Table 2.3 suggest a continuing North American/European cultural divide. Moreover, Gornick and Meyers (2003: 59) note that the American workforce reports the longest annual hours of any in the industrialised world (with an average of 1,966 hours a year), six weeks of work a year more than the European average, exceeding even the notoriously work-intensive Japanese (who average 1,889 hours a year). Whereas annual work hours are declining in most advanced economies they continue to rise in the US. It is interesting to make comparisons with Japan because it is widely perceived as quintessentially workaholic. Here the government has established a network of day-care facilities which open from 7 am to 7 pm in support of the growing number of dual earning households. Superficially this provision compares favourably with exemplary crèche and pre-school provision in France; the latter typically open from 8.30 am to 4.30 pm with 'wrap-around' services to cover lunchtimes and holidays. Yet it is meaningless to make this comparison outside the context of local cultures – such as those which compel Japanese parents to commute long distances and put in long hours. This is demonstrated in heavy demand for 24-hour childminding centres set up by private sector entrepreneurs to cater for early morning starts and late night

Table 2.3   Working hours, healthcare spending and taxation compared internationally

	Public holidays (days), 2003	Statutory minimum annual leave (days), 2003	Normal weekly working hours (with statutory maximum): 2000	Per-capita healthcare spending in US dollars, (% private spending), 1997	Taxation as per cent of GDP, 2002
USA	10	0[1]	40 (none)	$4095 (54%)	29.6
UK	8	20	37.5 (48[3])	$1391 (15%)	37.4
Canada	10	10[2]	40 (none)	$2175 (15%)	35.8
Australia	10	20	38–40 (none)	$1909 (33%)	43.7
Germany	13	20	37.5 (48)	$2364 (23%)	37.9
France	11	25	35 (48)	$2047 (26%)	45.3
Sweden	15	25	38.8 (40)	$1762 (17%)	54.2
Japan	15	10	40 (none)	$1760 (20%)	27.1

Notes:
[1] The average annual leave entitlement after ten years service in the private sector is 16.9 days (US Bureau of Labor Statistics, 1997)
[2] Eligible employees are entitled to at least two weeks paid annual vacation after one year and an additional week after a specified period (statutory provision varies between province).
[3] Some UK firms/employees can opt out of the 48 hour limit.
Sources: Incomes Data Services (2003) Working Hours and Holidays, www.incomesdata.co.uk/infotime/eutable.pdf; OECD (2000b) Health Data; OECD (2001) Taxation Data; OECD (1999) Working Hours: Latest Trends and Policy Initiatives, Chapter 5. www.oecd.org/dataoece/8/51/2080270.pdf.

deadlines (Watts 2002: 18). These are the 'gaps' which working parents have to plug in competitive market economies whenever the working 'day' and travel commitments exceed routine childcare provision. The role non-standard working and 'demand-led' cultures of work play in perpetuating gender inequalities is considered again in more detail in Chapter Four.

In summary what this spread of data shows is that there are significant differences *within* regime types such as between the UK and USA. For instance the UK maintains a National Health Service and provides a

universal cash benefit for all children up until the age of 18. This contra-
venes the liberal regime norm of welfare benefits that are modest, means
tested and restricted to those actively seeking employment. Indeed,
following the introduction of the UK National Childcare Strategy in 1998
more funding and a greater sense of priority has been given to meeting
the childcare needs of working parents. The shift is such that the Labour
Government's plans to further extend maternity and parental leave,
including the introduction of a Scandinavian style 'daddy quota'
(Smithers 2004) suggests a potential conflict between family-friendly
initiatives and a highly competitive ethos which challenges the likelihood of any fundamental change in workaholic business practices.
Notwithstanding the new rhetoric of European-style family support,
actual provision of childcare in the UK remains a private family matter.
This reluctance to intervene in the provision of childcare is crucial to the
question of work-life reconciliation. Jan Windebank (2001) demonstrates
this with respect to comparisons between dual-earner couples in Britain
and France. She suggests that the UK pursues a punitive universal worker
model: the state wants all working age adults to seek paid employment
but chooses not to assist workers facing costly barriers to entry (such as
childcare, transport and housing for those on low wages). Arguably too,
the logistical detail of work-life reconciliation is not limited to questions
of working hours, parental leave and assistance with the costs of childcare. More importantly perhaps it rests with the location of homes in
relation to jobs, schools and childcare and the ability to move comfortably and efficiently between these sites in order to co-ordinate events. It
is with this in mind that the next section considers the role of urban
planning systems in co-ordination strategies.

Urban planning systems

As with support for working families, it is tempting to look to Continental European cities for solutions to jobs-housing mismatches and
the damaging environmental impact of auto-mobility. For instance,
Beatley (2000: 172) observes the impressive strides German cycle-
friendly cities have made in promoting bicycle mobility. One of the
foremost bicycle-friendly cities is Münster (see Photo 2.4) where a size-
able proportion of the city's population live within the old centre with
access to a network of bicycle paths and traffic calming which provides
the cyclist with flexibility (including short-cut routes) that car drivers
do not have (Beatley 2000: 44, 172; Pucher 1997). This illustrates the
intervention of government in the private market (using incentives and
penalties to steer behaviour toward desired public goals) through
systems of land use planning.

Photo 2.4   Münster – cycle-friendly city

Arguably the impact of restructuring (and competitiveness) differs according to the mediating influence of planning systems, consumer spending, transport development and land availability. We can see this influence in the headline land-use indicators compared internationally in Table 2.4. This shows a strong association between those countries endorsing a liberal welfare regime and a housing stock where the dominant tenure is owner occupation. For instance, UK and US middle class families popularly expect quite early in their housing careers to own a property detached from other homes with a garage and a bit of land alongside. In fact UK and US residents share very similar housing tastes while, in contrast, Continental Europeans view private renting and apartment living the norm. This taste comes at a cost: UK middle class families are on average restricted to far smaller homes than both their US and European counterparts (Hardill 2002: 55). Britons have a taste for living at low density in a country where traditions of urban containment and concentrated economic activity create high population densities (second only to Japan in Table 2.4). This is despite limited high rise development. Historically these tastes have been encouraged by fiscal incentives favouring home ownership.

Yet it would be wrong to assume that the influence of planning is wholly consistent with discrete liberal/regulated regimes. Two illustrations serve to demonstrate this point. First, returning to the case of Germany, it might come as some surprise to see in Table 2.4 that running alongside commitment to mass public transit and cycle-friendly cites are very high rates of car ownership. Indeed, car ownership is rising faster in all European countries than the US (Orfeuil and Salomon 1993). The data shows that while the population density of Germany is similar to that of the UK the rate of car ownership is nearly 40 per cent higher. Moreover car ownership in Germany is six per cent higher than in the USA where population density is considerably lower. At the same time, greater investment in renewable energy together with strict environmental building codes help explain

Table 2.4   Key urban land-use indicators compared internationally

	Ecological footprint (hectares per person, 1996)	Population living in urban area (%)	Population density (people per square km, 1999)	Home ownership, 2002 (%)	Cars per 1000 population, 1999
USA	12.22	80%	30	65%	478
UK	6.29	89%	244.69	69%	373
Canada	7.66	81%	3.0	67%	459
Australia	8.49	–	3.0	69%	485
Germany	6.31	88%	234.86	43%	508
France	7.27	76%	108.09	54%	469
Sweden	7.53	84%	21.69	60%	437
Japan	5.95	–	337	61%	395

Sources: World Wildlife Fund (2000); World Bank (2002).

why the ecological footprint per person in Germany (the land it takes to produce, transport and collect waste from goods and services) is half that of the USA. Lower population densities in North America, Australia and Sweden contribute to larger ecological footprints (more on this in Chapter Six). Yet the far greater environmental burden imposed per person in the USA has to be explained as much by a culture of consumption and affluence as by a scattered population and lack of urban containment.

This feeds into the second illustration and the reason why we need to consider factors which cut across headline international differences in planning regime types. While living in Seattle for a period in spring 2000 I was struck each time I turned on the television by the words of a particular car insurance commercial. The advertisement went as follows. Peering through a pair of hands spread to form a make-shift view-finder, film director style, we see a middle class American family start their day: a car trip taking the kids to school, off to the shops, to work, to visit friends, returning to the house with gardening equipment – images of the kind of busy, mobile life and individual freedom taken for granted as the all-American dream. The voice-over to these everyday images was, 'picture your busy life and see how much you depend on your car'.

The following year there came to British television a frequently repeated advertisement for a popular family car, playing to the caption 'think before you drive'. While clearly designed to carry Mum, the kids and a couple of their school chums, this car was being promoted for discretionary use. The opening image was of a gleaming people-carrier apparently fully occupied by bobbing heads – which then pop out from behind the stationary vehicle, walking crocodile fashion, each child wearing a fluorescent safety vest over their school uniform. The viewer is told that purchase of this large family car comes with everything needed for the concerned parent to set up a Walking Bus. The children walk to school in a group along a set route picking up additional 'passengers' along the way, led by an adult 'driver' and with an adult 'conductor' bringing up the rear (www.walkingbus.com).

Of course advertisements like these present a caricature of consumer cultural difference. Americans are no more inveterate consumers than Britons are committed conservationists. That a car manufacturer can play on this concern without threatening a booming market is indicative of the way widespread car reliance reflects powerful connections between housing, employment, parenting and travel behaviour. This is despite much talk in UK planning of 'joined up government' and concern to reduce the volume of journeys travelled by private car each day. As we shall see in the following chapters, planners tend to view traffic congestion as an engineering problem rather than a consequence of changing gender relations or the product of 'time-squeeze' for working parents continually trading identities as parents, consumers and workers. An outline of the key differences between the UK and USA systems of planning in relation to housing, transport and urban containment is provided in Appendix B by way of context.

Finding the families

As a consequence of the rising number of dual-earning families the majority of children today grow up with two parents who work outside the home, some for very long hours. This research examines this trend with respect to a specific sub-population of middle class couples with children where both parents juggle earning and parenting responsibilities. Access to the target population was gained through a postal questionnaire used to refine selection of twenty households for each metropolitan area. The purpose of this method of sampling was to pick up variety in circumstance where it was constructive to do so (occupation, hours worked, age of children) while holding other variables constant (two parent families with children at home). This way the sample of one hundred households embraces a degree of variation in occupational status (from hourly paid janitors to salaried lawyers) and gender relations (couples engaged in different earning and parenting arrangements) while at the same time excluding both the most affluent and the truly disadvantaged. Consequently the research includes only a handful of Black and Asian middle class parents, though the proportion of non-white residents in the cities studied is as high as 46 per cent in the city of San Francisco and 34 per cent in Inner London (see Table 2.1). All but a handful of the households were dual-earning structures, variously combining full-time and part-time employment in different hourly paid and salaried occupations representing a cross-section of those undertaken by residents of the study neighbourhoods (see Chapter Four and Appendix C). A profile of the households interviewed by employment structure type and by neighbourhood study area is identified in Table 2.5.

A 'pilot' study was undertaken as a 'dry run' for the US component of the household research to look at both the technical and analytic aspects of qualitative data collection. This was conducted in the city of Portland in July and August 1999. Three further trips were made to the

Table 2.5 Household employment structure by city/neighbourhood

City/neighbourhood	Traditional	Flex earner	Flex career	Dual earner	Dual career	Total city
Total type	13	11	28	11	37	
London	3	4	4	1	8	20
Islington	1	1	1		1	
Hackney	1		1		4	
Barking	1	3	2	1	3	
Edinburgh	3	3	6	2	6	20
Newington	1		2		2	
Leith		1	3	2		
Craigmount	2	2	1		4	
San Francisco	3		4	4	9	20
Mission/SoMa				2	5	
Bernal Heights/ ExcelsiorAlameda/	1		3	1	2	
East Bay	2		1	1	2	
Seattle	2	2	5	4	7	20
Greenwood		1	1		5	
Kenmore	2	1	4	4	2	
Portland	2	2	9		7	20
Fremont			5		5	
Garden Home	2	2	4		2	

Notes on household structure typology:
Traditional = male spouse in full time employment, female spouse economically inactive (there are no 'role reversal' couples in the sample and fewer than five per cent in a representative population); **Flexible Earner** = male spouse in full time hourly waged employment and female spouse employed part-time; **Flexible Career** = male spouse in full time salaried employment and female spouse employed part-time (the sample does include a small minority of temporary 'role reversal' couples); **Dual Earner** = both male and female spouse employed full time in hourly waged employment; **Dual Career** = both male and female spouse employed full time in salaried professional employment (occasionally where there are 'cross-class' couples the household type is defined by the major earner, typically the male spouse).

US to conduct household research over the period 2000 to 2002. This provided scope both to live in each city for a two-month stretch and also return to each city at least twice to build up a picture of change over time. This was particularly valuable given the volatility of new economy employment captured in the selected cities; the dot-com boom and its subsequent collapse; and the impact global economic insecurity had on local employment and housing markets following the events of September 11 2001.

There are three reasons why relatively advantaged working families are the focus of study here. First, recent interest in growth in the population of two income families has tended to universalise the characteristics and experience of this group. By probing the opportunities, constraints, motives and behaviour of one sub-population, this book exposes the uneven distribution of costs to both private and public decisions. Second, it is in two income couples with children that tensions emerging at the intersections of housing consumption, labour market production and household gender relations are most pronounced. Lone parent families may be worse off materially and disadvantaged by lack of a 'second pair of hands' but they do not have to negotiate the terms of daily life with a potentially combative partner. Moreover, it is in heterosexual couples that weighty decisions are most frequently associated with heavily prescribed gender roles and power relations. Third, the ways that dual-earning households mediate change can have unintended consequences for urban structure and social cohesion. The obvious examples are with respect to residential location, school choice and travel behaviour. The solutions arrived at to satisfy competing preferences and complex co-ordination tend to undermine the assumption of more localised living implied by the new urbanism.

Notwithstanding this skew towards a white middle class nuclear family perspective, this book does not gloss over the concerns of diverse household types and minority ethnic groups. In the following chapters a panoramic view of the city is magnified through the household lens. Out of the corpus of detailed biographies and illustrative vignettes stretches an intricate web of life – with connections to workplace cultures through colleagues, informal childcare arrangements with friends and neighbours, to neighbourhood protest groups, through processes of gentrification to the lack of affordable housing for 'key workers' essential to a whole chain of urban service provision.

This way the research contributes to debates on rising inequality in two ways. First, it demonstrates that advantaged families rarely manage to combine paid and unpaid work democratically, or without significant stress (or damage to the environment). Consequently this book flags up the enormity of the problem: if balancing is hard for these families then how ever can those worse off cope? Moreover, if this inequality and lack of sustainability is a function of the 'successful' city and extreme market liberalism, are these models of 'competitiveness' really the ones to be emulated? It also highlights effects similar to those Ehrenreich and Hochschild (2003) refer to in their notion of a 'care chain' which can be global in extent. It suggests that more advantaged households tend to co-ordinate everyday complexity by offloading aspects of social reproduction onto less advantaged workers further down the chain: thus the childcare workers and shop assistants who are priced out of the local housing market are in some sense enabling those above 'to have it all' (for London see Cox 2000). Crucially, rather than explore unequal relations through social interaction at *different* points in this chain, the approach adopted here concentrates on variation at a *key intersection*. This approach is consistent for the cross-national focus on within-type extreme market liberalism, as well as a critical look at successful cities, and finally within-class variation in household coping strategies.

The 100 household interviews included individual employment biographies, maps and diaries of individual and household spheres of activity, together with narratives of the decisions made by couples concerning residential location, spatial mobility, all forms of work undertaken and networks of informal support making up daily routines. In-depth interviews, each lasting at least one hour, were conducted along similar lines to the well-established method of 'biographic' research (Wallman 1984; Campanelli and Thomas 1994; Halfacree and Boyle 1993; Jarvis 1999). Couples were interviewed together so as to engage directly with issues of spouse negotiation in the joint telling of both everyday routines and milestone events. While it was generally possible to maintain consistent interview conditions: in ten per cent of interviews the male spouse was absent for part of the interview, claiming a prior commitment. In one Portland interview it was particularly revealing to continue speaking with the female spouse alone. Once Jon Paine had left for his sporting activity Liz Paine admitted that her husband had earlier been rather too reticent in describing the way his job, which is more flexible and generally less demanding than hers, requires that he take primary responsibility for looking after their young son and attending to the evening meal during the week. She added that while he certainly does do all that he said he did 'he struggles with roles and how much he does (but) he works really hard to try to overcome that' (Liz Paine, dual career, Fremont – Portland) (pseudonyms have been given to all interviewees).

Summary

The purpose of this chapter was to identify the research approach and to explain the rationale for examining within-type rather than between-type variation. A research design was specified which combines extensive secondary data together with intensive household biographies across three scales of comparison: nation, city and household. It was argued that domestic social policy and planning regulations are inadequate as an explanation why men and women organise their working and domestic lives as and where they do. For some scholars any cross-national comparison is likely to be problematic simply because the scale of analysis is wrong. Catherine Hakim (2000) suggests for instance that studies based on headline trends over emphasise the role of national societal context in determining women's participation in paid employment and their propensity toward unpaid care-giving. Others stress that choice is not 'rational' and unconstrained but in practice shaped by 'social ties and socially negotiated moral rationalities' (Duncan 2003: 48). Thus, it is neither the state nor the individual alone but rather social and cultural ties which divide populations and steer behaviour.

In this chapter the argument that household coping strategies are embedded in local contexts of moral (cultural) and practical (environmental) constraint was demonstrated in relation to the UK and USA, two similar liberal market extremes, against a backdrop of international comparison. While the UK and USA are popularly identified within the same liberal regime type, evidence from comparative surveys of public attitudes suggests marked differences in support for government intervention in social and economic concerns. Britons tend to favour public intervention to redress economic inequalities and demonstrate a 'latent conservatism' to civil liberties, whereas Americans express hostility towards trade unions and 'big government' (Davis 1996; Jacobs 1992: 153). Moreover, the results of cross-national gender role surveys typically identify Britain as 'traditional' compared with more 'egalitarian' attitudes characteristic of US survey respondents (Crompton 1996). It is the task of the following chapters to explore this within-type variation and the unintended consequence of these local settlements.

Arguably, it is not possible to pursue an integrated approach with respect to a 'whole economy', as this project demands, purely on the basis of international comparison. This reinforces a widely held view within feminist research and cultural studies in particular that the nation state is only one of several contexts for action concerning the uptake of paid work: local labour markets, and neighbourhoods or social networks are equally influential (Duncan and Edwards 1997: 5). It is within the local milieu that notions of 'the right thing to do' are negotiated rather than there being an identifiable definition of ascribed duties for men and women 'out there' in the national psyche (Duncan 1995). We have to look at local contexts for the reason why, for instance, there are very uneven opportunities for work-life balance and selective willingness by workers in particular occupations and working environments to subscribe to family friendly initiatives.

Finally, we must not neglect cross-cutting influences based on consumer expectation, environmental awareness and the spread of new technology. For example it is questionable whether talk of 'normal' working hours is meaningful for internationally mobile knowledge workers. For this professional elite the ubiquity of portable ICT suggests a blurring of the boundaries of work and non-work which would defy working time regulation. Equally, we saw in the case of different national advertising campaigns above that travel behaviour (and the prospect of steering this toward soft modes) relates as much to local cultures and limitations as it does existing systems of transport and land use planning. Accordingly, this book fuses together two bodies of literature, those separately addressing issues of work-life reconciliation and the new urbanism. The aim is to instigate a more integrated approach to questions concerning the future of cities and the future of families.

3
Living and Working

Introduction

Party at Seattle day-care

A significant feature of 'success' defining the five featured cities is a reversal in urban population loss. The image of these cities has been altered by a rise of materialism combined with local authority place-promotion and a shift toward the public display of business and social 'networking' (Pacione 2001: 7). In London, for instance, the rapid pro-liferation of a 'cappuccino culture' was such that Mayor Ken Living-stone established a special squad to stop the encroachment of city pavements from bar tables and chairs (Burdett 2000: 68). Viewed this way it is tempting to explain the increased symbolic importance of these cities in terms of gentrification; by the replacement of working class by middle class residents and growth in city-friendly sectors of the economy such as finance, new media, culture and tourism (Graham and Guy 2002: 370–1). Indeed, for two decades social scientists have engaged in heated debates concerning the changing fortunes of selected inner city neighbourhoods (for a good overview of this see Lees 1994; 2000). Attention has variously focused on shifting gender relations and the formation of new household employment structures, the emergence of 'pioneer gentrifiers' including 'yuppies', 'dinky's' (dual incomes no kids yet) and dual career families (Rose 1989; Warde 1991); demand by city professionals to cut the cost (in time and money) of commuting to outer suburbs as well as to realise the 'rent gap' between properties occupied by working class tenants and those improved by upwardly mobile owner occupiers (Mills 1988; Smith 1996; Karsten 2003). Notwithstanding this well rehearsed debate, this chapter questions the relevance of gentrification to the complex matrix of livelihood found in the five featured cities.

Thorns (2002: 46) summarises the shifting 'logic' behind changes in residential location in terms of three epochs: the zenith of the industrial city when households worked to live with and for the family; the suburban boom when work was viewed as a route to consumer satisfaction; and the post-industrial city (typically expressed through gentrification) where work and consumption are at the centre of life. Critics point out that neither a 'work to live' or 'live to work' view adequately represents either the pre-industrial separation or post-industrial blurring of production, consumption and social reproduction. What is useful in this chronology, however, is the way it makes connections between changes noted in Chapter One in the mode of production (and, with this, household gender divisions) and the growth and status of cities. Often the transformation of the built environment hinges on a particular mode of production, occupation or consumer taste, such as with the Square Mile in the City of London in the mid 1980s and the South of the Market area in San Francisco in the mid 1990s (McDowell and Court 1994) (see also Pryke 1991; Zukin 1991; Budd and Whimster 1992). Emerging in the wake of new sectors, new jobs and new ways of working are material changes in the use, status and cultural constitution of urban space. This in turn alters the basis on which individuals and households make decisions where to live, how to meet conflicting demands upon their time and the need to move frequently between different sites of activity. It is for this reason that this chapter focuses on living *and* working, on housing *and* employment, with these connections made explicit in the case of new hybrid 'live-work' environments.

We saw in the previous chapter how, with renewed commitment to the compact, mixed-use city, urban regeneration associated with 'gentrification' might be interpreted as a material solution to work-life balance for affluent city workers (Butler and Robson 2003: 9). It is entirely logical within the new urbanism, for instance, to extend the concept of mixed-use development within individual buildings as well as streets and neighbourhoods (Rudlin and Falk 1999: 97). Buildings designed to harness tools of ICT for synchronous living and working simply update the idea, and elevate the status, of 'living over the shop' (LOTS) as an exercise of spatial rationalisation. Why waste time travelling each day from an apartment equipped with telephone and personal computer, only to sit down to work with identical equipment at a remote office site? This line of thinking, coupled with knowledge of at least one world-famous electronics business emerging from the garage of an ordinary family home,[1] explains the big attraction of hybrid live/work development schemes to city leaders in the five featured cities.

Of course just as many urban villages are so-called as a marketing device, so the definition of live/work is equally fuzzy. It is nevertheless instructive for the purpose of understanding daily life in the featured cities to unravel the connotations and contradictions behind this surge in hybrid development. This is because the rationale for constructing live/work 'shell' units, which owners or tenants can tailor to their own requirements,[2] closely resembles the demand for flexibility we are accustomed to reading about in the labour market practices of the new economy. Indeed it is evocative to place the 'planning' story of live/work spatial rationalisation alongside the 'social policy' story of work/life reconciliation. Managing two jobs or careers within a fixed household arrangement throws up similar problems to combining multiple activities in a unified space. What distinguishes the promise of both is the way they appear, through the integration implied by the hyphenation of terms, to overcome the complexity of people's daily routines. In practice we find that live/work schemes rarely achieve this assumed space-time efficiency. An obvious problem for the dual career household is that inevitably a live-work activity for one partner may be a 'live only' for the other. Mixed-use endeavours are thwarted, in part, because they fail to match the complex and fluid state of contemporary employment structures and lifestyles.

Sharon Zukin (1988) first introduced the phenomenon of 'loft living' to the gentrification debate in the late 1980s with respect to the transformation of SoHo, New York. For a long time this was considered a fairly unique coincidence of warehouse renovation and artist concentration. Now we see live/work lofts springing up in every city, built to look like industrial space if none already exists, clustered together through the designation of specific 'cultural quarters' (see for instance Scott 2000; Zukin 1995; Hall 1998; Landry 2000). Efforts to cultivate such a concentration of loft-style property are evident in Portland's Pearl district and developers in Seattle are hoping to emulate this 'positive model of an urban village' in a 380 unit live/work scheme proposed on the site of a former car dealership in Ballard (Seattle Press 2004). Elsewhere in Seattle, the Pioneer Square historic district is the focus of efforts to provide affordable 'artists housing' in retail districts through live/work schemes (Seattle City Council 2003). In London live/work developments are so heavily concentrated in the Hackney area that the local authority has adopted Supplementary Planning Guidance on the issue (Rudlin and Falk 1999: 97). Conversion of the Gainsborough Studio's on Poole Street in Hackney is a classic example which combines 200 apartments with up-market design businesses and a film studio. Elsewhere in London the philanthropic Peabody Trust has built affordable housing specifically for people in the early stages of setting up a business in the West Ferry Docklands live/work scheme (The Peabody Trust 2004). Developers of Leith Lofts claim to be 'bringing the loft concept to Edinburgh' by regenerating two listed industrial warehouses to provide 28 open-plan loft 'shells' (Leith Lofts 2004). But of all the featured cities it is in San Francisco where proliferation of this property type has had greatest social and environmental impact. Here live/work developments accounted for more than 20 per cent of dwellings built between 1994 and 1998, the vast majority concentrated in a single area South of Market Street popularly dubbed SoMa (US Census Bureau 1999). Much of this chapter therefore focuses exclusively on the way working families living in this one San Francisco district co-ordinate daily life.

This chapter begins with my own observations of urban renewal in the San Francisco South of Market area over the course of two decades. This provides the basis for identifying parallel shifts in the supply of labour and the demand for housing. The intersecting pressures of a small but influential new media sector, a culture of intense work-orientation, competition for land and a latent bohemian politics are together captured in narratives drawn from the San Francisco household biographies.

Discussion draws in particular on vignettes representing those households living in the central Mission and South of Market area (SoMa) (see Figure 2.4). Here conflict over land and lifestyle at the urban scale are coconstructed through the struggle by individuals to balance the competing demands of 'life' and 'work' at the household scale. For example, recent planning battles have been about whether this neighbourhood is commercial or residential as much as they have been about white-collar versus blue-collar interests. No single stakeholder has dominated transformation so as to completely extinguish pre-existing claims of belonging. We shall see also that dual income households carry with them attendant work-life issues in the blue collar and right through the middle classes. Related factors range from house-price inflation, the quality of public services (especially schools) through transport and congestion problems to work location, as well as aesthetic and cultural choices. Viewed holistically, households engage in a complex round of solutions to a range of problems. The net outcome is their 'perch' in the city which, given the compromises inevitably involved, tends to be both temporary and precarious.

Let's go to San Francisco

As a student living in San Francisco in 1985 I took a job working three days a week for an up-market contract furnishing business. My boss was in the classic mould of the entrepreneur who grew a successful Dun and Bradstreet-listed company out of a one-woman band. Making my way to work I was aware that this business, situated alongside other identical single-storey warehouse buildings between the port, the railroad and a major freeway intersection, occupied premises on the 'wrong side of town'. Separating this site from the nearest transit stop was a desultory parking-lot landscape. Yet, once breached, the reward was an exhilarating contemporary work-space (I recall walls of glass and sand-blasted brickwork). Our neighbours were trendy architects, oriental carpet dealers and up-market cabinet makers. Behind every non-descript exterior were displayed all the trappings of what David Brooks (2000) was later to define 'bourgeois bohemianism'. Though unaware of it at the time, I was witnessing the first phase of a redevelopment so extensive that, 15 years later, I was to find here new multi-storey buildings and basement parking for the exclusive use of penthouse loft dwellers.

It is tempting to imagine this was the start of a linear upward trend in neighbourhood status, land value and infrastructure investment. Instead the intervening period unleashed boom and bust cycles characteristic of the way, since gold-rush days, renewal of San Francisco's building stock has never quite kept pace with the rise of new product technology and the rendering of other labour market practices obsolete (Brechin 1998; Walker 1996). Hotels and lodgings built to accommodate freelance miners and dock-related itinerant workers existed in a state of neglect in the South of Market area long after maritime activity declined. The coincidence of surplus de-industrialised space and proximity to good transport links prompted artists, designers and contract furniture dealers in the early 1980s to establish inexpensive showrooms. Just as downtown office workers began to comment on the number of florists and coffee shops cropping up south of their usual stamping ground, the local economy faltered. Fears for the collapse of Bank of America, a major regional financial services employer, precipitated a deep and prolonged slump in the commercial real estate market (Walker 1996: 78). Sales of designer furniture evaporated overnight as newly built office buildings sat vacant for months on end. My boss let me and her other staff go, handed back the keys on her showroom and once again began the process of building up a business from scratch from her kitchen table at home.

Recovery of the local economy was barely underway when the city was struck by the 1989 Loma Prieta earthquake. This inflicted serious damage to infrastructure networks. Faced with an opportunity to rebuild parts of the city, including a stretch of waterfront opened up by the collapse of an unsightly elevated freeway, City leaders sought to mobilise widespread renewal. Attention not only turned to rebuilding the physical fabric of the city but also the financial and skills base. At this time San Francisco had little to compete with the powerful high-tech industrial base of neighbouring Silicon Valley. Thus it was that San Francisco's new media boom of the mid and late 1990s emerged as a direct result of figurative and economic reconstruction, as venture capitalists identified a growth sector to capitalise on the way San Francisco's cultural cosmopolitanism acted as a magnet to draw in creative talent (Walker 1998a).

The new media industry began on a small scale in the area of South Park, an oval of grass originally surrounded by town houses designed to emulate a London Square. As the industry grew, the South of Market area provided obvious scope for expansion. A city centre location boasting a heady blend of high and low culture was attractive to new media workers on whom the creative industry relied (Graham and Guy 2002). Brandishing the claim that San Francisco could only retain new media growth by significantly increasing capacity for flexible studio

Photo 3.1   San Francisco Howard and 6th – awaiting the wreckers ball

space, City planners issued special building permits allowing live/work schemes to be developed on a large number of vacant industrial sites in the area. These permits attracted lower level fees and exemption from planning restrictions requiring that ten per cent of all new dwelling units were made available on an affordable (below market) basis. The very speed with which buildings and land were appropriated under this initiative wrought palpable conflict. A number of suspected arson attacks on live/work developments were attributed to local hostility at continuing displacement ('e-viction') by upwardly mobile dot-com workers. At one former warehouse on the corner of Howard and 6th, paintings, trestles, clocks and sofas were suspended perilously from every vacant window – a graphic reminder that they were simply waiting to be pushed out by the wrecker's ball (see Photo 3.1) (see also Solnit and Schwartzenberg 2000). As a consequence of this liberal zoning the profile of this whole area changed rapidly and to such a dramatic extent that reference has been made to this as the third Gold Rush.

A cynical reading of this pro-growth planning policy is that City leaders had for a long time been looking for ways to make downtown expansion acceptable to local residents. Vigorous opposition to this pro-growth alliance took the form of street marches and public demonstrations in the run up and aftermath of the November 2000 Presidential elections. Two hotly contested local propositions hinged on the extent to which new office development, then seen as necessary to ensure San Francisco could compete with neighbouring Silicon Valley, would be permitted to encroach further on the still largely residential Mission, South of Market (SoMa) and Potrero districts. This was a passionate issue equating to far more than a proliferation of glass and steel. For some, a southward expanding central business district threatened the erosion of San Francisco's diverse artistic heritage and a homogenisation of the local art scene (Graham 2000). Proposition K represented the pro growth initiative of Mayor Willie Brown who firmly believed the way to reduce property prices was to increase supply. To make growth appear more palatable he intended to increase the density of development downtown (upward expansion) to minimise further incursions (outward expansion) in formerly residential areas. Opposing Mayor Brown was a group of 'slow growth' residents (mainly artists) who together put forward Proposition L. This would tighten planning restrictions to limit office construction in some neighbourhoods and ban it in others. By fighting a close-run contest funded largely by goodwill alone, the grassroots initiative can be said to have won a moral victory. Nevertheless, as it turned out, neither proposition passed into legislation.[3] Recession started to bite in 2001 and rising office vacancy rates once again replaced shortage as the developers' complaint.

In practice live/work developments never functioned as planned and were priced beyond the reach of the target population. The presumption in favour of mixed-use (residential with commercial) was openly abused with most functioning as up-market condominiums. Those who occupy these new units today are seldom artists, or even new media workers, or, more significantly those that work in the city (Solnit and Schwartzenberg 2000: 103).

Variations on a theme of gentrification

We see in this recent history that the term gentrification is rendered meaningless when universally applied to a myriad property types (artist colonies, new industrial, loft-living, retail and leisure) (Bondi 1991; Butler and Hamnett 1994). This reflects the way gentrification debates have been silent on the process of industrial buildings, manufacturing driven out by services, or by new media, as well as the cross-sector gentrification of residential by industrial and visa versa (see Pratt and Ball 1994). In the latest comprehensive review of the state of the art of the 'gentrification debate' Lees (2000) stresses the need to explore the complexity of gentrification. In particular, she points to topics that have been poorly researched: the relationship between first and second wave gentrification (super-gentrification), of relationships between race and class in gentrification, and the legitimation of gentrification in recent urban policy. This chapter starts to address the first and last of these to some extent.

Arguably the San Francisco South of Market (SoMa) district is one example where the language of gentrification inadequately explains the integration of social and urban transformation in recent years (Roschelle and Wright 2003: 153). The story is not simply one of invasion and succession, social polarisation or the arrival of chic coffee bars and restaurants (though these visible symbols of place-making play their part). Accompanying the progressive shift from warehouse storage to showroom display to new media and e-commerce was an unofficial invasion of derelict buildings by artists, many of them squatters, seeking large studio spaces and proximity to the bohemia of the Haight and the rainbow politics of the Castro. Consequently from the outset this 'cultural quarter' encompassed two largely incompatible visions spanning a digital divide: those of the financial savvy of the downtown and the software coding expertise from neighbouring Silicon Valley on the one hand and the struggling studio artist on the other. Certainly, a pre-existing poor community was first 'invaded' by 'artists', then by 'new media workers' and finally colonised by 'loft dwellers', but no single invasion (or vision) was absolute.

It is instructive to pick out of this organic process three rounds of renewal associated with shifting housing and labour market characteristics. Evidence of each is clearly identified from analysis of the household biographies, as summarised in Table 3.1. In the first round of renewal the traditional tensions of economic exclusion are present but complicated by rent control and the relationship of occupiers to the local labour market. More generally there is economic exclusion through rising rents, property transfer to owner occupation and private developer incursions. The Florin's, for instance, are not forced by rising rents to leave the city, but they are to some extent 'trapped' in an apartment too small for their family needs. As sitting tenants with protected rent, they pay half what they would have to pay if they vacated their apartment and moved to a bigger property, paying the 'going market rate'. Just as many welfare recipients are caught in a poverty trap, this well paid dual career couple are stalled in a housing trap – they are neither squeezed out nor permitted scope for upward mobility.

Table 3.1 Three dimensions of gentrification in San Francisco

1. Economic exclusion
'San Francisco's now become sort of like Paris in that you have to have money to be here and enjoy the amenities. Now the ring is also very rich, you have to move out to like Stockton to get the cheaper (rents)' Mr Florin

2. Successive waves of incomer 'othering'
'and now it's (overrun), everybody knows about it, it's been discovered'
Mrs Frame

'I think this is one of the last neighbourhoods to go (...) (now) there are more white people moving in who are just, you know, it's happening all over the city, more of the Yuppie types'
Mr Flynn (white and middle class).

'it was socially a more tense place to be, because of the rising rents and feeling pressed out and that, but the transition of the neighbourhood, there was resentment towards the people coming in (...) and we were perceived as being part of that, even though, you know, certainly we were in some ways, but like we had, I had been living in the Mission for a much longer time (...) I felt sometimes frustrated because I was white I would be included in that group and I really had been living, you know, I'd lived in a warehouse space in that neighbourhood and been part of that community for a while'
Mrs Flower

3. 'Gentrifiers' occupy multiple, competing positions
'one of our friends that we met in the park he's a teacher and he's like scooting over to work for some Internet teaching thing because he can't afford to pay his rent, and that's nuts, it's nuts, well it's nuts that teachers can't afford to live in San Francisco and they are actually having to give them housing subsidies so that they can be here and it certainly pisses me off that I can work in this community, be part of this community in the Bay Area for a while and I can't afford to stay here'
Mrs Flower.

Ross and Tilly Fabien exemplify the predicament of those 'crossing over' to the new economy, as freelance artists now also benefiting from dot-com employment.
Tilly: it's sad what's happening here (people being priced out)
Ross: it sucks, like the parades, 'get the dot-com's out', and now I see both sides of the fence
Tilly: now we're also dot-commers all of a sudden. It's like, oohh, dot-com scum, oh no, sshh, that's us, we are the enemy, how did that happen?
Ross: yeah, there we are, right on this fence.

Source: Authors interviews with one hundred working families across five cities

In the second round we see the effects of each wave of incomer attempting to preserve a sense of 'their' 'discovered' San Francisco neighbourhood, 'othering' subsequent incomers as outsiders and viewing all change to the built environment as destruction. Analysis of these cohort-specific incomer-identities highlights a number of contradictions. There is the question, for instance, at what point does an incomer become permanently resident? Those households moving into blue-collar neighbourhoods before the first coffee shops opened invariably distance themselves from this transformation, though as owner occupiers and sophisticated consumers they benefit from such development. Equally, households moving into the city in recent years claim to do so for the experience of ethnic and cultural diversity, while unwittingly compromising this by their arrival in large numbers. Mr and Mrs Fraser, for instance, 'like an interesting culture, a diverse culture' where they can 'walk to buy a newspaper, to go to a shop', yet within their SoMa live-work complex they are surrounded by prospering white professionals such as themselves. The activity of walking to local shops is consigned to a weekend leisure pursuit as each parent commutes daily to demanding, full-time, Silicon Valley jobs. (These competing identifications are further elaborated below.)

In the third round it is evident that residents who enter into city life according to different waves of in-migration also occupy multiple, potentially competing, positions according to their politics, work-mode, residential experience, consumption and lifestyle. Added to this are contradictions brought about by the practical difficulties associated with raising a family in an increasingly costly and congested city as well as attempting to meet both individual and group household goals. An extract from the Flower household biography illustrates this point:

> We see something that's completely different being valued, economically, by society, so it's like, I mean both of us would be more than capable of doing well in that (new economy) industry if that's what we wanted to do with our lives (...) but we've made value decisions that those aren't what we want to do and then we see our friends getting into these big companies and doing e-trade so they can pay their rent that way. Yikes, you know, it's like you either participate in this almost slutty way (or you ship out), you know, like they keep their liberal progressive values (...) but then we also have values for like good food and, you know, community, which don't always come in those same packages

A matrix of livelihood

Just as there is a tendency for all urban renewal to be explained by the catch-all process 'gentrification', so changes in the nature of employ-

ment are too readily defined by the 'new economy' and ICT development (Graham 1998). San Francisco's urban renaissance is as much
about a *fracturing* of middle class interests as it is the colonisation of
once affordable blue-collar neighbourhoods by 'yuppie' professionals.
Certainly, global competition and internet technology have changed
the nature of work, not least the length, timing and consistency of the
working 'day' (Jarvis 2002: 344–45). Consequently as Charles Jencks
observed in 1996 'the city never sleeps'. But this masks the parallel existence of many very different ways of making a living. In contrast with
the hype in recent years about 'the booming economy of bits and
bytes', new media and e-commerce actually constitutes only ten per
cent of all San Francisco jobs while tourism and hospitality account for
as much as 50 per cent (Landry 2000: 137; Mitchell 1995). Of course the
connection here is that emphasis in the new media sector on networking through social interaction has helped cultivate an affluent café
society as well as 'a new layer of the exotic and more poverty than any
other part of the Bay Area' (Walker 1996: 81). We see this complex
intersection manifest in the way countervailing notions of flexibility are
defined not only by class, race and gender but also, far more subtly, by
occupation specific modes of working. Not surprisingly, those working
to meet all-night, caffeine-driven deadlines are usually identified as
single men (Bronson 1999; Hafner and Lyon 1996; Coupland 1995).
Absent from most of these accounts are partners, children and elderly
relatives – indeed anyone for whom emotional attachment and moral
responsibility might constitute what is ruefully called a 'drag unit'
(Darrah and Freeman 2002; see also Ullman 1997). Consequently the
city is witnessing the rise of a new (persistently gendered and unequal)
occupational stratification defined by multiple intersecting modes of
work.

The cultures, ethos, tools and environments of paid work are not
only shifting but in many cases incompatible when viewed from a
household perspective. Conditions of work in San Francisco's many
new media firms would be unrecognisable to those more used to the
routines imposed by legal or financial service occupations, where variations in product cycle and identity percolate through to practices of
time-keeping, surveillance, personal communications and business
travel (Darrah et al. 2000). In all these respects household level home-
work-family reconciliation vary. At one end of the spectrum professional working parents who are asked to work long hours and travel
on business at short notice seek to out-source aspects of social reproduction through markets for emergency childcare, grocery delivery
and 'lifestyle management' concierge services. Low wage service

providers are drawn into these new markets, experiencing in turn a host of non-standard contracts and shift-work. All can experience difficulties combining jobs, 'balancing' home and work, and co-ordinating activities, locations and schedules. 'Flexibility' for one spouse or household generates fresh obstacles to co-ordination for another especially those working further down the chain of social reproduction, as discussed in Chapters Four and Five. There are geo-graphies to this pecking order. In San Francisco, a new generation of urban 'loft-dwellers' now lives, but rarely works, in the city. The clean-ers and day-care providers employed by these households, on the other hand, work in the city while travelling back each night to homes far out on the East Bay and central valley. Arguably, the ease with which partnered employees can share earning and parenting is determined in part by the viability of them combining (whether by choice or constraint) the spatial, temporal and cultural expectations attached to work in a particular place and occupation.

One way of illustrating the significant impact competing modes of work can have on dual earning household arrangements is to contrast those representing three broad economic spheres functioning in paral-lel in the city today. First to be identified are 'modern' (craft) produc-tion and personal services such as those employing printers and janitors. Second there are 'established' professional services, such as those employing lawyers, medics and teachers. Finally, there are 'new' knowledge-based and creative industries such as those employing digital artists, soft-ware coders and bio-technicians. Because of their separate historical, social and spatial constitution, each economic sphere charts a subtly different set of locations, cultures and modes of work. By way of example, lawyers, doctors, software coders and digital artists all might be driven to work very long hours, but they each do so according to quite different imperatives and with marked implications for spouse employment (Jarvis 2002). The contrasting features of each of these economies are summarised in Table 3.2 drawing on evidence from the household biographies. Complicating these broad categories are pre-existing divisions between hourly-paid workers, salaried employees, freelance workers and entrepreneurs: characteristics which further define labour market experience. Moreover, individuals within these contrasting economies occupy positions spanning public, private and voluntary sectors, each offering different conditions and rewards. Table 3.3 captures a measure of this complexity with respect to the paid work occupation combinations identified in the twenty working families interviewed in San Francisco. (Appendix C lists similar infor-

Table 3.2 Contrasting features of three modes of employment in San Francisco

---

1. Modern
'I work four ten hour shifts and then I get Friday, Saturday, Sunday off (...)
they wanted to get more production out so they run a ten hour shift during the
day, ten hours at night and then on the week-ends they do three twelve hour
shifts (...) It was their choice but it's been working out good so we only put
(son) in (day-care) four days a week and I have him on Friday's which is fun
(...) If I need the overtime (pay) I can do it'
*Mr Flynn, hourly paid printing press operator working for a large financial services
provider.*

2. Established professional
'Generally, as a new attorney, any attorney, you are required to put in 2,000
(billable) hours (a year), so that's 40 hours a week, 50 weeks a year, but you
can't possibly bill every hour you work on the job, so what that works out to is
65, 70 hours a week'
Mr Floyd, attorney.

'I've always worked short hours for a litigator and every once in a while I heard
something about 'well, he does good work but his hours are a little short', you
know (...) I probably work at least 50 hours of which 40 are billable'
Mr Florin, environmental lawyer.

'I was working in a semi-management position and I had to be there at least
9 hours, they expected 9 hours out of me every day, and with the commute it
was a 12 hour day, it was an extra 3 hours a day driving, and not only that it
meant getting up early, going to bed early'
Mr Fender, middle manager, financial services.

3. New economy
'He rolls out of bed in his pyjamas, walks to his studio, sits down at the
computer and starts working (...) (several hours later) I'll go into his studio
and he'll still be in his pyjamas, just totally immersed in the work like he's
completely focused'
*Mrs Fabien describing her husband working freelance from home as an Internet
illustrator.*

'So I was considering dong more of a (freelance job), working for a consulting
company for the biotech industry which would allow me more independence,
more flexibility, more part-time, but, I just realised it's not (possible), first of all
the idea of working from home that didn't (appeal), I need the stimulation of
working with all these people and the idea of not knowing, not getting that
regular paycheck, not having the security and having to think about the next
thing all the time, I thought that would add a lot of stress and then I just
thought, I'm going to end up working full time anyway because that's my
nature'
Mrs Fraser, biotech licensing co-ordinator.

'There's a very strong emphasis at this particular company on, you know, on
what they call 'face time', in being in, and every time my boss talks to me (...)
about all the people there, all the editorial staff and their various weaknesses

Table 3.2   Contrasting features of three modes of employment in San Francisco
– *continued*

and strengths and who he's thought about firing, you know, the thing that comes up the most often in his evaluation of the people around us is their work ethic which he defines by how hard they work, how long they work (…) but, the company is {A}.com which is a parenting site, a pretty successful one too, a lot of the people on staff, especially on the edit side are working mothers'
Mrs Florin, Internet journal editor.

'The job at {A} lasted, oh, about two years, these were relatively good jobs, these were as good as they get in the games industry, as stable as they get (…) long hours, flexible time, expecting you to work in crunch mode, what they call crunch mode, a lot, when you're working overtime, weekends, generally working long hours (…) and it would happen, it just went on for months, seven days a week, we were on a juggernaut death march where we couldn't, we knew we had a big hit, we just had to finish it, we couldn't stop'
Mr French, videogame producer.

Source: Authors interviews with one hundred working families across five cities

Table 3.3   San Francisco household spouse employment combinations, organised by ideal-type modes of employment

Economic sphere/ contract types	Working hours, work culture/mode, mobility imperatives	San Francisco case: household structures	Difficulties balancing with spouse employment and the needs of dependents
'New economy': knowledge-based, high-technology, multimedia, ICT, research and development			
1. Freelance: – 1a. contractor – 1b. home-based 2. Employee: – 2a. temp/contract – 2b. standard	Variable weekly (long) hours/business travel/ variable work-place; 'presenteeism', creative collaboration often precludes tele-working; individual workers have little control over work schedules determined by global clients and product cycle 'critical path'.	FLORIN (Dual) 4b + 2b FRENCH (Flex) 2a + 1b FRASER (Dual) 2b + 2b FABIEN (Flex) 2a + 1b FROST (Dual) 2b + 5b	Difficult to sustain two careers of this nature without significant recourse to marketised forms of social reproduction; extreme intensification; hyper-mobility.

Table 3.3   San Francisco household spouse employment combinations, organised by ideal-type modes of employment – *continued*

Economic sphere/ contract types	Working hours, work culture/mode, mobility imperatives	San Francisco case: household structures	Difficulties balancing with spouse employment and the needs of dependents
'Established professional': legal, financial, organisational and administrative service delivery			
3. Self employed: 4. Private sector: – 4a. temp/contract – 4b. standard 5. Public sector – 5a. temp/contract – 5b. standard	Routines and practices of engagement are often heavily circum- scribed by need for client contact and 'face-time'; where clients are part of the global market, sign- ificant 'out of hours', 'on-call' work might be expected – this work might invade the home via phone, fax and email. Early career development typically requires job mobility and possibly international secondment.	FENDER (Dual) 4b + 5b FORD (Dual) 4b + 4b FULLER (Flex) 6 + 4b FARMER (Dual) 5b + 5b FLOYD (Dual) 4a + 5b FOSTER (Dual) 4a + 4b FLOWER (Trad) 5a	Difficult to sustain two careers of this nature; spouse employment likely to be sacrificed if frequent job relocation required ('trailing spouse'); while a high degree of autonomy is possible, this is often circumscribed by meetings that cannot be rescheduled and business travel
'Traditional': production (craft) and personal services			
6. Self employed: 7. Private sector: – 7a. standard/ salary – 7b. hourly paid/ shift – 7c. temp/irregular 8. Public sector: – 8a. standard/ salary – 8b. hourly paid/ shift – 8c. temp/irregular	Standard/salaried contracts typically entail regular hours, relative security and generally good bene- fits (particularly in the pubic sector) but below average real wages. Hourly paid work typically entails shift-work, 'on-call'/ paid overtime.	FOX (Dual) 6 + 5b FOYLE (Dual) 8b + 5b FLYNN (Flex) 6 + 4b FRAME (Flex) 6 + 6 FRANK (Dual) 7b + 4b FIELD (Trad) 7b/c FILBERT (Trad) 7b FLAME (Dual) 6 + 8b	Real wages typically trail those of more globally integrated/ high-performance occupations; shifting male spouse hours of work can consign female spouse to low status/ part-time employment; evening and weekend work might require access to childcare out of normal hours.

Source: Authors interviews with twenty households in San Francisco

mation for the eighty households interviewed in the remaining four cities by way of comparison.) Cross-reference is made to individual spouse employment, along with reference to one of three simplified employment structure types ('Dual', 'Flex' or 'Trad') (see Table 2.5 for an explanation of each employment structure type) (see also Jarvis 2002).

Tackling the implications of particular combinations of work in dual earning structures is much like peeling the layers of an onion. Working hours and times, occupation, work-place, terms of employment, routine tasks, irregular scheduling, overnight travel and relative time-sovereignty together shape the specificity of employment (Doyle and Reeves 2001). The difficulties dual earning households experience balancing diverging, competing and shifting modes of working are summarised in the fourth column of the table. This part of the matrix indicates some of the practical constraints imposed on the 'where' and 'how' of daily life for households exposed to work in different spheres of the economy. Most households are located in the matrix according to membership of a single economic sphere such as 'established professional'. Others straddle spheres, in the manner of 'cross-class' couples (McRae 1986). Mr Flynn's hourly paid 'modern production' job as a press operator, for instance, accompanies Mrs Flynn's standard contract 'established professional' job as a high school teacher. Yet here too there is scope for influences to percolate through from the pace-setting new economy to paid work routines and practices in older industrial processes. Mr Flynn describes the difference made to his working hours and job commitment shifting from a small firm of printers, handling community art reports and music scene posters, to the in-house print facility of a multinational corporation. He felt far greater commitment to the product of the former but struggled with the shifting working hours and fluctuating income. This ambivalence toward the 'brave new world of work' (Beck 2000) echoes a common theme of the household biographies generally.

The coder, the janitor, his wife and her career

Successive rounds of renewal and efforts to combine spouse employment in potentially competing occupations pose fresh challenges for work/life reconciliation in two income households. We see evidence of this in the biographies of five working families each living as unwitting neighbours in San Francisco's Mission district. Presented though a series of vignettes, this holistic reading of the data demonstrates the closely bound nature of 'life' and 'work' in the story of San Francisco's recent transformation.

First to be introduced are Steve and Lois French who live in a modest painted stucco town house at 4010 South Street.[4] While claiming to embrace a politics of egalitarianism, Steve and Lois make very unequal contributions to household income and domestic labour. Steve is employed outside the home for anything up to 60 hours per week while Lois fits in up to 15 hours earning a small income as a freelance journalist working from home. They justify this traditional division of earning and parenting roles by highlighting Steve's commitment to long hours working in the multimedia games industry. This case reinforces the findings elsewhere in feminist research that suggest the potential for the 'new economy' to deliver greater gender equality through informality, autonomy and flexibility largely exists as an unfulfilled promise (Gill 2002; Stanworth 2000). The blurring of spatial and temporal boundaries to patterns of working (the ability to work at home or on the move at any time of day and night) *suggests* the possibility of fitting round the school run and trips to visit the doctor with a sick child. Yet this is *not* the case where in practice the working 'day' is extended rather than usefully broken up to suit the demands of routine household co-ordination (see Perrons 2003 for the UK new media picture and Perrons 1999 for the mixed blessings of flexible working in the European context).

We see clearly in the case of Steve and Lois French the way that men and women participate in the new economy and assume the mantle of flexibility differently and in ways which tend to perpetuate structural inequalities in pay, promotion and caring responsibilities. This persistent inequality is partially explained by gendered norms and expectations (such as with investments in education and choice of occupation) which pre-date family formation. So it was that Lois 'chose' to pursue a career which would adapt well to the family as a 'greedy institution' (Coser 1974), whereas Steve never questioned the centrality that his quest for 'the next big idea' in new media would take in his life. Persistent inequality can also be explained by deeply entrenched patriarchal attitudes in the work-place. Consequently, while Lois French works on her computer from home in chunks of time jealously carved out from her caring and domestic responsibilities, Steve is assumed by his employer to be 'always on', unencumbered by competing commitments on his time, to meet each ever tighter project deadline (for this mode of working in the UK high-tech industry see Henry and Massey 1995).

As an early writer of video games, Steve can trace the intensification of a work culture built on the perennial buzz of creative problem-solving to changes in technology and increased competition:

> In the early days of the game business, ten to fifteen years ago, projects only lasted six to nine months and you were done, end of the game, now they last three, four years and back then they had smaller teams. When I first started in games, one person could do a game and I did one game all by myself including the art, most of the sound, probably the music really, now games take 20, 30 people, 3, 4 years. Crunch periods have gotten, probably percentage-wise they're not any bigger so a crunch period in the old days, on a nine month game the crunch period might be two months, you know, but on a four year game a crunch period's now a year!

He describes the 'crunch mode' as being a phase when 'you're working overtime, weekends, generally just working long hours'. There is a glint of almost manic enthusiasm in Steve's eye as he describes the year of crunch mode he has just experienced.

> We were on a juggernaut death march (laughs) where we couldn't (stop). We knew we had a big hit, we just had to finish it and we didn't, we couldn't stop, we couldn't even look round and plan for how long it was really going to take because if we did that we'd probably all quit (laughs), so, yeah, it was kinda one of those things, put the blinders on (...) I was leaving at 8 every morning, well, five days a week leaving at 8, coming back, um, at the earliest at 9, often coming back after midnight (...) we would have maybe two hours off on Saturday say from 11 to 1.

While Steve sometimes works on scripts at home, the activities involved in designing a new game generally require that he attend the office every day both 'to lead his team by example' and to work on story-lines in collaboration with other designers. Both the nature of this collaborative endeavour and Steve's commitment to the creative process mean that 'he may be home late from work, very late, every night for a week' but there is also 'a frustrating randomness' to daily working hours. This reinforces the critical function Andy Pratt (2002: 40) found among a larger group of San Francisco new media workers (the vast majority of them men) of tacit and situated knowledge. This explains why, though the technology would allow him to write scripts and produce code at home, Steve is required to share his skills and work interactively. The importance of 'being there', ready to run with a solution as it emerges, even if this is at the tail-end of the day, discourages creative workers from leaving the office punctually, or in extreme events at all, for fear they will miss out on the next big idea (see for instance Reich 2001; Massey 1996). Whether real or imagined, this perception that creativity by necessity involves 'burning the midnight oil' makes few allowances for life beyond the project, far less to the daily needs of dependents.

Two blocks further up South Street I call on Paul and Irma Fox. Climbing a short flight of steps at number 5280 I step over what at first glance looks like a sack of garbage. When the sack moves I know it shelters one of the city's many rough sleepers. Yet this is not one of the Mission's 'stepover' single resident occupancy hotels (so labelled because you have to step over homeless to gain access) (Ostler 2000). This is the one-bedroom rented apartment Paul and Irma share with their son Toby who is three. Paul is a janitor who cleans local state schools as an independent contractor, working variable hours and times between the hours of 4 pm and 8 am each day. Irma works full-time (days) as programme director for a non-profit social services agency. She explains that hers is 'good career' but one which '(is) never gonna pay a lot of money'. As noted previously, many otherwise advantaged dual earning families have lost ground in recent years to the way the new economy sets the pace in the competition for accessible housing and associated neighbourhood amenities. Real wages for professionals working in the private sector, especially knowledge based high-tech, biotech, multimedia and e-commerce, where benefits include bonuses and stock options, far outstrip those for college educated professionals working in the public sector. This huge pay differential encourages a degree of adverse selection whereby those workers most attracted to the salary and perks of e-commerce, for instance, rushed to join the bandwagon in the late 1990s (as Cassie Flower observed of her friends above). It is unclear to what role adverse selection (or plain greed) played in the wave of dot-com closures following the global downturn in electronics investment at the end of 2000.[5] Either way, many jobs performed as a 'vocation' in the public sector (such as social work, caring and education) simply do not transfer easily into better paid jobs in the private sector.

Irma has considerable autonomy over the content and schedule of her work, though she often has to be 'on call' outside normal working hours. On the one hand this flexibility allowed Irma to take Toby in to work with her when he was six weeks old until he was six months old. On the other hand she would not have had to nurse an infant while at the same time fulfilling the demands of a responsible job if she had access to paid parental leave (which we know from Table 2.2 is not available to the majority of US workers). Despite maintaining two incomes and off-shifting their hours of paid work to minimise recourse to paid childcare, Paul and Irma find themselves falling behind relative to sharply rising housing costs. They feel 'squeezed out' because they 'have no choice (but) to leave the city' if they are to make room for their family. They explain that others they know moved out as they had children, mostly to the East Bay. While they have resisted pressure on them to do the same, they now talk of relocating to Sacramento:

Irma: It's sad because I love it here, it really is kind of, for me it's heartbreaking, it's not like, well yeah, let's leave, it's more like we are kind of, we are trying to make some realistic choices

Paul: the only reason we consider moving out of the city now is just because, now we're stuck for housing. Our little boy is sleeping in a closet up there and as he gets bigger, this is a one bedroom (rented apartment), you can see like straight up there that's the bedroom up there, there's the bathroom there and he's next to it in a little, what was a walk-in closet.

Irma: so we took the doors off, put up a curtain, painted it, it works for now but not that much longer.

This couple see no alternative but to move out of the city and make a fresh start elsewhere. Any prospect of a reduction in the gap between public sector incomes and the private sector housing costs appears to be a pipe dream. It is such that Mrs Fox wryly suggests that it would take 'the big earthquake and the housing market to crash' for them to remain in the city they love.

Bridging the digital, cultural divide

On a parallel street, several blocks closer downtown, are Guy and Greta Florin who live in a privately rented two bedroom Victorian apartment with their two sons. Moving to San Francisco from the East Coast as students 12 years ago, Guy and Greta each at first pursued 'established' professional careers in law and publishing, occupations which were relatively ubiquitous. Greta switched to on-line publishing six years ago and has since worked for a series of e-commerce companies. Guy's legal work, though not strictly part of the new economy, involves environmental planning concerns which are specialist to the Bay Area. Like Paul and Irma, Guy and Greta have also adapted the internal arrangement of their rented apartment to accommodate their two sons age four and two. Greta explains:

> This (apartment) is ok for the immediate future (but) it will feel too small when the boys are bigger, I mean, they're both sleeping in the living room now, you know, we've turned the small second bedroom into an office so they're sleeping in ostensibly the living room, this is ostensibly the dining room but, you know, they're still little so it's ok for (now).

Making space for an office at home contributes to this couple's ability to juggle two careers together with family life so as to co-earn and co-parent. Guy explains that the hours he currently works away from home in a downtown law firm are less than expected of him at this stage in his career. In order not to fall behind in security, pay and promotion, he 'makes up' for short days by undertaking a significant 'second shift' at home at night. He explains:

> If I have a major project or something, what happens is I end up making a huge number of photocopies at work, spending about an hour preparing to write a brief or a memo at home, the kids go to sleep, and that evening Greta does the dishes and clean up ('yeah' Greta sighs) and I get to work at 9.30 and I work until 2 or 3 (...) but I'm here, and I'm here between 5 and 9 each evening and, you know, I'm not missing dinner and bath time and the kids bed time and so on.

This narrative illustrates the closely bound nature of 'life' and 'work'. It shows how one couple organise their home space and domestic life to reflect material constraints experienced in the local housing market, institutional constraints with respect to spouse work practices (including the need to complete additional paid work from home) and moral obligations towards children and spouse. On the surface of it this is a concerted (and rare) attempt to establish a dual-earner-dual-carer arrangement. Guy suggests that (unlike Steve French) he actively resists pressure to be the last to leave the office at night though it means he brings work home with him to catch up on at night because he is still expected to undertake a set volume of business. The suggestion that Guy is still obliged by the 'macho' culture of his occupation to put in longer hours than Greta means that although both parents come home to put their sons to bed it is Greta who conducts the domestic second shift, cleaning, paying the bills and ordering groceries on-line. By contrast, the previous case suggested a degree of role reversal where Irma is better qualified and better paid than her husband. Nevertheless, as we shall see in Chapter Four, the degree of asymmetry in domestic and caring responsibilities is far greater in conventional traditional male breadwinner and dual earning households where mothers work reduced hours than it is in situations where fathers are the secondary breadwinners.

The Florin's suggest a necessary ambivalence towards the changes that have taken place in the six years they have lived in South Street. On the one hand, Greta acknowledges that her engagement in the new economy has brought significant material advantage and increased the commitment she holds to her paid career. On the other hand she highlights a frustrating treadmill effect whereby, despite improved earnings in a dual career household, a yawning gap remains with respect to opportunities to improve their housing situation. Moreover, the advantages of Internet employment are tempered by increased personal risk. Though she refuses to contemplate working with the most volatile pre-IPO[6] companies – feeling she is 'too old to do a start up' – Greta has experienced high job turnover through Internet firm failure. By accepting this level of risk the Florin's effectively tie themselves to the constraints of the long hours and intrusion of work into their home associated with Guy's more secure legal career. When the Florins' second child was born, for instance, both Guy and Greta wished to reduce their working hours. Guy recognised he had 'always worked short hours for a litigator and every once in a while heard something about "well, he does good work but his hours are a little short", because the hours (in law) are a little excessive.' He worked a minimum of 50 hours of which 40 were billable. The only way he was able to break out of this requirement was to become an hourly paid employee, a move which, as Greta explains, 'lost (him) all his benefits, all his vacation time and a considerable amount of his seniority in the workplace'. The experiment was short-lived because his job satisfaction eroded as he was 'taken off all the interesting projects'. Guy is now back working 'normal' long hours. Greta, on the other hand, has been far more successful in negotiating an upper limit to her full-time working week as well as the ability to work occasionally from home.

In a neighbouring street live Ross and Tilly Fabien. Until recently Ross and Tilly both worked full-time from home, Ross as a freelance graphic designer and Tilly as a fine art painter. Then Ross took up his first salaried position as artistic director of an Internet search engine, switching allegiance to the new economy. For Ross this move introduced a whole new routine: commuting to an East Bay office each day, participating in a 'corporate' culture and regularly travelling away from home on business. The shift from two precarious, home-based, open-ended modes of working to a combination of one fixed (though typically 'demand led') plus one flexible schedule provided this couple with scope to sustain two careers and raise a family in the city. Tilly explains that 'having one steady income' for the first time meant she was able to pursue her painting career without needing to supplement her income with 'commercial work'. It provided important financial security just as Tilly was expecting their first child.

The shift Ross has made from working as a lone freelancer at home, to close interaction with other designers in an open-plan 'shed', neatly illustrates the diverse modes of working which underpin the length, intensity, location and flexibility of the working day in San Francisco's new economy. When he worked freelance from a computer terminal at home, just like many software developers, Ross found himself so interested and absorbed and at the same time isolated that he was overtaken by a 'fugue-like' concentration. Tilly describes how working this way effectively removed him from his environment so that he was emotionally unavailable to meet a domestic crisis or practical concern:

> He would roll out of bed in his pyjama's, walk to his studio, sit down at the computer and start working (...) (several hours later) I'd go in to his studio and he'd still be in his pyjamas, just totally immersed in the work like he's completely focused.

Now, like many high status creative workers, Ross spends long hours interacting with fellow workers in a relatively unstructured and fuzzy work process deemed to incubate creative thinking. The former mode involved introspection, the latter high levels of interaction. Each mode imposes quite different constraints on Tilly's working life and the opportunities Ross has to manage his working hours, times and availability (emotionally and physically) for parenting. This resonates with English-Lueck's (2002: 51) observation that 'the presence of a networked computer at home simultaneously grants an adult the privilege of working near family, and distracts that person's attention from the people in the home environment' (p. 51).

The Fabien's offer a discretely different account of the moral and institutional constraints they experience balancing home, work, family and community. They exemplify the predicament of those 'crossing over' to the new economy, as freelance artists now also benefiting from dot-com, digital art, employment. By shifting his mode of work, Ross effectively crossed the great cultural divide which today represents 'two competing visions' of San Francisco (Redmond 2000). Yet the crossing remains incomplete. They now effectively live and work at one and the same time with a foot in both worlds. They maintain close links with their former experience of San Francisco as a world of artist colonies and political activism. Yet at the same time, engagement with the new economy has brought with it altered household arrangements and elevated status in the competition for housing and a more secure perch in the city.

Managing life away from the loft

Mark and Zoe Fraser permit access to their visitor via video intercom. Walking into their fourth floor loft space it feels as though here at last there is a strangely abundant amount of light and space. Indeed, explaining how they chose to live (but not work) in the city, Mark claims, pointing at the large windows overlooking the street: 'it's about access to San Francisco, to the physical space'. Both Mark and Zoe commute to Silicon Valley jobs, each driving for over an hour a day. They stagger their schedules to maximise their hours at work while minimising the time their three year old daughter Polly spends at day-care. Zoe leaves the loft at 6.30 am, before the others are awake. She generally misses the worst of the traffic at this time and can be at her desk by 7 am. Mark gets Polly ready for day-care and drops her off just before 8 before he drives 30 miles south to his office in Redwood City. Zoe leaves work at 4.45 pm so she can get back to San Francisco to collect her daughter by 5.30. This way Polly averages between nine and ten hours day-care. Mark usually comes home from work sometime after 7 pm.

Both parents are regularly required to fly to the East Coast on business, sometimes for several days at a stretch. It is only by virtue of their relative seniority that they are each generally able to schedule their business travel so as not to overlap time away from home overnight. Their jobs require 'a lot of interaction with the people (they) work for'. Moreover, Zoe claims that she would 'hate to work at home' in their live-work loft. They observe that few of their neighbours work from home in this particular live-work development. They openly admit to 'exploiting the loophole' in regulations providing them the opportunity to become owner-occupiers in the heart of the city, though this type of development was 'intended for (other) people' not those like themselves who buy live-work lofts simply to live in. They experience long combined hours working away from home (a total of 122 hours per week between them on average including travel). It is of little relevance to them that they both commute to Silicon Valley as it would never appeal to them to make this their home.

A common feature of both their careers has been a high (voluntary) job turnover. Zoe claims that 'three years is a long time to be in a job, in either (of our) industries (...) I've never been in a job for three years in my life'. Though they have both actively pursued career advancement through job mobility they have 'explicitly ruled out' taking a job outside the San Francisco Bay Area. Mark emphasises that: 'when we look for work, neither of us looks for jobs outside the area, basically'. Zoe emphasises strong commitment to her career and the role this plays in ruling out a disadvantageous relocation:

> I'm in the biotechnology area which is in this (geographic area), and he's in the telecommunications hi-tech area and both of (these occupations) are very good here so it's hard for us to consider moving because we need to be in a place where both of us can really pursue our careers and that rules out most places, you know, biotech is only in a few centres. Our careers are very, very important to us, it's not as if we'd move some place where the cost of living is lower and he would be able to work and I wouldn't really worry about it. It's not that I have to work, it's that I really love it so this is the best option for us.

Mark and Zoe experience the boundarylessness of the portfolio or protean worker: continually updating skills, friendships and knowledge of events to build their careers (and maintain continuous employment). For them, aspects of 'work-work' (however tenuously connected to current employment) dominate the 'rest of life' through a variety of face to face business and social encounters which generally take place outside the home. They can only achieve this lengthening of the working day because both conduct aspects of family-work while away at the office (telephoning each other to co-ordinate late meetings and childcare cover). Because the Fraser's find this blurring problematic and have chosen to exclude work-work from their home they accept a lengthening of their working 'day' as the price to be paid to retain their home in the city as a haven.

Willing workers or greedy firms?

A core concern of this book is to integrate debates concerning the growth and development of cities with those about the changing nature of work. Too often both prioritise the role of technology, viewing ICT as variously resolving problems of co-ordination or sowing the seeds of cultural destruction. At one extreme it is argued that the need for physical co-presence will be so radically reduced people will not need to travel: they will simply work from home and shop on-line. Not only does this remove points of friction from the daily time-space co-ordination prism (needing to be somewhere at a set time), it removes cars from the roads and curbs land-take for new office development. At the other extreme tools of ICT are seen to make it easier for people to co-ordinate with others while on the move so that, rather than eliminate movement, it allows more movement and activity to be packed into the working day. The suggestion is that rather than release workers from fixed imperatives, the possibilities of work are all the time and everywhere. Tools such as portable computers, e-mail, mobile phones and fax more often extend already long days by forcing additional business communication into the car and home at weekends (Jarvis et al. 2001).

Both propositions are largely mythical, perpetuated by the fact we are usually introduced to new media and high-tech workers as individuals operating in an emotional vacuum. In reality of course many find a mate and some even choose (much later than once they would have done) to raise a family. In practice remarkably few workers interviewed regularly work from home as a substitute for time spent travelling to and from a specified place of work. Many actively resist the notion of working from home even on a part-time basis. Others are precluded from doing so because of the collaborative nature of their work or demands made upon them to provide 'face time'.

In both planning and social policy circles debates about work/life balance and the design and function of cities tend to stress the dualistic nature of 'life' and 'work'. It is nevertheless interesting to note a perceptible shift in recent years from the practice of hyphenating terms (live-work and work-life) to use of the forward slash symbolic of the 'blurring' of boundaries (live/work and work/life). This traces a parallel shift in language from 'juggling' work and family to *reconciling* work with the rest of life (Gross 2001: 189). Initially the relationship was perceived as one of conflict on the basis that they are 'separate' spheres of commitment (to partner/children, to an employer, to 'the market') usually located in distinct spaces and places. Critics of this notion of separate spheres pointed out that some forms of paid work have always gone on at home just as mothers who go out to work continue to plan family meals and rush to the aid of a sick child. Household research demonstrates how fluid and unstable the spheres of home and work are, where work variously encompasses 'work-work', 'life-work' and 'family-work'. Yet it has become fashionable to associate the post-industrial city with a 'live-to-work' mentality centred on positive enjoyment of 'creative' work, busy leisure and pre-occupation with a myriad gadgets designed to enable busy workers to increase their busyness (Thorns 2002; Reeves 2001: 81/2; Brooks 2000: 203).

Critics of this view point out we are no more liberated from drudgery in the new economy than our grandparents toiled purely to make a living, never reaping satisfaction from a product well made. Debate hinges on explanations for why people appear so harried today. There are those who blame unregulated labour market competition and the 'greedy firm'. Others suggest we are a lot of 'willing workers' because we find our jobs today so much more interesting than in the past. In this respect Richard Florida (2002: 150) points to an important distinction between people complaining there is not enough time to do all they might wish to do in a day and them actually being overworked. The greedy firm thesis is perhaps best demonstrated in Juliet Schor's book 'The Overworked American'. Arlie Hochschild's book 'The Time Bind' also reinforces this argument. Schor (1992) claims that the shift towards longer working hours is explained in part by growth in the proportion of salaried workers for whom expectations of unpaid overtime (as an expression of commitment) are the norm. Steve French and Guy Florin exemplified this in the narratives above. Another explanation is the steady reduction in the hourly rate of pay following 1970s global market restructuring. To reduce costs, businesses have shed jobs and used technology, deregulation and the erosion of trade union power to require workers to do more for less. In order to maintain current living standards, these employees must now put in longer hours (typically holding multiple jobs). The argument is that for both hourly paid and salaried workers, standards of living have largely been maintained through movement away from the male breadwinner model. Economic restructuring has effectively exploited the cultural change whereby more women have entered the labour market and remained economically active during stages of their life-course such as early motherhood when domestic and childcare demands are greatest.

In contrast, the willing worker thesis is clearly evident in much of the post-industrial new economy literature, notably that by Richard Florida describing the emergence of a dominant 'creative class' and that by David Brooks (2000) describing in the case of San Francisco a class of Bourgeois Bohemians or 'BoBo's'. Here the argument is that for those in demanding and interesting (creative and knowledge industry) jobs, work is pleasurable and has such intrinsic status and identity benefits that it is not possible to differentiate work from life as two dis-crete sides of an equation to be balanced. Brooks (2000: 200) claims that in earlier industrial times people's preference for leisure and plea-sure (playtime) was greater because they were 'stuck in boring jobs'. He adds that the 'Protestant Work Ethic had been replaced by the Bobo Play Ethic, which is equally demanding'.

There is nothing new about the suggestion a 'willing worker' dispo-sition explains long working hours. Dennis Hayes (1989: 30) for instance talks about the enchantment and thrall of work for com-puter devotees in his account of the underside of the quintessential post-industrial powerhouse that is Silicon Valley. Indeed, it was in the context of the workaholic willing worker, rather than concern at the 'greedy firm', that the phrase 'work-life balance' first emerged in the mid 1980s. Initially the mythical notion of balance appeared in business magazines (such as Industry Week) in articles recognising that family and personal interests provided a healthy counterweight to professional activities without which the willing worker threat-ened to burn out or lose their creative edge. The suggestion was that workers should occasionally be prized away from their desks to engage in compulsory playtime for the good of the firm.[7]

The problem with this polarisation, where claims are *either* of greedy firms *or* willing workers, is it neglects evidence of uneven development and profound inequality. In the research presented in this chapter for a sub-population of relatively advantaged working families there is evidence of both self-exploitation and externally imposed structures of constraint (Ross 1997; Pratt 2000). The notion of a networked colony of new economy firms in San Francisco wrongly conveys the impression that material renewal and lived experience are unidirectional. In practice, a complex matrix of social worlds (Clark, 1996) underpins these contested cultural and territorial transformations. The tendency of this dualism between a firm and individual worker perspective neglects some of the most important logistical and emotional obstacles to daily life which have to be negotiated within the household – an institution which is growing increasingly complex. In addition to the trend toward long working hours, for instance, there is also evidence of more intensive parenting practices, increased consumption (which itself takes time) and busy leisure (some would say leisureless leisure) – all adding to the sense we none of us have enough time in our lives.

Summary

In San Francisco, perhaps more than anywhere else, land and housing 'anti-gentrification' movements necessarily reach beyond issues of property, class and wealth distribution. Spatial exclusion does not simply operate at the level of the neighbourhood or street but functions instead as a complex co-habitation of spaces, a co-mingling of cultures, in a semi-permanent state of competition and transformation. Those groups seeking to 'Take Back San Francisco'[8] (as a space for creative and non-profit interests) are typically white, middle class and anti-establishment – as are the dot-com 'enemy' said to have appropriated land and lifestyle values. Aside from a race or class-based invasion then, this conflict hinges more particularly on a clash of cultures associated with competing modes of work. This historically bourgeois city is witnessing a fracturing of middle class interests along lines of engagement in public, private and voluntary sectors of modern craft, established professional and new media spheres of the economy.

Increasingly, cultures of work and working time arrangements shape the possibility for working families to sustain two jobs or careers over the long run. Arguably, it now takes two good salaries to secure a perch in the city, but the commitment frequently required by these careers ultimately threatens the durability of this combination. Despite pooling two or more wages, many middle class working families are being squeezed out of accessible central city neighbourhoods. This is not to say that jobs in the new economy have a monopoly on boundaryless, insecure, portfolio or long hours working. Certainly, there are practices such as 'fugue-like' creative thinking and crunch-mode working which emerge as particular features of the new economy. Yet while some activities involve introspection, others require high levels of interaction, where water-cooler brain-storming or evenings spent socialising in bars, scribbling the solution to an engineering problem on the back of an envelope, provide vital dimensions of productivity. All this is to say that diverse modes of working underpin the length, intensity, location and flexibility of the working day. Different production imperatives cross cut myriad consumption preferences. Consequently the stories told here of land and lifestyle conflict break with existing coffee-shop coup notions of gentrification. Instead the evidence suggests that waves of construction wash over and incorporate previous rounds of labour market restructuring.

The development of live/work loft space was one response to the boom economy which in turn served to heighten the pace of transformation. We see how within the space of a dozen street blocks there exist very different local actualities to people's lives. In different ways each of the households introduced in this chapter struggle on a practical level to piece together elements of housing, employment and family life. Of course, the difficulties confronting these working families are unlikely to generate great sympathy. Many would like to have the Fraser's problems. With two good salaries, rewarded with bonuses and stock options, they are incredibly advantaged. Yet, here too, personal circumstances are relative. With a second child on the way, they would like to move to a house with a yard 'suitable for a family' but find that the next rung of the housing ladder is beyond their reach. They face what is for them a stark choice. Either they move a long way out of the city in search of affordable family housing, compromising their ability to jointly participate in paid work and parenting, or they meet the challenges of raising a family in a place geared towards the unattached professional. The point is not to suggest that such private struggles warrant public assistance. Rather, regardless how uneven the distribution of resources (such as income, assets and pairs of hands), there are no simple winners. Moreover it is easy to see how competing modes of working in dual earning structures can exacerbate inequalities *within* households, undermining efforts to achieve democratic earning and parenting arrangements.

This chapter demonstrates how transformations in the nature of work and the urban fabric are co-constituted. We consequently need to view processes of urban transformation and everyday co-ordination as an integrated whole. Masked behind the popular banner of 'gentrification' are conflicts not only between ethnic and class identities but also between business and residential, commercial and industrial interests. There is a powerful sense in which intersecting modes of work impact on the future structure, growth and cohesion of the city, at the same time that transformations of the built environment (and the politics of power, space and legitimation which regulates this) establish fresh obstacles to the reconciliation of work with the rest of life. Only through this analytic lens can we begin to grasp the complex warp and weft of advantage and disadvantage that comprises the cloth of everyday life.

4
Flexibility

Introduction

> The price of success for women at work can be high: the
> average female manager is less likely to be married and more
> likely to be childless than her male counterpart; half of all
> women managers are childless and they are twice as likely to
> have been divorced or separated as their male colleagues. The
> majority of male managers' wives are there to be supportive,
> whilst the majority of female managers are in a dual earner
> relationship if they are in one at all (Wilkinson 1994).

August 1999 I started phoning my sample of working parents to
arrange in-depth home-based interviews. Ideally this had to be when
both parents were home together and not preoccupied with food
preparation or getting young children to bed. This was a tall order.
There was barely an hour on weekday evenings after children were
asleep before exhausted parents, who had to be up anytime from 5
am, would succumb to sleep themselves. At least this was the case
where both parents worked 'normal' office hours. Others who
worked opposite shifts enjoyed only fleeting moments in each others
company. On occasions my efforts at data collection were hampered
by unexpected events. One time I arrived for a scheduled interview
only to be warned that, as Mr Snaith had just been made redundant,
now was 'not a good time to talk'. Over the course of 18 months
conducting interviews I learned of birth, death, separation, redun-
dancy and numerous unspecified 'family dramas': all testimony to
the magnitude of reconciling the demands of work with the rest of
life.

The problems of routine juggling revealed themselves in the typical response – 'I'll have to check each of our calendars'. Indeed, arriving at one interview, there on prominent display on the kitchen wall were a series of carefully colour-coded charts identifying days and times of the week when each family member had places to be and tasks to perform. Sharp time-management of the sort I encountered would be the envy of any multinational corporation. Of course I noticed this correspondence between domestic and business practice precisely because the realms of home and work overlap to such an extent today. Scholars in the USA pejoratively attribute this blurring to the 'workification' of life (English-Lueck 2002). The blurring of home and work occurs in the way aspects of 'home-work' can be managed simultaneously with 'work-work' by time-sovereign professionals who have access to the Internet (Doyle and Reeves 2001). Some working parents pay bills, purchase gifts, and order groceries on-line from the office over lunch. Moreover, those who choose a day-care facility with a web-cam installed can monitor the quality of care and stimulus their child receives each day while they are at work (Parent Watch 2004). At the same time, a blurring of the boundaries is caused by the expansion of paid work and the way business responsibilities breach the sanctuary of the home via ubiquitous tools of ICT. It is estimated that in the USA 43 per cent of employees regularly commit to unpaid overtime (Casey et al. 1997: 20). Much of this is work performed on a personal computer at home as a 'second shift' at night, as we saw in the case of Guy Florin in the previous chapter. Unpaid overtime also stems from facets of professional employment which do not conform to a '9 to 5' model of the working 'day'. Arguably, it is not the contracted 35 to 40 hour full-time working week which many professional women find irreconcilable with family life. It is instead the expectation that they attend additional functions out of hours and travel away from home on business when regular childcare is unavailable. If a partner or parent is not available, waiting in the wings to pick up out of hours childcare, the likelihood is that future prospects for pay and promotion will have to be sacrificed to reduced status 'mother-friendly' employment. The practical realities of extreme cultures of work and expectations of hyper-mobility go some way toward explaining the failure of a dual-earner-dual-carer model. Something has to give way under these pressures and it is typically gender democracy.

This chapter compares household solutions to everyday co-ordination across the UK and US samples. It considers whether variation is determined by particular state-market-family arrangements – modifications to extreme market liberalism; or associated with the working conditions of specific occupations or sectors; or quite simply the result of uneven access to income, housing, and neighbourhood advantage. The emphasis placed on everyday co-ordination distinguishes this project from the existing social policy perspective where scope is limited to working hours and childcare provision. A more holistic approach flags up two neglected dimensions of flexibility in work/life reconciliation which this chapter sets out to address. First, it highlights the way earning, parenting and childcare preferences intersect with housing history and consumption practice. Second, it demonstrates the importance of asking the question 'flexibility for whom?' from a household perspective rather than with respect to the individual, industry or firm. It is only from a household perspective that we learn with what degree of stress the terms and conditions of specific occupations, working hours and contract types *combine* for partnered employees in dual earning households (Jarvis 2002). These two theoretical developments are expressed in relation to five household meta-narrative types. On the basis of this analysis it is possible to identify a number of cross-national differences in household solutions to everyday co-ordination as well as characteristics which are common to particular household groupings on the basis of lifestyle and resource entitlement.

Flexibility for whom?

Whether 'flexibility' is institutionally imposed or personally realised is a moot point. For example, the advent of 24 hour shopping is a boon for the professional working mother who works 'normal' office hours but less rewarding for the low wage mother employed to stack shelves through the night. The key question here of course is choice: the extent to which non-standard working hours aggravate co-ordination problems (through lack of childcare options starting very early in the morning or ending late at night for instance) or allow partnered employees who wish to care for their children at home to do so by working opposite shifts. As we see in the biographies, parents rarely have a lot of choice over the hours, terms, and conditions of their own, or their partner's, employment. This way the evidence presented in this chapter builds on existing criticism of both highly individualistic models of decision-making and structurally determined accounts of household employment structure. Instead it is argued that preferences are fluid and as such need to be viewed biographically and in relation to the unequal distribution of household resources and assets. While the cultural constitution of earning and parenting behaviour is well articulated in the feminist literature, the *infrastructural* logic of this –

that defined by material, institutional and moral capabilities in Chapter One, remains underdeveloped.

Flexibility is the watchword for parents to be able to cope with unexpected events. This is because care-work is rarely seamless (whether for young, elderly or disabled family members); instead it involves a 'privately arranged hotchpotch' of care (Smithers 1998). Local time-use innovations and ICT can help reduce scheduling difficulties. The extension of shop opening hours including 24 hour grocery shopping, improved on-line shopping services, introduction of breakfast and after-school clubs as well as childcare for shift-workers, for instance, go some way towards improving the flexibility working parents have to meet multiple, competing responsibilities. Nevertheless it can be argued that too much emphasis on the role of time and technology results in a narrow understanding of flexibility. Focusing on working hours and time alone fails to address unequal household resource distribution (lack of transport, lack of kin support, poor local public services). Neither does it account for the way individuals absorb workplace cultures which then percolate through the physical placement of individuals in households and social networks which also serve as conduits of lifestyle affirmation.

Previously it was stressed that flexibility for partnered employees in dual earning households depends on the partner (their willingness to resist extreme cultures of work) as much as on family-friendly initiatives per se. Arguably, a democratic dual-carer model of dual earning is unlikely if both parents work long and variable hours. There is limited flexibility in this employment structure to accommodate unexpected events. As one Edinburgh father observes: 'stressful things are the things you can't predict like illnesses and having to travel away, where you have to change the routine' (Mr Eaton, dual career, Edinburgh – Craigmount).

Adopting a household approach to flexibility, this chapter considers the integral role of unequal resources and assets, the consumer treadmill, informal networks of reciprocity and local urban context. The analysis flags up cross-national differences. It shows that flexible employment typically equates with reduced working hours for women in the UK. By contrast the US business case for flexibility rests with new markets for childcare and personal services. Each form reproduces a different structure of inequality. In the UK there is a tendency for family-friendly policies to be interpreted on the ground as 'mother-friendly' and for these to deliver part-time contracts for women with reduced pay and status (Brewer 2000). This reinforces traditional gender divisions and unequal

access to life-chances. One consequence is a well established feminisation of poverty in old age. Far more UK working women work part-time
than their US counterparts at all stages of the life-course. On average
24 per cent of childless working women in Britain work part-time
(including those planning a family and those whose children have
grown up and left home). That rate nearly doubles to 44 per cent with
one child and rises to a remarkable 65 per cent for those with two or
more children. By contrast in the USA, just 9 per cent of childless
working women work part-time while 15 per cent of those with one
child and 24 per cent of those with two or more children work part-time
(OECD 2003). This difference persists despite a similar restructuring of
the labour market and house price to income ratio's typically requiring
two earners for a mortgage in dynamic cities (as discussed in more detail
in Chapter Five).

Equally, the extent to which the US approach to work/life reconciliation relies on private market solutions is neither fair nor efficient. The
high degree of market penetration is apparent from a cursory look at
entries in the telephone business directory (yellow pages) for day-care,
childminders, nurseries and pre-schools. There are not only many
more entries under each of these headings in San Francisco, Seattle and
Portland compared with London and Edinburgh but the services
offered are far more extensive. Private day-care providers routinely
advertise 'before and after school transportation', '24 hour day care
and transportation – newborn to five years', 'day and night care', 'easy
freeway access' and there are facilities staffed by registered nurses for
the care of mildly ill or infectious children. High levels of market provision ensure that the 'patch-work' of activities and schedules making
up a typical day are stitched together in a more seamless whole for
affluent US families. Mr and Mrs Slocum, for instance, rely on a
national childcare franchise to take their daughter to and from school
by mini-bus and entertain her on purpose-built premises out of school
hours. In the UK it is more usual to find day-nurseries open from '8 am
to 6 pm' with very few advertising transport, sick-child or overnight
provision. Of course the high cost and shortage of these elite services
leaves the majority of US families at the mercy of the same ad hoc
informal solutions familiar to UK parents. More importantly perhaps,
many parents resist the idea that novel concierge markets can, or
should, make it possible for them to continue working through any
number of domestic crises – such as when their child is sick or
unhappy at school. This point is picked up again with respect to the
career egalitarian household type below.

However conceived, what normally passes for 'flexibility' in employment practice is no match for the complex reality of everyday co-ordination in dual earning households. From the household research we learn that it is typically female spouse employment which must be squeezed into day-care opening hours or sacrificed to the needs of a sick child. More equal arrangements are evident in US dual earning structures but here too, in those households with fathers working very long, irregular or shifting hours, mothers typically limit the hours they work and avoid promotions which might inhibit their ability to leave work on time each day on a regular basis. Moreover, the 'scheduling work' mothers routinely undertake has grown in scale and complexity to take account of both family members and service providers. As Mrs Strong admits:

> If you plan it right you can work it (the hours) to your advantage, you can try to get the meeting rescheduled, arrange for the person who wants to meet you at 7am, you know, that kind of thing, but I've found that takes a lot of forethought, a lot of energy.

Where more democratic arrangements exist in US dual earning couples, they can simply amount to the practice of dipping by turns into paid vacation and sick leave rather than a strong belief in shared parental responsibility. This suggests a shift towards equal access to male-stream careers, as a function of equal opportunities labour laws, rather than a cultural shift in parenting norms and behind the scenes gender role expectations. Even in affluent dual career households where working mothers no longer perform routine childcare and domestic tasks themselves, they rather than their spouse invariably take responsibility for co-ordinating the work of others.

Preference, biography, entitlement

Preferences are not limitless in the manner of a 'wish list'. Instead they cohere in socially viable and pragmatic combinations in relation to specific cultural settings (Kuran 1991; Wildavsky 1987). In the household setting, intimacy and repetition create a high degree of stability (whereby each spouse might anticipate each others view or action in a given situation). Yet preferences remain subject to change, shifts and modification (Hertz 1986). Individual preferences evolve because they are interdependently linked with those of others – the 'linked lives' to which Bailey et al. (2004) allude in the context of migration decisions. Preference formation and decision-making draws on imperfect information which is selectively processed. Specific examples of this 'dissonance' are introduced with respect to travel behaviour in Chapter Six (see also Sen 1993). In effect, the households are 'cognitive misers' who use past experience and cultural or normative 'cues' to economise on their need to process new information in making choices and decisions (Meeker 1971). Nevertheless the biographies also reveal evidence of new challenges to this efficiency (such as in the conversations Sally Philpott has been having with her friends below). Noting a shift towards intensive parenting, for instance, Diane Richardson (1993) argues that parents have now acquired an additional responsibility, namely the intellectual development of their children. This typically works through the choice of school and extra curricular activities which will provide 'the right opportunities' (bright and motivated children and parents and teachers who value education) rather than direct tuition, though data on home-schooling for the USA shows that this too is on the increase (Lyman 1998). This highlights the added burden of time and effort imposed by extreme market liberalism and a system of wellbeing which emphasises self-reliance and self-help in gaining accessing to healthcare, education and security in old age. Middle class families in particular feel they can no longer take for granted that their neighbourhood school is right for their child and instead will anguish at length over information from a number of different sources (on the question of middle class 'consumption' of education in the UK see Allatt 1996). The sheer volume of information processed in this climate is much greater (taking up more time and energy) though as we shall see it is no less selectively processed.

By asking how far shared parenting and democratic household arrangements are limited by free choice (willing workers, born housewives) or structures of constraint (greedy firms, absent fathers), this analysis contributes to theoretical debates seeking to explain preference formation and the supply of women's labour. Some scholars argue from a human capital perspective that women part-timers are by nature different from women full-timers because they invest in family-oriented rather than work-oriented capabilities (Hakim 1991; 1996). This approach reflects a popular thesis of 'individualisation' in an age of sovereignty – of time, information and consumer choice (Beck and Beck-Gernsheim 2002). Others suggest that this polarisation of status is peculiar to Britain where increasing numbers of partnered women take up part-time employment because they experience a squeeze on their time from husbands working longer full-time hours (Bosch 2004: 623).

In Denmark, by contrast, men have reduced their full-time hours alongside extended part-time hours for women. The result is a convergence which has helped to change the family division of labour (Bosch 2004: 622). In feminist scholarship the notion that men and women make choices concerning employment and parenting as free agents is firmly rejected. Instead the influence of tradition or habit, cultural norms and unequal gendered power relations are emphasised. As Ferber and Nelson (1993: 6) observe, choices are made in situations 'fraught with issues of dependence, interdependence, tradition and power'.

It is constructive to critically examine why Catherine Hakim (2000) rejects the structural argument that particular welfare regimes influence women's labour force participation cross-nationally. According to her 'work-lifestyle preference theory' women who maintain continuous full-time employment do so because they are as committed to the world of work as men and quite exceptional in this respect. The majority of women are primarily committed to family and this explains their location in low paid occupations, supplementing household income. A third type variously shifts between full-time and part-time employment as 'adapters' or 'drifters' (for a competing analysis of part-time female employee labour market orientation see Walsh 1999). Superficially, recognition of a typology of female labour force supply improves on structural welfare regime models which have difficulty explaining within-country variation in women's employment. Yet this understanding of lifestyle preference poorly reflects the fluid and complex narratives discussed below. It assumes that women 'naturally' have a choice whether to work or not whereas men do not because 'there are no major constraints limiting choice or forcing choice in particular directions' (Hakim 2000: 18; cited in Duncan 2005). This notion of lifestyle preference lacks any sense of contextual constraint (McRae 2003; Duncan 2005). It would suppose that women in the USA are unaffected by the absence of a system of paid parental leave and if instead they had access to the six months of paid maternity leave new mothers in the UK are entitled to it would have no impact on their behaviour.

Feminist critics point out that heterogeneity can be better explained by the way identities are socially and geographically constructed (Duncan 2005). This critique is extended through the five household meta-narratives below. While earning and parenting behaviour are usually scrutinised on the basis of female spouse work-histories alone, this project pays close attention to combined housing and labour market biographies. This is an important difference to stress. Usually, male employment is taken to be a constant while female employment is the variable of interest. Simon Duncan makes this point in his definitive UK geography of patriarchy when he declares men's employment to be conceptually uninteresting because few pursue other than continuous full-time employment (Duncan 1991a: 423). It is true that few fathers in the sample are employed part-time or engaged in more than temporary role reversal. Yet the narratives suggest considerable variation in men's *commitment* to employment and fatherhood. We learn that some father's *resist the treadmill* of long working hours specifically to prioritise parenting and family time. Moreover women's attachment to paid work can change quite dramatically as a result of external shocks, such as in the wake of debilitating fertility treatment or a traumatic birth. Seven of the families interviewed had the best laid plans for a 'normal' period of maternity leave severely disrupted by unexpected problems: premature birth, birth defects requiring surgery, and limiting long-term sickness. Mrs Easington, for instance, describes in her biography how commitment to her career was transformed by the experience of a stillbirth. When she went on to deliver two healthy daughters she did not question her instinct to reduce her hours of employment. Likewise Mr Easington demonstrates strong resistance to the 'macho' culture of long hours typical of the civil engineering environment in which he works.

We know from UK and USA labour force surveys that while dual earning couples are the new norm only a minority (10–20%) represent the dual career type most likely to feature equal career salience. A similar size minority represent households with both parents working full-time, but in less skilled, sometimes poorly paid jobs. By far the majority, especially in the UK, are one and a half income couples practising asymmetric parenting. This profile is confirmed by the household analysis – but it is also complicated by evidence of far greater heterogeneity than would otherwise be imputed from secondary data (see also Ferri and Smith 1996). While superficially the household share identified as *career egalitarian* (14 per cent of dual earning couples interviewed) corresponds with the 10–30 per cent of women British sociologist Catherine Hakim defines as work-centred career planners (a category widely associated with non-childbearing behaviour), the narrative findings dispel any straightforward correlation between employment status and childcare provision. Likewise the 37 per cent of households characterised as following the *path of least resistance* do not correspond with either the 20 per cent of women

Hakim identifies as home-centred, or the 60 per cent of women she labels 'drifters' or 'adaptive' who combine paid work with strong commitment to motherhood (Hakim 2000: 158).

In sharp contrast to the strong individualism and assumed rational choice Catherine Hakim employs to explain lifestyle preference above, most mothers and many fathers in this research suggest an uneasy ambivalence towards their earning and parenting roles. This further demonstrates the fluid and contradictory nature of preference formation. For Mrs Eider 'there was always an assumption' that she would go back to work 'because we were both working on that basis' while Mr Shearer claims that being a teacher is a major source of his wife's identity – her 'whole life' and it is he who has reduced his commitment to a 'career'. Alongside similar statements, Mrs Fraser's suggests her career commitment is conditional and contingent despite maintaining on paper an uninterrupted work history. She explains:

> In order to make this work (having a career, being a working parent) you have to be really happy because you have to put in a lot of energy and you have to be really positive and if something happens in your career where things are not going well with the job and its not satisfying then the whole thing kind of falls apart because you just don't have the energy to do the things you need to do, you're not as happy as you need to be to keep it all together, not as motivated (Mrs Fraser, dual career).

Similarly, while Sam and Sally Philpott share a history of strong and equal career commitment, Sally suggests that she is more drawn to the role of a stay at home mother as her children get older. She explains this change in attitude with respect to the way the task of parenting has shifted from that of physical caring to mentoring. She admits that she 'wasn't into the baby thing. I never in a million years thought about quitting my job or scaling down'. But now that her children are older and capable of 'mature discussion' she feels a stronger inclination to be actively involved in their day-to-day lives. She is considering cutting back her hours so she can 'be off by 3 o'clock to pick up (her daughters) from school'. From articles she has read and discussions she has had with other mothers she has gained the belief that '(the hours of) 3 to 6 (pm) are very experimental times for young teens'. She consequently has 'much more desire to be home with them now in the teenage years' and has been saying to her husband 'we're selling this house, we are going to scale down and I'm not going to worry about making a home payment and I'm going to be picking up my kids each day when they get off school'.

Examples such as this, repeated across the sample, demonstrate the way moral choices are locally embedded: not only culturally constituted in relation to local middle class norms, but bound up in networks of everyday practice. We see this clearly in the biography of Mr and Mrs Smith, a quintessential *resist the treadmill* dual career couple. It is Mrs Smith's personal preference only to have her children cared for by a family member. This is a value which she shares with her parents who live close by. Mr Smith emphasises that he does not hold strong views on childcare but he defers to his wife and her family because they are prepared to put into practice what they believe in:

> Her family is in a similar mind-set – it's her family that does the childcare. My family are not as close and my parents are much more career-minded so they are not really available.

It is Mrs Smith's family that are willing to provide childcare so their values are revealed (or realised). In this example we see the meshing together of preference, biography and entitlement. It is not sufficient to explain this integrated household strategy (of simplicity, co-parenting and extended family care) on the basis of a moral choice or a fixed preference. What emerges in practice also functions through the access this household has to particular resources (transport, personnel, local knowledge). In effect this echoes what Pierre Bourdieu calls 'the logic of the situation' – whereby preferences are constituted in relation to that which is possible (Bourdieu 1977: 73–74, see also Bourdieu 1990).

Understanding flexibility from a household perspective

Some indication of the long hours many parents work today is apparent in data presented for the sample of working families in Table 4.1. In all five cities, working father's average more than 40 hours per week and working mothers typically exceed this normalised full-time threshold too. These averages mask significant variation whereby some parents on full-time contracts work as few as 32 hours a week while others routinely work 60 hours or more. Taking journey to work time into account, assuming a five day week, working fathers average 47–51 hours while mothers employed full-time average 43–46 hours a week away from home. Six fathers officially work 'part-time', though four explain that the long hours

Table 4.1 Usual hours in paid employment for working parents interviewed in five cities

Usual hours in paid work per week	London	Edinburgh	San Francisco	Seattle	Portland
Male spouse:					
Full time	45[1] (n=18)	43 (n = 19)	43 (n = 18)	42 (n = 19)	47.5 (n=20)
Part time	35 (n=2)	20 (n=1)	25 (n = 2)	30 (n = 1)	
Female spouse[2]**:**					
Full time	40.3 (n=9)	40.1 (n=8)	41.2 (n=13)	39 (n=11)	41.2 (n=7)
Part time	20 (n=8)	21.5 (n=9)	13 (n=4)	23 (n=7)	19 (n=11)

Notes:
[1] Mean values (followed by sample size)
[2] female spouse samples do not add up to 20 per city because the population of working families surveyed included a small number of women who are economically inactive.
Source: Authors interviews with one hundred working family households across five cities

they put in at the office bear no relation to those they are contracted to work. They variously work longer hours than contracted as a consequence of their work-orientation or in anticipation of securing full-time status in the future. By contrast mothers working part-time, notably those in the UK sample, typically do so to accommodate parenting and domestic responsibilities.

Of course this survey data tells us nothing about the imperatives driving parents to put in additional hours at work (see Jarvis 2002). In the previous chapter we saw how different cultures and modes of working help differentiate the 35 hours a week employee from the 60-plus 'workaholic'. A detailed breakdown of all the spouse labour market combinations (Appendix C) shows that in just over half of the dual earning families parents are engaged in the same industrial sphere as one another. Yet within this common arrangement, private sector, *demand-led* employed fathers are frequently partnered with public sector employed mothers and, in Britain, with mothers undertaking low status, part-time (school hours) employment. When we focus attention on *how* partnered men and women co-ordinate everyday life, a range of coping rationalities emerge. Structures of constraint in local housing and labour markets are always present in these biographies but so too are preferences concerning family and friends, moral and political values, consumption and social status. Although in this sense the biographies are idiosyncratic, it is possible to identify five meta-narratives as representative of sub-sets of all one hundred households interviewed. These groupings reveal themselves in the way each household co-ordinates daily life. Pseudonyms are applied to all household interviewees and all identifying features are removed to preserve anonymity. To help locate each household in relation to the city/state in which they live the pseudonyms follow a system of coding: those starting with an 'F' represent San Francisco households; 'S' for Seattle; 'P' for Portland; 'L' for London and 'E' for Edinburgh.

Career egalitarian

At one extreme there are dual career households with both parents working full-time, often commuting long distances and travelling away from home periodically on business. Referred to here as *career egalitarian* households, the one shared goal is to maintain two equal careers, regardless how they compare in terms of pay and status. Typical of this group is Mrs Fraser's claim: 'our careers are very, very important to us: it's not that I have to work, it's that I really love it'. Of the households interviewed, fourteen display *career egalitarian* characteristics, all comprising the dual career employment structure, representing one in three dual career households overall. The characteristics of this type are most pronounced where both parents are employed in project-oriented creative or knowledge industries. They are also rather more evident among US than UK couples. As suggested in Chapter Two, one reason why women in the US tend to work full-time after maternity leave is the lack of social protection. Scott and Dunscombe (1992: 38) point out that healthcare insurance in the USA is costly and generally only available to full-time workers (Scott and Dunscombe 1992: 38). Equally, the local transmission of gender roles and parenting standards can be said to exert a powerful cultural influence on a mother's decision to reduce her hours or drop out of paid employment in the UK. In this way mothers who take up full-time employment can experience castigation for not 'being there' for their children (Pfau-Effinger 1998). Arguably, whether household earning behaviour is influenced by fiscal, economic or socio-cultural factors, there exists distinct variation in childcare practices by race, class, occupation and region (Sainsbury 1994).

Career egalitarian households are most likely to find themselves geographically removed from extended family and consequently rely heavily on private markets for childcare, home improvement and domestic help. Yet individual employees in this group are not the most mobile, neither do they work extremely long hours but, from a household perspective, they do exhibit the longest *combined* hours working away from home. This relative lack of mobility stems from the fact that family life has been established on the basis of mutual career salience. It is taken for granted that neither spouse will threaten this symmetry by chasing promotion which would require relocation or excessive business travel. Most *career egalitarian's* identify with a 'hub' metropolitan labour market because making this a permanent home allows each partner scope for job mobility without ever having to confront the thorny subject of whose career is primary (Jarvis 1999a: 231). As Mrs Fraser observes 'it's hard for us to consider moving because we need to be in a place where both of us can pursue our careers and that rules out most (other) places'. By maintaining two good incomes, these households are materially among the most advantaged of all the working families, but when it comes to unexpected domestic crises they can feel stranded. Migration has removed them from kin who might otherwise have provided emergency childcare and, spending little time at home, their social contacts tend to comprise full-time workers like themselves rather than neighbours who might be at home during the day. Dual career couples consequently find it difficult to participate in an informal economy of favours. Instead they must cope within the dyad.

One in four *career egalitarian* household employs a day-nanny while the majority take their pre-school children to the home of a registered childminder or a private day-care facility. Parents employing a nanny in their own home benefit from a relatively straightforward exit to work each day. They are saved the frantic rush to get their children up and out the door on time, whisking away sleepy children still in their pyjamas, consuming breakfast on the way, sharing in the stop-go stress of grid-locked roads or the coughing crowd of the commuter train. But securing the exclusive services of a live-in or day-nanny is the most expensive form of childcare provision and not without the worry of this arrangement falling apart at short notice. The biographies suggest that working parents consider a nanny affordable (or indeed 'essential') only in the London and San Francisco samples. The Fraser's have twice employed a nanny for one year for each of their two children before switching to a private day-nursery. The couple explain their choice of childcare in terms of the benefits of home-based help for an infant who is prone to sickness and not yet adjusted to a strict daily routine. For the older toddler their preference is for more structure and educational content than home-based care provides. Mr and Mrs Lord have stuck with home-based care for their school age children because of the convenience of this arrangement. By continuing to employ a nanny while their children are at school they are guaranteed their children will have clean clothes and tidy bedrooms as well as someone to care for them if they are taken ill. By also catering for the children's after-school activities, Mr and Mrs Lord are saved the complicated negotiations other parents routinely encounter, identifying on a daily basis which parent is best placed to leave work early. Mrs Lord stresses that for her it was crucial to find a solution to the extra-curricular activities and work-load this entails – organising costumes and uniforms, party gifts and sports kit. This hints at the emergence noted elsewhere of a new servant class fulfiling the role of 'substitute wife' (Cox and Watt 2002).

Managing domestic crises within a dual career structure requires both partners have considerable autonomy over their working life. Genuinely democratic household arrangements are rare *precisely* because many occupations and sectors simply do not allow the level of autonomy required to achieve this give-and-take. As we know from the previous chapter, cultures of work (and options for flexible employment which do not involve demotion) largely determine individual capacity to cope with disruption to daily routines. Those parents like Mr and Mrs Locke who own their own business are in a rather unique position by the scope they have to take a sick child into the office with them and even use their staff for emergency care-giving. Mrs Locke explains how she plugged a gap in a school run arrangement by asking her office junior to 'become nanny for two afternoons a week'. Another time when their children attended a school close to the office, if neither parent could get away from a meeting they 'would ask one of the female staff to just nip out and go pick them up – it would be half an hour of their time'. Mr Locke admits that 'if we were in proper jobs, as employees, however senior we were, it would be very difficult to do what we do'. He goes on to suggest they have cultivated for themselves a very convenient lifestyle by virtue of the fact that they 'have complete control'. Elsewhere employees like Mrs Shearer have to 'get creative and figure out other ways of (ensuring seamless childcare)' where family and work commitments collide. This patchwork of care is considered in more detail below with respect to the challenge of 'minding the gaps' in social reproduction work.

Career Egalitarian households are the most likely to make regular use of paid childcare, employ a home help or cleaning service and shop for groceries on the Internet. They are party to the burgeoning growth of such novel concierge services as dog-walking (see Photo 4.1), and chil-

Photo 4.1   Novel concierge services – San Francisco 'doggie day-care'

dren's party planning. Yet when it comes to family well-being parents identify strict limits to market substitutes. First choice for non-routine childcare cover remains that of one or other parent. Mrs Scully explains that while her Seattle public sector employer pays for access to the Tender Loving Care sick children's day-care facility, most times if her son is really ill she would stay home with him because she would be 'just too worried' to hand over responsibility to anyone else. The TLC service addresses the perennial problem working parents face when their regular day-care provider excludes a mildly ill or infectious child. Many working parents would welcome access to a childcare facility open 6.30 am to 5.30 pm, staffed by registered nurses, paid for as a recognised benefit by their employer. Yet while this perk is welcome and innovative it does emphasise that in the USA flexibility is above all else about improving productivity. From the employers perspective the aim of family-friendly initiatives is to militate against time lost from key employees to domestic conflicts. In contrast most parents seek the choice *not* to have to be there at work but instead to be allowed time off without penalty when their family needs them. The choices available to working parents in the US differ markedly to those routinely offered in social democratic regimes where mothers and fathers are equally entitled to take paid leave for sick dependents. In the Scandinavian countries generous family leave entitlements are designed to protect working parents from excessive work/life conflicts on the grounds that this sustains the universal worker over the long term. Arguably the US and the UK calculate the costs of work/life reconciliation far more narrowly and over the short term.

Resist the treadmill

At the other extreme, a very small number of households actively resist what they view as the 'treadmill' of working long hours and the compulsion to organise family life to maximum time-efficiency. Here the dominant narrative is to seek 'a more family oriented, gentle paced life' (Mr Ellis). A politics of shared parenting is emphasised through reduced earning by both parents. What is most notable in the context of academic discourse concerning the dual-earner-dual-carer model is how few working parents achieve this ideal, whether by accident or design. Just six working families (6%) achieve an egalitarian division of labour by opting for a 'slower pace of life'. The small size of this group suggests that it is not enough to *idealise* a slower pace of life. This strategy also requires that dominant cultural norms associated with being always present at work and 'keeping up with the Jones') are strongly resisted. This might explain why little evidence of this narrative type was found in either London or San Francisco. Here it is likely that extreme cultures of work and conspicuous consumption are harder to resist. Though speculative on the basis of the small samples interviewed, this appears to reinforce the notion that some regions function as an 'escalator' for the enhancement of social and economic upward mobility (Fielding 1991: 3). Those professionals migrating to the escalator region do so specifically to benefit from dynamic upward mobility (by chasing promotion prospects and looking to take out a large mortgage) rather than to resist these pressures from the perspective of alternative values.

For *resist the treadmill* households, long working hours are ruled out by a conscious decision to consume less (especially in terms of housing) and to live 'against the grain' of locally established material norms. Closely associated with efforts to curb the 'workification' of life is strong belief in restricting childcare to the family circle. This is illustrated in the case of Mr and Mrs Sargent who both work reduced hours so that they can share responsibility for parenting, working opposite shifts. Mrs Sargent (a nurse) works two nights a week on a rotating schedule (Friday and Saturday one week, Wednesday and Thursday the next) and Mr Sargent looks after the children the days when Mrs Sargent is sleeping. In this arrangement Mr Sargent (a physiotherapist) averages 34 hours a week serving two separate part-time contracts while Mrs Sargent averages 16 hours working for one hospital. Between them this couple work 50 hours a week – what many individuals routinely work in a single contract. As with all the biographies, the decision to co-parent forms part of an integrated response to opportunities and constraints in housing, employment, transport and leisure – rather than functioning as an isolated work-oriented versus home-centred labour market preference. This is illustrated in the web of decisions Mr and Mrs Sargent made when first setting up home together:

> Our intention, when we got married, was to buy less house than we could afford so we were never strapped with a huge mortgage or driven by debt, so we just live simply. We're on a baseline survival income (...). Right now we are at 50 hours a week of combined income and that probably won't change for the next fourteen years or when the kids are bigger. If it was up to (Mrs Sargent) she'd never work another day in her life, she's not that vocationally oriented, even though she has a professional skill, and I'm the same way, but we need her income because of the way we've split our work (...). I treasure, I absolutely treasure my time off and doing the things I love to do outside of work and if you're part time it's easier to get time off (because) nobody misses you.

In another case Mr and Mrs Smith each work 30 hours per week for the same Seattle public sector employer on a job-share arrangement. Like the career egalitarians they 'always had the ideal that (they would) both be involved with parenting, that (they would) both work'. The difference is they are not prepared to purchase substitute day-care to boost the time they are available to work outside the home. Mrs Smith explains this in terms of her strong belief in family-focused childcare. She would 'only want people taking care of them that love them as much as (she) love(s) them'. Though Mr Smith claims he would have been willing to have the children in day-care the cost always scared him. He happily went along with his wife's value system because it suited his preference for living a simple, 'less frenetic' life:

> We try and cut back on things like (we only have one car) so that we don't have to work more (to pay for a second). We've also resisted doing the soccer team and that kind of thing. That gets you into a whole world of driving that I don't approve of. I think it's irresponsible to demand of parents, to be a good parent, you have to be in this driving everywhere culture.

Again Mr Smith's anxiety to keep family overheads low suggests an integrated approach to life which encompasses choices made about where to live (close enough to relatives to exchange informal family support); how to journey to work (by bus because it doubles up as time to read) and personal politics. Where usually attention is paid only to career salience and parenting norms, these other intersecting threads of preference arguably play a crucial role in the way work is reconciled with the rest of life.

Elsewhere we see how preferences evolve to accommodate changes in circumstance. This demonstrates the way parents are continually reinventing themselves through their biographies and the compromises they make together in relation to collective goals. This is evident in the case of Mr and Mrs Eaton who both work 'reduced hours' in their respective professions (working 30–40 instead of 45 plus hours per week); Mrs Eaton as a general medical practitioner (GP) and Mr Eaton as a software developer. It was not their original intention to restrict their careers in this way. Instead the Eaton's describe a process whereby they slowly adapted to the unforeseen challenge of raising a child with congenital learning difficulties. The difficulties they have gaining access to specialist childcare and education heavily circumscribe this couples ability to provide and co-ordinate care within a dual career structure. In order to help meet his son's special needs, Mr Eaton recently quit his job with a large firm of engineers and decided instead to try working freelance from home. He claimed that the male dominated environment in which he worked as an engineer extracted high levels of unpaid overtime and travel at short notice which he found particularly family unfriendly. His employer appeared to associate flexitime options and leave for sick dependents with 'mother friendly' policies more suited to employers in female dominated service sector occupations. In this case, the demands of his employment combined poorly with the nature of Mrs Eaton's profession, where fixed patient appointments and on-call work limited her ability to 'drop everything' to plug gaps in routine care. In this case we see clearly how preferences are formed in the context of constraint. It would be wrong to suggest that resisting the treadmill of long working hours is entirely a matter of life-style choice. For the Eaton's the desire to make more time for a child with special needs is not synonymous with a preference for downshifting.

Keep a lid on the hours

Three other categories of co-ordinating behaviour can be clearly distinguished between the two extremes so far introduced. Closely allied with the career egalitarian type are those (also pursuing a shared parenting ideal) whose priority is to 'keep a lid on' the hours they work. Mrs Egham is typical of the employees in this group by her claim that she and her husband both limit the time they put into their public sector careers:

> I definitely knew I wanted to go back to work full-time (and) we both felt, it's a 35 contractual hour week we work and although we both do more than that it's not as if we are working 50, 60 hours a week. We can be quite disciplined about it (Mrs Egham).

Similarly, while Mrs Pink took for granted that she would go back to work full-time, eight weeks after giving birth, she claims to have stayed longer with her current employer than might otherwise be the case because the good relationship she has with her boss provides her with scope to take a long lunch if either of her sons has a doctors appointment.

This *keep a lid on the hours* narrative typifies one in five households across the sample. Most of this group of twenty are dual career structures but some represent a 'flexible career' structure combining full-time male with part-time female spouse employment. While presented as a shared household narrative, unlike those who *resist the treadmill*, keeping a lid on the hours tends to operate through asymmetric responsibility for co-ordinating childcare and domestic life. Not surprisingly, working mothers more often adapt their full-time careers to fit day-care opening hours than do working fathers. Nevertheless, this juggling type is characterised by agreement that both parents should curb excessive modes of working (long hours, long distance commuting, and regular overnight business travel).

The mix of childcare provision in this group is closer to that of *career egalitarian* than *resist the treadmill* households with most parents relying on private day-nurseries or registered childminders for routine care but some also having family members help out occasionally. These households typically split the morning and evening routine, with mothers usually doing the evening pick up because they are deemed better able to 'cut off (their) working day on time' (Mrs Liddell) whereas fathers might work longer into the evening to make up for a late start dropping children off in the mornings. Most couples identify one spouse, by the nature of their work, as being better able to leave work at short notice to respond to unexpected crises. While it is usually mothers in this type who claim to plug gaps in routine childcare, women who are teachers appear least able to meet this function. We see this in the case of Sam and Jill Parker who both work regular day-time hours, fitting conveniently around paid childcare opening hours. Sam's full-time local government job requires extensive local travel and some overtime while Jill works fixed hours, three days per week, as a teacher in a local school. Though Sam works longer hours than Jill he has more autonomy over start and finish times. Jill explains that her husband's flexibility is crucial for her to be able to continue working part-time because the days when she does work, she cannot abandon the children in her care without advance notice. Similarly, though Nick and Rose Paris both trained as teachers, Nick sought promotion to office-based teaching administration in part because it would provide the family greater flexibility in terms of employment mix. Residential location and journey to work is another factor influencing the relative adaptability of spouse employment to family demands. For example, Mr Sayer is better placed to leave work at short notice, though he is the major earner, because his wife commutes over an hour south of Seattle to her place of work in Tacoma, participating in a car-pool arrangement which means she does not have access to her own car to travel independently outside normal working hours.

As with each household narrative type, coping strategies reflect structures of constraint as well as childcare preference. While Ted and Holly Frost are fortunate by the relative autonomy they have to limit the hours they spend away from the family home (Ted as technical manager for a large computer firm and Holly as a university professor) they feel powerless to resist the pressure to put in a 'second shift' on the computer at night when their children are in bed. As a consequence neither of them sleep enough on a regular basis. Indeed this is a common characteristic of parents interviewed for this research. Ted and Holly try to dovetail their working hours, sharing out who does the school run, who takes the children to after-school activities, trying not to overlap the days they each work late. In the school holidays they employ a nanny in their home on a part-time basis. When their children were very young they were cared for variously by Holly at home, in a private day-care, in a private pre-school and then later in evening day-care after school. So they have tried many different options, often employing several at once in the all too familiar patchwork.

For this narrative type, the question 'who does what' changes daily according to a continually rolling calendar of events. Mr and Mrs Strong, for instance, are both employed full-time as engineers in the construction industry, Mrs Strong in the public sector (a management position) and Mr Strong in the private sector (a skilled manual position). If one of their two children wakes up sick with a fever and needs to stay home then both parents will 'look at (their) calendars and whoever has the higher ranking meeting goes to work'. But if their son 'has a peanut (allergy) emergency' while at school then Mrs Strong will 'drop everything to go do (the) parenting' because she is recognised by the school as the parent to contact first. Both parents use up equal amounts of their individual paid vacation, taking turns to provide childcare through the school breaks. This strategy means they spend very little time together as a family but it does minimise their reliance on commercial out-of-school childcare. This case illustrates very clearly how round the clock care is maintained through a complex check-list of situation-specific, gendered contingency arrangements, drawing on a range of resources and personnel.

All hands to the pump

A fourth group comprises those households less committed to equal career opportunities than they are convinced they need two wages or salaries to get by. Here it is a case of 'all hands to the pump' – to raise what is considered a necessary household income.[1] Although similar in size to the previous type (encompassing twenty three households), *all hands to the pump* behaviour is witnessed in a range of employment structures: dual career, dual earner and flexible earner/career combinations. High housing costs are commonly cited as reason why both parents work outside the home in situations described as stressful with respect to childcare and commuting. Here the claim is 'you don't have a choice' (but to both earn). Larry and Kim Pacey are typical of this group. They are paying off large debts (especially relating to student loans) and rely on their combined employment benefits to provide adequate family health insurance. They claim that what Larry earns as a teacher would not sustain a household in Portland because they made it onto the property ladder in the 90s 'when prices really went crazy' and took on a 'crippling mortgage'. Larry in particular was very concerned about the financial responsibilities of starting a family and his inability alone to provide the necessary measure of security:

> I just shook my head the whole time saying there's no way just one of us can work and the other one stay at home. I mean even if I was the stay at home dad (as the lower earner), just living in Portland is so expensive, our mortgage – it would be impossible.

In this household group the mix of childcare is evenly split between private market and unpaid family (usually spouse sequential schedule) provision. Again, routine and emergency provision for childcare is a function of localised situations of constraint. Cultures of work associated with particular occupations and sectors continue to exert a strong influence. Mr Sand, for instance, is the one his son's day-care always calls on in an emergency because, owning his own entertainment business, he works evenings and weekends to dovetail with his wife's fixed hours as a dental hygienist. Mrs Sand goes on to explain how as a household they rely on one of them having this flexibility:

> Because with children, this whole thing, it has to be flexible and he is the flexible one as far as our relationship goes. He can pick up our son if he's sick or take him to the doctor if he's sick or do those things, if things need to be done at home, he is more flexible because he is a business owner

Uneven divisions of labour are typically justified in this type on the basis they are the result of efficient use of household personnel. Of course this retreat into 'rational economic' justifications for action frequently masks unresolved tensions surrounding persistent gender inequalities. Because these households claim to be struggling financially, the partner who brings in the most money (usually the male spouse and this by working the longest hours) contributes least to childcare and domestic responsibilities. The analogy might be drawn here with a civil war in which men and women fight side by side against a common enemy, the understanding being that only when the war is won will women seek their own liberation. Bill and Mary Peet illustrate this tacit impasse whereby ideals of gender democracy are shelved for the good of family finances. They combine two jobs and childcare, sharing one car, by working sequential schedules. Mary is employed part-time as a hairdresser working shifts which start after she has seen the children off to school. Bill works nights, meeting the children home from school in the afternoons after catching up on sleep. While sequential scheduling allows Bill and Mary to share the school run it remains the case that Bill's job is afforded primary status. The subordination of Mary's employment is manifest in the number of times Mary has switched job to fit around changes in Bill's working schedule and the need for Mary to work locally, freeing up the family car to facilitate Bill's access to irregular and anti-social working hours.

Mrs Skyla also suggests a legacy of male breadwinner expectations in the following narrative. This is despite the fact that she is technically better qualified than her husband and contributes income from two part-time jobs totalling 32 hours employment outside the home. She also has responsibility for managing round the clock care both for her invalid mother (who shares their home) and the couple's ten year old daughter. For this she employs a home-help who doubles up as a childminder after school. Mrs Skyla explains this division by valuing her husband's monetary contribution far more highly than her own co-ordinating (managerial) role.

> he makes better money, he works the long hours, he's the one that puts in the overtime, he's the one that works Saturdays, that kind of thing (...) and then I add money but my money has never been close to his money (but) I do the, OK, where is everybody, how is everybody doing, so I check everybody's emotions and (he) takes care of all the hard work. (...) I'm more of a scheduler, having thought it out ahead of time, so I schedule the care-givers and I'm responsible for school activities

Arguably this denigration of non-financial household contributions mirrors the dominant value system of market capitalism. Nevertheless, the impression this narrative gives of traditional gender role specialisation in a dual earning arrangement is complicated by more fluid and varied coping practices than would otherwise be anticipated on the basis of divisions of labour observed at any single point in time. In the past Mrs Skyla has been the sole breadwinner and supported her husband through periods of unemployment and ill health. Moreover, housing strategies assume an equal if not greater function than employment structure in this household biography, as will be demonstrated when we return to this case in the following chapter.

The path of least resistance

The final and largest category, comprising 37 per cent of the sample, is characterised by conditions under which the job or career of a primary wage earner (typically male) imposes significant barriers to (female) spouse employment. All but one of the thirteen male breadwinner households appear in this group, as do two out of three flexible (one and a half income) households. A small number of 'role reversal' households are identified, where women are working full-time alongside a part-time employed spouse, but these arrangements are rarely considered to be permanent. The dominant narrative for couples in this type is the claim they are following a 'path of least resistance' to avoid more stressful juggling of paid employment and unpaid work. For Steve Poulter, for instance, maintaining a good quality of life is about eliminating sources of tension and stress associated with two competing careers. Arguably this path cultivates gender role specialisation and as a result, paradoxically, a shift from the stress of 'juggling' to the suggestion of increased marital tension. It is in this type that we see the effect of women being more successful at improving their access to paid employment than persuading men to assume more responsibility for family care and domestic labour (Brannen and Moss 1991; Preston et al. 2000). Laura Poynter 'complains', for instance about her husband's 'lack of availability and involvement (with the kids)'. Mark Poynter rarely makes it home from work before his children are asleep. He is an absent father despite migrating away from the San Francisco Bay Area specifically to escape 'high burn-out' hours and a 'high powered' pace of life, to set up home in a part of Portland that 'is not the city' close to extended family. In this relocation it was recognised that Mark's career would take priority with respect to employment and proximity to Laura's parents would take priority with respect to housing. Although this arrangement reflects gender specialisation it continues to function through an integrated biography. This way the *path of least resistance* narrative does not simply reveal itself in traditional gender divisions of labour but is mutually constituted alongside concern to function within an extended family, preference for neighbourhoods with a 'small town' feel and reliance on private motorised transport. This narrative consequently provides the antithesis of *resist the treadmill* behaviour and politics, despite sharing similar belief in family-oriented childcare.

Most women in this type admit to having adopted a more traditional home-maker role than they would otherwise have chosen for themselves. They explain that this is as a result of their spouse working long hours, awkward or irregular hours, working away from home or travelling away frequently on business. Some like Abi Summer, married to a merchant mariner, have given up all thoughts of outside employment while their children are young. The terms of Bob Summer's employment are that he sails four weeks together (working a 12 hour daily shift) then returns home for two weeks before returning to his ship and this schedule rotates through the year. These conditions heavily circumscribe the opportunities Abi might otherwise have to take up paid employment. Indeed, Abi describes herself as 'a single mother with a part-time husband'.

Others, like Mrs Lonmore, continue to work for pay but in 'mother track' part-time employment. Here it is important to differentiate the 'short' hours generally worked over two or three days in this group from *all hands to the pump* mothers in part-time employment who typically average closer to 30 hours over a five day week. Mrs Lonmore, a qualified lawyer like her husband, recognised that 'something had to give' when she had her son in her late 30s. She made the deliberate switch from private practice law to public sector administration. As a consequence of 'taking her foot off the accelerator' in her career, she can juggle home and work to compensate for the heavy demands of her husbands career. She assumes full responsibility for managing routine and emergency childcare as 'quid pro for the fact that I work in the Civil Service and I can down tools at 5 o'clock in a very lowly position, whereas you can't get away with that sort of thing when you are at (husband's) level'. By this classic 'career sacrifice', Mrs Lonmore has made sure that her job provides sufficient flexibility to accommodate childcare and domestic events because the culture and conditions of her husbands work fails to offer this room for manoeuvre. Nevertheless, when we pick up the threads of this case again in Chapter Five, we find that Mrs Lonmore's subordinate income contribution is off-set in part by her instrumental role in managing alternative household assets.

The preceding analysis makes a strong case for not straightforwardly reading off gender roles and relations from women's employment status. Sometimes the meta-narratives coincide with household employment structure, but many times they do not. A major problem with cross-sectional survey research is the tendency to over-determine gender roles and parenting practices on the basis of paid employment status alone as a measure of career salience, financial autonomy and moral rationality. In the household biographies we find a consistent meta-narrative beneath which temporary or periodic changes can occur in employment structure. The biography of Steve and Amy Poulter highlights this point. Reflecting on the tensions of balancing two careers and the cost of full-time day-care for their daughter, Steve claims that their quality of life 'stinks'. After their daughter was born they pursued a dual career structure, on the implicit understanding that Steve's career, which calls for time-consuming continuing education, assumed primary importance. Their response to 'constantly dealing with the same old stresses' differentiated their lifestyle and strategy from that of the career egalitarian who would seek remedy in shared parenting arrangements. Though Amy is at pains to point out that it is she who does all the 'buzzing around', picking up and dropping off at day-care, Steve argues that 'it's not healthy for this marriage to have both of us working'. Now expecting their second child, Amy is quitting her public sector career to stay home full-time. Here a consistent *path of least resistance* meta-narrative is maintained through temporary experimentation with shared earning (but not shared domestic labour) in a dual career structure. Within this narrative, female spouse career salience is preferred but only considered sustainable if it does not disrupt male spouse career.

Comparative perspectives

The household biographies demonstrate that business leaders, individuals and families understand flexibility in quite different ways. Moreover, it is in this respect that the UK and the US samples differ quite sharply. A sense of contrasting cultures at work is conveyed by Mrs Philpott, a Human Resources manager in Portland, in the way she responds to potential recruits who ask about options for flexible working hours.

> These college graduates I interview, (they say) 'so do you have a four day week at your company?' and I'm laughing, oh my gosh, you need to go the high-tech route, you need to go to Europe, you know, it doesn't happen in the wholesale business, it doesn't happen that way in America (Mrs Philpot, Dual Career).

In the UK, in contrast, a perceived Americanisation of the labour process is actively resisted on a number of fronts. The Trades Union Congress (TUC), for instance, has been instrumental in challenging the UK opting out of the European Working Time Directive[2] by highlighting the damaging effects a culture of long working hours has on health and wellbeing (TUC 2002). On balance too, the UK households more actively resist the *combined* long hours of the *career egalitarian* type. Doing so in the absence of any incentives for parents to share the personal costs of social reproduction typically takes them to a default position which assumes a more traditional asymmetric gender division of labour.

In Chapter Two it was observed that firms seek competitive advantage through numerical flexibility (scope to hire and fire freely and with minimal cost) and adaptive flexibility (requiring workers to switch rapidly between functions as production demands). In this respect most employers differentiate between conditions of work imposed on hourly paid wage 'earners' versus the relative autonomy of those in salaried 'careers'. This distinction is particularly clear in the USA where it reflects the official designation of production workers (such as fabricators, cleaners) as non-exempt from overtime laws, for whom overtime payments are due for working hours totalling more than ten hours per day or 40 hours per week. Professionals (such as software engineers and managers) who are exempt from restrictions to them working overtime are instead likely to put in unpaid overtime. This distinction is again reinforced by working parents who are themselves employers. Mr and Mrs Saunders are partners in a small engineering firm with forty employees. Mr Saunders raises the issue of the distinction between 'two groups' in the firm, 'unskilled labourers and skilled engineers':

> Being a small employer it's very difficult (to offer flexible working). We give levels of flexibility. There's hourly paid people that are doing factory built things and they have to be there (so) the flexibility is, on a day to day basis, pretty limited, or we'd like it to be so. In general terms they can pick their hours but they need to stick to their hours. Our engineers though are more flexible but then we have workloads that come through (at short notice) and keep them (working overtime). We have guys that stay 24 hours a day sometimes. They'll sleep on a futon in my office. It just happened the other day, this one guy, you know, then he took today off to go with the kids. It (flexibility) depends on the position and some places it works and some places it doesn't.

This demonstrates what has come to be viewed as a distinct North American model of flexible employment whereby so called 'family-friendly' initiatives are encouraged along the lines they are good business (Googins 2000). While some employers offer excellent benefit packages as a means by which to compete for the best workers, others can fill vacancies without making any commitment to its workforce. Those workers who do not hold the asset of skills which are in short supply are in a poor position to negotiate favourable terms (Potts 2002: 63). This illustrates the basis of extreme labour market divisions in the USA where uneven access to healthcare, holiday and sick leave entitlements compound already fundamental inequalities in pay.

In the UK, women are more likely to reduce the hours they work outside the home after maternity leave. Moreover, UK families are more likely to benefit from stronger kin capital to plug gaps which emerge in routine care arrangements because of greater residential stability. An army of 'granny nannies' are the 'linchpin' in family coping strategies (Prasad 2000; Wheelock and Jones 2002; for the USA see Hair Hunts 1998). Nevertheless, this traditional mode of coping is coming unravelled in situations where couples gravitate towards the 'hub' London labour market to satisfy two competing careers. While a dazzling range of private 'concierge' services have opened up to meet the demands of these time-squeezed professional migrants, access is limited to the very affluent (at most ten per cent of the working families interviewed) and as we see repeatedly in the biographies, when it comes to family welfare, parents are reluctant to rely on market substitutes. Census data shows that private childcare was purchased by just 55 per cent of US and 35 per cent of British working families in 2000/1. Added to this we find that overall rates of market provisioning differ little between single earner and dual-earner families (Rubin and Riney 1994). This is because much social reproduction is performed as a 'labour of love' (Folbre and Nelson 2000). Women no longer choose between work *or* family but instead manage the conflicting responsibilities of work *and* family. Mothers are consequently hardest hit by the 'time squeeze', widely observed to experience 'role strain' carrying a 'dual burden' of paid employment and unpaid domestic and caring work. In this respect national portraits based on welfare regime types perhaps over determine the extent to which private markets deliver US welfare. Working parents in both countries similarly 'tax themselves' in time and money far more heavily than households without responsibility for dependents (Folbre 2001: 202). The continuing importance of family-care in dual earner families reflects not only the influence of parenting norms but also financial constraint. Affluent dual earner households are in a position to purchase support services such as high quality childcare and domestic help. Yet their solutions to co-ordination problems rely on low-wage childcare providers and cleaners for whom private childcare is prohibitively expensive, even where they themselves form part of a dual earner of multi-job household (Land 2002a).

Minding the gaps

The suggestion that families rarely sit down to enjoy a meal together fuels speculation that family life suffers as a result of more parents seeking employment outside the home and working longer hours. Families have gained the income women earn from paid employment but lost the time they are available for unpaid caring and domestic services in the home. Understandably there is concern that less time is given over to the care of children and elderly relatives. At the same time of course it can be argued that very low income families are unable to improve their situation by becoming dual earners because of the prohibitive cost (in cash and support terms) of childcare. Here we see a debate in which the rise of the dual earner household is viewed by some commentators as harmful (Hoffman 1989). Amitai Etzioni points to rising consumer expectations and preference for income over time as explanation why children are spending more time with non-parents or on their own as 'latch-key kids'. He defines the problem as a 'parenting deficit' (Etzioni 1993) (for a critique of the Communitarian position see Fraser and Lacey 1993). For example the school day is shorter in the USA than it is in the UK and this generates a 'gap' of some 25 hours per week between the normal full-time working week and the school schedule. This gap is of greatest concern for parents of 'tweens' aged 8–14 who mostly rely on self-care. It is true that market failure contributes to a 'care deficit' in the five high cost cities, because affordable, good quality commercial childcare is in short supply (Wilkinson 1994: 35). Yet there is no evidence in the household biographies of an erosion of family obligations. On the contrary there is the suggestion of intensive parenting (Hattery 2001) especially where parents *keep a lid on the hours* or adopt a *path of least resistance*. These narratives in particular suggest time and energy is transferred from paid employment and invested in children's education in response to perceived failings in public provision (Stephens 1999). Nick and Rose Paris, for instance, went to extraordinary lengths to put their children through a co-operative pre-school where parents are required to participate directly in class-room activities. Rose had her mother watch her two younger children while she went to 'parent help' at her eldest daughter's school. Her sister and husband, who have children of a similar age, also live nearby and it was on this basis all four parents decided to participate directly in their children's pre-school education. This required creative time management as Rose explains:

> we patched together the four of us and my mom and dad, you know, six adults got these kids through pre-school that year where, you know, brother-in-law took, he stayed home on Mondays and worked Saturdays that year and my sister took Fridays off and I was home, you know, at noon, and my folks did Wednesdays and (husband) took days off and to help.

Evidence that parent participation in schools is on the increase in the US contradicts Robert Putnam's thesis that, under pressure to earn and consume with greater intensity than ever before, American's are withdrawing from unpaid community enterprise and 'bowling alone' (Putnam 2000). Of course, this form of voluntarism is far from altruistic. Rather it represents an investment in family cultural capital and the 'privatisation' of community. The danger of the extreme market model is that while the supply of care is relatively unchanged it is qualitatively altered by the way it is now defined as a private commodity. Thus 'receipt of care' and the cultural capital of parenting 'investments' assume the same patterns of exclusion and inequality found with all other market commodities. Joan Tronto (2004) makes this point forcefully in her critique of US neo-liberalism. She claims that what is being lost is any sense of collective responsibility and shared endeavour. Contrary to the assumption of a 'trickel down' effect Tronto (2004: 2) argues that 'when unequal citizens only care privately, they deepen the vast inequalities and the exclusion of some from the real prospects of being full citizens'. We see this in the way middle class parents feel increasingly compelled to sign their children up for a host of extra-curricular activities, seeing this as the best way to improve their children's chance of future success. This is especially characteristic of the US sample where parents are particularly instrumental in fulfiling the aspirations they have for their children.

Co-constituted alongside the privatisation of care is the popular expectation that technology will provide solutions to the time-squeeze. Undeniably, labour saving technologies have played a fundamental role in freeing up time from domestic drudgery for mothers to spend with their children. But a more recent trend suggests that the tools of ICT are increasingly used to close the gaps which open up as a consequence of more parents working longer hours away from home. This was suggested above in the use of web-cam surveillance of infants in day-care. It is equally apparent in the way mobile phones are used by parents to check up on older children who take care of themselves after school each day (Furedi 2001). Undeniably working parents have gained significant time efficiencies in recent decades, as witnessed by the widespread popularity of telephone and Internet banking. New technologies can eliminate certain time-fixed constraints and shift them temporally (for instance recording a television programme) or spatially – to eliminate the need to travel to a specific place in core opening hours (shopping or booking a holiday on-line). The majority of households interviewed owned a personal computer and more than half had access to the Internet at home. This parallels OECD data which indicates that on average 55 per cent of UK and 58.4 per cent of US individuals made use of the Internet in 2001. Yet surprisingly few of the sample families (5%) routinely shopped for groceries on-line for home delivery. To put this low figure into context it is important to note that interviews with the US families coincided with the collapse of several big name Internet grocers. The on-line giant Webvan which had purchased HomeGrocer.com in 2000 declared bankruptcy in 2001. Instead, most of the parents shopped on the way home from work or as a family at weekends. Although shopping on-line has really taken off since the household interviews were conducted, this sector accounts for just one per cent of the total US grocery market. While OECD data for 2002 indicates that in the UK 20.9 per cent and in the USA 22.5 per cent of individuals order goods and services over the Internet, more than 35 per cent of all shopping visits are made to eBay and Amazon for the purpose of discretionary rather than obligatory purchases (OECD 2002b). Several of the San Francisco families marvelled at the stress-free convenience of shopping for groceries on-line, where the alternative is to fight for parking and trolley space in congested city stores with a toddler in tow. From Portland too, the local media reported great excitement in 1999 at the time-saving potential of Internet shopping and home delivery (Trevison 1999). Nevertheless it is questionable whether selecting food on-line offers more than a limited solution to the time-squeeze. This is not least because time-shifting rarely *saves* time but instead increases the intensity of social-reproduction work, making it possible to pack more 'home-work' around a longer working day (Southerton 2003). It is questionable too whether on-line shopping reduces the 'ecological backpack' associated with increasing food miles, as goods are dispatched from depots further away than the local supermarket and delivered on demand rather than economies of scale in door to door journeys.

In short, just as the commodification of care exacerbates social inequalities, this expanded role of technology negatively impacts on the environment, increasing the volume of energy consuming and polluting private car journeys. The harried working family increasingly relies upon private motorised transport for the convenience of multi-tasking. Sally Philpott, for instance, equates 'car time' on the school run with 'quality time' as a daily interval dedicated to conversation with her kids. This way, interactions which might once have taken place at fixed family meals are now conducted on the move. The impact of the time-squeeze on travel behaviour is discussed in more detail in Chapter Six. Where the Internet obviously has transformed the lives of the middle class families interviewed is with respect to processing information for household decisions (concerning local schools, childcare facilities, and big-ticket consumer purchases). It helps make aspects of financial management and space-time co-ordination more efficient (banking on-line, arranging business travel) but it does not eliminate the need to co-ordinate movement between places and discrete activities.

Summary

What distinguishes the research presented in this chapter is the way the terms and conditions of both parents' employment are scrutinised within a whole household economy framework. Whether a partnered mother of young children remains in employment, and if so for how long, and with what capacity to 'drop everything' at short notice, is not determined by individual disposition alone. Rather it is a matter of negotiation and compromise alongside spouse employment. More crucial still, ongoing preference *formation* is bound up in an integrated biography whereby employment structure intersects with housing and consumption aspirations, migration and mobility constraints, family goals, social and kin networks, moral choice and lifestyle politics. The point to stress is that household employment structures are not the function of fixed or 'given' preferences but rather, like housing careers and moral rationalities, the result of locally embedded and socially constructed biography-building. We saw this above in the way Mr and Mrs Sargent bought 'less house' to 'resist the treadmill' and accommodate shared parenting through male part-time employment. Likewise, the house Mr and Mrs Edwards wanted to buy as a project for renovation stretched their finances to the extent that to secure the necessary loan Mrs Edwards had to significantly increase her hours of work for a time in a situation where, following the 'path of least resistance', she bore responsibility for patching together childcare arrangements, ensuring everyone was where they had to be on time each day.

A particularly powerful illustration of this intersection is conveyed in the case of Sharon and Jamie Fuller who describe their housing situation as the anchor point to their current mode of living, including how they organise childcare for their six year old daughter. For several years now they have lived with Sharon's mother in the house she owns. They view the arrangement as mutually beneficial whereby Sharon's mother 'helps somewhat with childcare when we get in a pinch – the fall back is grandma' and she is helped in turn by them '(taking) her shopping and to her doctors appointments' because although she walks unaided she is unable to drive on medical grounds. As Sharon explains: '(the house) is actually three things; it's that we have this on site support system; then there's my mother's situation – she's actually told us she wouldn't stay (on) in the house if we didn't live with her because there's always a danger that she could fall or something; and then the other thing is the housing market – we won't buy until my mother sells this house or she dies and I inherit my one fourth (share)'. In the event they no longer live with Sharon's mother it is understood they would move out of the Bay Area. They have never yet owned their own home and though both are currently working, Jamie as a freelance photographer and Sharon as a part-time public sector attorney, each have experienced periods of unemployment. Viewed as a potted biography (included as Appendix D to offer a detailed illustration) this case shows how time and again over the life-course housing, employment, gender and generation intersect.

Notwithstanding the centrality of childcare in the lives of this population (as reflected in the weight of evidence in this chapter), other family welfare issues are high on the agenda too. As the Fuller's biography also highlights, many couples in this sample are of the 'sandwich generation' (Agree et al. 2003). They delayed starting a family until their careers were 'on track' (or they had repaid student loans), often in their late 30s, at which point they now face a double dose of family leave requests because their parents health is failing at the same time as their offspring are prone to the usual childhood ailments. This reinforces the argument made throughout this chapter that it is not a single or straightforward trade-off between work and family or work and 'the rest of life' which working families are confronted with today. Mothers and fathers make sense of their lives, and construct their biographies, in continual dialogue with family and friends. Individual preferences and group compromises function through a relatively stable but not immutable local cultural milieu. The meta-narratives of work/life reconciliation working families follow have to accommodate intersecting preferences in spheres of home, work and family life. Neither are these meta-narratives pre-scripted or independently-authored. Always present in the biographies are structures of constraint – including the neglected difficulties of combining different sets of working arrangements within the confines of geographically fixed and temporally ordered resource capabilities (Jarvis et al. 2001). National promotion of neoliberal policies alters the climate of incentives and disincentives in which individuals make sense of their aspirations. This is reflected in evidence of cross-national difference in both household employment and cultures of work. Nevertheless it is not possible to typify national modes of work/life reconciliation on the basis of policy difference alone. Local cultural variation, including religious affiliations, promotion of new-right 'family values', and identification with social and environmental movements, also exert a powerful influence.

5
Equity

Introduction

Homeless in San Francisco (central reservation, Van Ness Avenue)

A recurring theme of this book is that behind the picture postcard image of successful cities are profound inequities. Staying at the down-town Berkeley YMCA[1] from August to November 2000, I was shocked to discover how many low-wage workers called this budget hotel accommodation home. I also observed men and women sleeping rough. Indeed, by 2003 street homelessness had attracted such public concern that the issue dominated the San Francisco mayoral race (Calvan 2003). I regularly met the same 'guests' in the one communal kitchen and this way got to know the work routines of two African American men, Sol and Dino, both long-term residents of the YMCA and experts in the art of living frugally. It was Sol who advised me not to store food in the open shelves provided. Instead, he had a brown paper sack (the sort routinely provided by US supermarkets) as his 'larder' and used this to carry sugar, peanut butter and other condiments to and from his bedroom, along with a small cool-box. Most meals consisted of ramen instant noodles, hot-dogs and Pop-Tarts: those heavily processed foods which require only basic kitchen preparation. That both men were unhealthily overweight was a consequence of them camping out rather than over-eating.

One Tuesday morning I overheard Sol ask Dino, 'is this your weekend?' 'Yeah' Dino replied, 'I've just got off, I've until tomorrow night'. Sol laughed: 'this is my Sunday night then I'm back on tonight'. Exchanges such as this concerning their topsy-turvy working life brought home to me better than any text-book that wages are insufficient as a frame of reference to explain inequality and uneven development (Smith and Wallerstein 1992: 254; see also Sennett 1998a). Those trapped in casual and degraded employment struggle to secure mainstream accommodation as much because they possess only weak social capital associated with poor quality jobs as by the absence of a living wage. Viewed over the long term, the weekly cost of living in a budget hotel, motel or commercial hostel far exceeds what most middle class students pay for a room in a shared house or studio apartment rented from a private landlord. The difference is that marginalised workers like Sol and Dino struggle to raise the cash deposit, acquire a credit rating or cultivate the sort of character reference necessary to enter the mainstream. This argument is well rehearsed by Barbara Ehrenreich (2001) in her gritty window onto the hard-working maids, cleaners, nursing aides and Wal-Mart sales staff found crowded into motel rooms (and the occasional car or van) across the USA.[2] She observes that 'there are no secret economies that nourish the poor; on the contrary, there are a host of special costs. If you can't put up the two months' rent you need to secure an apartment, you end up paying through the nose for a room by the week' (Ehrenreich 2001: 27). Polly Toynbee 2003 presents an equivalent exposé of life in low-pay Britain in '*Hard Work*'. Likewise, Fran Abrams (2002) describes how she tried to survive on the UK minimum wage of £4.10 per hour in London, Aberdeen and Doncaster and only in the latter was she able to break even, then only by taking shelter in a damp caravan (trailer) (Abrams 2002, cited in Perrons 2004: 41 and 53). In each of these experiments, housing costs are identified as the most common barrier to a sustainable low-wage livelihood.

Switching from Sol and Dino's downtrodden badinage at the YMCA to my interviewees' up-beat, high-pressure biographies and their comfortable, though not ostentatious, middle class homes, felt jarring at times. Against a backdrop of inner-city deprivation it might seem odd, perhaps even offensive, to write a chapter on equity based on the lived experience of relatively advantaged two-parent working families. We know from valuable accounts of urban poverty in the US, such as William Julius Wilson's 'The Truly Disadvantaged' (1987) and 'When Work Disappears' (1996), that the depths of disadvantage are increasing, just as the heights of consumer sovereignty are celebrated more vehemently in the West than at any place or time in history. Considerable attention has consequently been paid to the *polarisation* of the UK and US populations between 'work rich' and 'employment deprived'[3] extremes. Yet, as shown in the extreme case above, you can be ostensibly 'work rich' in the simple sense of being employed and holding multiple jobs, yet at the same time disadvantaged in the competition for housing and neighbourhood services.

Competition for the trappings of a comfortable Anglo-American lifestyle takes place in relation to the infrastructure of everyday life (overlapping material, institutional and moral constraint, as introduced in Chapter One) and an uneven distribution of household assets and resource entitlements. With respect to the notion of 'entitlement' it is constructive to rehearse the highly regarded explanation economist Amartya Sen provides for the cause of famine. Sen (1981) explains that famine is attributed less to an absolute shortage of food than failure of socially constructed food entitlement (whether in relation to self provision, market purchase or informal exchange)[4]. Feminist economist Nancy Folbre makes a similar point when she stresses that pure income advantage is not the primary structure of constraint (Folbre 1994: 66). While labour market earnings and household income represent the dominant (often the only) measures of inequality in conventional analysis, questions of household life-chance are viewed rather differently in this chapter. Here the aim is to consider how working families cope with fierce competition for housing and childcare provision. Orthodox economic theory characterises the decisions 'revealed' by household action as a straightforward trade-off (for instance Becker 1976) but this model is arguably flawed (for a review of the literature see Gardiner 1997). Biographical analysis by contrast affords greater insight into the role of competing identifications as well as negotiation and compromise. Instead of a simple trade-off, working families face complex dilemmas where choice is circumscribed, contingent and deeply embedded in structures (material, institutional, moral) over which they often have little control. Moreover, individual preference (to live in the city for example) has to be negotiated in the wider household context including that of spouse employment (pay and promotion prospects) and shared family goals (good schools for the kids), interactions which generate compromise and unintended social costs (such as to the environment as we shall see in Chapter Six).

The earlier chapters have shown that inequalities persist *within* households, on gender grounds, even where those *between* middle class households diminish. Recognising that working families comprise a heterogeneous sub-population, not least by race and class, the household research was designed to limit the number of variables under observation. This made it possible to look at the influence of within-class variation in housing *careers* and employment *conditions*. The research repeatedly demonstrates that it is the same dilemmas which stand between a quality of life imputed on the basis of household income and that which is tolerated in practice. The most commonly experienced dilemmas relate to housing affordability, the growing emphasis on self-reliance (especially in health and education) and childcare shortage. Added to this list are transport and school choice, dilemmas which are discussed in Chapter Six in relation to the bearing they have on questions of environmental sustainability. In this chapter, biographical vignettes are introduced to demonstrate empirical connections between the overlapping spheres of housing amenity, employment quality, and gender norms first identified in Chapter One. To make the point that inequalities are reproduced *through* these connections, discussion focuses in the second part of this chapter on household data for London alone, thus allowing close attention to the detail of one case study.

Social capital

The social capital that is frequently missing for those in precarious employment such as Sol and Dino is something akin to what Tom Wolf called the 'favour bank' in his novel 'The Bonfire of the Vanities' – I'll do this for you now in the expectation that down the road you or someone else will return the favour (McDowell 1997: 3). Moreover, social capital is what Albert Hirshman (1970) describes as a 'moral resource' whereby the supply of favours and information or opportunities increases rather than decreases with use and becomes depleted if not used (but for a critique of this position see Baron et al. 2000). Consequently, those who have social capital tend to accumulate more, just as is the case with conventional capital. The stark divide which results from this cycle of reinforcement is illustrated by Mr Spring's observations as a volunteer youth worker.

> I do a lot of volunteer work through our church doing various things that would not have been possible had I had a regular job

and (...) we have a very professional church, in fact, if you're not an attorney or a nurse you don't really belong there and, I think about it in terms of people who come from disadvantaged backgrounds, perhaps even more important than not having money, the disadvantage they have is they don't have these networks we take for granted or don't even realise exist. I grew up in a professional family, my dad has worked for Boeing for 46 years and he's in management and all these kids I went to school with their parents were all professionals and now I know half a dozen attorneys, half a dozen architects, I know engineers, doctors, all these people. (Mr Spring, Dual Career, Seattle – Greenwood.)

Mr Spring explains how the cultural benefits he gained from a middle class home and education helped him to realise his ambition as a writer and consequently provided him greater autonomy over his working life, including scope to undertake voluntary work and in this way, through the professional congregation at his church, to keep expanding his social network and social capital. This also demonstrates how social networks serve as lively conduits of information, such as that which might result in a new job, or influence the choice of where to send a child to school (Granovetter 1974; Astone and McLanahan 1991; Devine 2003). After housing equity and income security it is access to social capital which best defines relative advantage. Inequalities between families are particularly apparent with respect to the strength of social networks and resources of local knowledge associated with trust ties and shared norms. We have to critically examine the assumption that middle class families have greater control over the way they manage their lives, simply on the basis of income status (Gardiner 2000). We saw in the previous chapter how the ability to consume 'less housing' as a strategy to eliminate pressures of time-squeeze in *'resist the treadmill'* households is possible only for those with sufficient resources (including access to informal economic assistance) to exercise this option. Scope to purchase domestic and childcare services in *'career egalitarian'* households provides at best a partial substitute for proximity to social and kin networks. Nevertheless, those employed to help middle class families have still fewer resources to reconcile their own pressures of work and the desire to improve *their* children's prospects.

The tendency for social capital to function through like-minded special interest groups, such as the church congregation, means that class inequalities such as those separating Mr Spring from the unemployed youth he counsels, remain deeply entrenched. We see clearly how Mr Spring's advantage of birth continues to attract advantage over the life-course. Yet these characteristics of stratification (race, class and gender) are not alone responsible for highly unequal living standards in the five featured cities. Though well endowed in social capital, Mr and Mrs Spring experience relative hardship in relation to the local housing market. 'Trapped' to an extent by rising house prices, they juggle home-working and childcare in a one-bedroom apartment. It is the purpose of this chapter to scrutinise some of these more subtle *within-class* dimensions of uneven development and inequality. First it is important to place the sub-population of working families interviewed into a broad national context.

Neo-liberal inequalities

Neither the UK nor the USA has much to be proud of with respect to poverty and income inequality. Poor children in the USA are worse off in real terms than poor children in all of the 12 other OECD countries and the UK more closely emulates this model than it does greater efforts at the redistribution of wealth in other European countries. Cross-national comparison usually employs the Gini coefficient whereby higher levels indicate greater inequality ranging from 0 (all workers are equal) to 1 (one person has all the earnings). Using this measure, Jesuit and Smeeding (2002: Figure 1) find the USA in 1997 to have a Gini index of 0.372 and the UK in 1995 to have a Gini index of 0.344. By contrast, in 1995 Sweden had a Gini index of 0.221 and Taiwan a Gini index of 0.277.

The US 'official' poverty line is set at around 40 per cent of the median household income whereas 50 per cent is generally considered the norm elsewhere. European Union countries have accepted a line of 60 per cent of the median. When we turn to consider the income distribution of the five featured cities in Tables 5.1 and 5.2 we find 26 per cent of US households and 24 per cent of UK households on average below 50 per cent of median income. Most striking perhaps is the fact that UK poverty levels in 2004 are nearly double those witnessed in the late 1970s. Moreover, contrary to the common association of poverty with unemployment, 39 per cent of those in poverty today represent working families. Couples with children run twice the risk of income poverty compared with those without dependents (DWP HBAI data, cited in CPAG 2004; see also Flaherty and Dornan 2004). The UK and USA have witnessed large increases in both poverty and income inequality. Inequality grew fastest in the UK as a consequence of severe restructuring over the period 1977 to 1991 but it remains the case that inequality is higher still in the USA (Atkinson 2002; Galbraith 1998;

Table 5.1 Income distribution (percentage) in three US cities, 2000

Income distribution	San Francisco	Seattle	Portland
Total	100 per cent	100 per cent	100 per cent
Less than $10,000	9.8	6.4	9.3
$10,000 to $14,999	5.0	4.2	6.1
$15,000 to $19,999	4.2	4.3	6.2
$20,000 to $24,999	4.3	5.0	6.8
$25,000 to $29,999	4.4	5.3	6.6
$30,000 to $34,999	4.6	5.6	7.0
$35,000 to $39,999	4.5	5.4	6.3
$40,000 to $44,999	4.7	5.4	6.0
$45,000 to $49,999	4.1	4.9	5.1
$50,000 to $59,999	7.6	9.2	9.6
$60,000 to $74,999	10.1	11.9	10.7
$75,000 to $99,999	12.1	13.6	9.9
$100,000 to $124,999	8.3	7.6	4.6
$125,000 to $149,999	4.9	3.9	2.2
$150,000 to $199,999	5.3	3.4	1.7
$200,000 or more	6.1	3.8	2.0

Source: US Census Bureau 2000 (based on 1999 incomes) Data for each locality is at county level (San Francisco County; King County; Multnomah County).

Galbraith and Berner 2001). As Toynbee (2003: 10) observes, the USA may be working, but it has double the poverty rate of most European countries.

Another important feature of the new stratification is a growing income divide between top-end and low-end jobs, as illustrated in Chapter Three with respect to the San Francisco sample. In part this gap reflects the rules of competition, where the firms in the private sector knowledge economy offer 'super star' salaries in order to attract the 'brightest and the best'. This tends to mean that professionals following a vocation in the public and voluntary sectors (those in education, social work, environmental conservation and overseas development for instance) earn a fraction of the salaries commanded by professionals in the private sector. Further amplifying income

Table 5.2 Income distribution (percentage) in two UK cities, 2000

Income distribution	Greater London	Edinburgh
Total	100 per cent	100 per cent
Less than £12,999	11.2	24.6
£13,000 to £18,199	19.7	25.5
£19,000 to £23,919	20.7	17.4
£23,920 to £35,775		22.5
£35.776 or more		10
£23,920 to £49,607	38.4	
£49,608 or more	10	
Median income	£32,224	£21,943

Source: ONS New Earnings Survey 2000. Note, annual incomes are calculated from weekly earnings. In the City of London, ten per cent of the population earn more than £78,000 per annum.

inequality among professionals is the practice of financial service employers paying bonuses massively in excess of annual salaries. This sets 'city' earnings apart and places added pressure on the housing market through demand for additional residential property as a commercial investment. Freeman (2002) suggests that bonus payments can distort the average earnings index by as much as 1.5 percentage points in a single month. At the lower end of the occupation scale comparisons between 'well paid' private versus 'secure' public sector jobs are complicated by the fact that employees on low wages fare especially badly in the private sector. Those who lose public sector employment through compulsory competitive tender (CCT) can find themselves re-employed by private sector contractors on poorer terms and lower pay. Increasingly it is recognised that what workers earn in essential services might represent a statutory 'minimum' wage but it does not constitute a 'living wage' (Jarvis et al. 2001: 13).[5]

The five featured cities also share in common the co-existence of economic success and urban decline in relative proximity. London's Canary Wharf is frequently cited as an example of an affluent corridor development imposed on, and irreconcilable with, a district experiencing persistent social and economic deprivation (Potts 2002: 62). It is a matter of enduring debate whether increasing earnings inequality is the result of an expanding professional elite or a deepening underclass (see for instance Hamnett 2003; Perrons 2004). Interestingly, Buck et al. (2002: 156) conclude in the UK context that while inequality in London is distinctive, for working families it is better explained by the role of the housing market than as a consequence of occupational polarisation. In a volatile market, uncertainty not only surrounds housing affordability but also the accumulation of equity. Housing wealth is not only geographically uneven (with house price rises in some regions double or treble those found elsewhere) but also lacking any regard for inter-generational equity. A 30-something couple buying their first home in London in the early 1980s would have had an easier time securing a mortgage and finding a place they could afford than an identical couple at the same point in their housing career a decade later (CML 2004). In the US context, Downs (1989: 87) estimated for the late 1980s that home equity was the single most important component of net wealth for 70 per cent of owner occupiers. Today as more families mortgage themselves to the hilt the same could be said about the single most important component of debt. The US HUD estimate that households 'cashed out' some $139 billion of accumulated equity in 2003 and used this to service credit card debts and make home improvements. The volume of equity release business increased from approximately 2.5 million refinanced loans in 2000 to more than 15 million in 2003 (US HUD 2004). With evidence that more and more families rely on their home to provide both lump-sum investments and security in old age, concern must be with the volatility and suitability of private housing investments as a substitute for public social security.

Taking a whole household economy into account, inequalities between working families are crystallised in relation to housing ladders and care chains. Chris Hamnett (1999: 156) reminds us, 'there is not a single national ladder, but a large number of locally specific ladders, each with very different characteristics and opportunity structure'. Likewise, a general population of working families are sub-divided in a myriad ways by race, class and gender but are seen to connect as links in a chain – through socio-spatial divisions of capital and labour. What they all share in common is the reality that in extreme market economies child-rearing is a private concern and children valued as a private rather than a public good. As Nancy Folbre (2001) observes, parents tax themselves heavily for the privilege of raising the next generation of workers. Using the McClements equivalence scale, a team of economists from the UK Institute of Fiscal Studies estimate that families raising children at home need to earn £9,000–£19,000 (depending on age and number of children) more than a childless couple with an income of £20,000 just to enjoy the same living standards (McClements 1977 from Goodman et al. 1997). As a consequence working families of all description – well-paid professionals to low-wage workers – face added pressure to work longer hours both in paid employment and in unpaid social reproduction work. The private costs of children are thus closely associated with gender inequality and uneven development (England 2000). The following sections demonstrate this with respect to housing affordability and self-reliance.

Housing ladders and care chains

Employment status offers an ambiguous measure of life-chance in cities like London and San Francisco where, in a booming economy, a super-rich minority dominates competition for single family owner occupation. None of the sample of working families interviewed here are close to being super-rich. Those who hold enviable 'housing wealth' do so because they bought their home at a low point in the economic cycle; or they acquired an inheritance or cash gift from relatives and this provided a deposit they could not accumulate on the basis of their salaries alone. Much of this housing wealth is more imagined than real and could only be realised through death or by down-shifting out of a dynamic labour market. Others in the sample, in similar occupations, on comparable salaries, have been less fortunate in their timing or lacked that essential windfall. One in three working families interviewed relied upon financial assistance from extended family, or benefited from inheritance, either to enter owner occupation or move from an apartment to a single family dwelling. Moreover, one in ten own a second home, usually as a source of rental income. Of course owning a home is by no means essential – but in extreme market economies it is increasingly important as a vehicle for providing a pension safety net and a popular route by which middle class parents launch their offspring's independence. Capacity to make a living and manage everyday life in such a competitive climate depends upon access to good health, ownership of superior skill and social capital, and windfalls such as inheritance. Those without these resources risk falling behind – and this comparative disadvantage automatically transfers to the next generation.

The biographies demonstrate how, in a climate of neo-liberalism, housing wealth plays a critical role in determining whether, and how successfully, individuals and households can cope with risk and attend to future (unknown) welfare needs. By way of context, a recent survey of UK home-owning parents of adult children (conducted by MORI for the Joseph Rowntree Foundation) found that parents expected to make a gift or loan of £17,000 on average to help their adult children become homeowners in what is viewed a hostile market for first-time buyers (MORI 2004). In contrast, 'hidden households' lacking access to family support can experience periods of 'sofa surfing'[6] (staying with friends or family) or live in overcrowded housing or find themselves trapped in unsuitable rented accommodation. Such hardships are illustrated in vignettes for the Slater, Pound, Lewis, Lacey and Fox families. These findings resonate with UK and US secondary data that suggest one in three cases of homelessness today are 'hidden' and involve families in work with dependent children (for Scotland see McKendrick et al. 2003). This challenges the stereotype of the unemployed, mentally ill or substance abusing single man. It also dispels the myth that all two-wage households, because they are 'work-rich', necessarily have opportunities for social mobility.

Housing affordability

Reduced housing affordability occurs in two ways. First, it results from an *absolute* housing shortage pushing up costs, through housing demand increasing more rapidly than the construction or release of additional housing supply. Second, it results from a mismatch between the type and price of housing available relative to incomes within the area. The usual method of measuring affordability in a particular market is to consider the house price to income ratio. This method is used in Table 5.3 to indicate levels of affordability in each of the five case studies. The figures demonstrate that average house prices exceed

Table 5.3 House price/income ratios for the five featured cities, 2000

Locality	Median house price[1]		Median household income		Income to price ratio	
	1995	2000	1995	2000	1995	2000
Greater London	£96,073	£177,949	£19,396	£32,224	4.9	5.5
City of Edinburgh		£93,968		£21,943		4.3
San Francisco County		$396,400		$55,221		6.7
Seattle (King County)		$236,900		$53,157		4.5
Portland (Mult- nomah County)		$157,900		$41,278		3.8

Notes:
[1] US Census data based on valuation for specified owner occupied units
Sources:
UK ONS (2000) New Earnings Survey; Land Registry for England and Wales (2004); Edinburgh Solicitors Property Service (ESPS) (2004); US Census Bureau 2000 (income data for 1999).

median earnings whereby the ratio of average house prices to earnings is higher than the standard multiple of three times income allowed by the main banks for the purpose of granting a 25 year mortgage. Even allowing for joint income households the problem is acute. Furthermore, any test of affordability based on averages is likely to underestimate the scale of the problem. House prices and incomes vary widely and, as we shall learn in more detail in Chapter Six, sub-markets for jobs and homes are poorly aligned such that low wage earners may be in a sense trapped in high-cost housing markets by lack of transport (see also Jarvis et al. 2001: 8; Hamnett 2003: 155).

We gain some sense of the shortage of housing, especially affordable housing, from difficulties local employers have recruiting staff. Employers in the private sector can increase pay or offer special pack-ages to compensate workers for high costs of living in a particular region (as in the case of London 'weighting'), ultimately passing this cost on to the consumer. Those in the UK public sector with national pay bargaining (such as nurses and teachers) and those in ubiquitous private sector jobs in both the US and UK (bus drivers, shop assistants, cleaners and the like) are unable to defray the cost of differential wages. These shortages tend to be met in the USA through irregular employment, hidden homelessness, and overcrowding – hardships concentrated among ethnic minority economic migrants. In the UK the changing role of the social rented sector has had a major impact. In 2003 the Joseph Rowntree Foundation reported that even those UK households with two moderate incomes could no longer break into high-cost housing markets as first-time buyers (Wilcox 2003). Pro-jecting a shortfall of 1.2 million homes over the next 20 years, the Royal Institute of Chartered Surveyors point to the massive drop in social and affordable housing following the 1980 Housing Act as pivotal to the current crisis (RICS 2003a). Consequently a 'housing underclass' is observed today that includes not only traditional candi-dates for social rented housing but also moderately paid professionals (RICS 2003b).

The UK government is experimenting with a number of schemes designed to alleviate affordability constraints but these tend to be restricted to specific markets (London and the south-east; first-time buyers) and particular occupations (public sector nurses and teachers) (Monk 2000; see also the Barker Report 2004).[7] Yet it is clear from the household biographies that affordability problems span a whole range of situations. A study by the University of Washington (Carlson et al. 1999) highlights the way the crisis in housing affordability (both of owner occupation and private rented accommodation) has risen up through the socio-economic hierarchy. Not only are very low income households squeezed out of accessible housing but firms report difficulties retaining skilled staff, especially those with families, who can no longer afford to live within commuting distance of where they work. Large employers, such as the University of Washington, are forced to consider intervening in the market as lenders or even direct housing providers to recruit and retain staff.

Another way of measuring relative housing affordability is to consider the impact a tight market has on conditions of housing hardship *on the ground*. This project, for instance, found surprising evidence of overcrowding and hidden homelessness. In Chapter Three we found the Florins using their living room as a bedroom for their two sons. Also living in the same San Francisco neighbourhood were Paul and Irma Fox, with their son sleeping in the walk-in closet of a one-bedroom apartment. It was shown in Chapter Four that Mr and Mrs Fuller and their daughter would be effectively homeless if required to compete in the Bay Area housing market, but for the option they have to live with Mrs Fuller's mother in the house she owns. Below we will see that in the Lewis home, three children crowd into a single bedroom. In Seattle overcrowding is a way of life for Hank and Ruth Slater where sub-let rental income props up precarious employment and inadequate insurance against unemployment.

Behind the façade of a modest three bedroom Greenwood home, Hank and Ruth Slater and their two sons all sleep in rooms originally intended for living and eating. Stepping inside their home is like chancing upon a misplaced discount bedroom furniture store. The couple supplement their earnings from two jobs by letting out their ground floor bedroom to Ruth's sister and her young child. The two basement bedrooms are home to Hank's 80 year old father and all the furniture he retained from when he previously owned the whole house. Thanks to a make-shift kitchen and bathroom arrangement, Hank's father has a relatively self-contained 'apartment' for which he pays rent out of his pension. Three family units (four adults and three children) share a single family dwelling in this otherwise unremarkable middle class neighbourhood.

Mr and Mrs Slater came to live in the Greenwood house because Hank's father offered to sell it to them to get them out of the trailer (caravan) where they were living as newly-weds. This exchange followed a precedent set by Hank's grandparents who sold the house to Hank's father as a way of helping him into owner occupation and funding their own retirement. The monthly costs of the Greenwood house were high but Hank and Ruth were happy to gain a foothold in 'real property' at last. Despite securing a college degree in his 20s, Hank's employment history revealed frequent job changes and periods of unemployment. It was to plug frequent gaps between temporary contracts that Hank set up his own business as a carpenter and handy-man. Over time this grew from weekend 'moonlighting' to a full-time business.

The income Hank earned from his carpentry business fluctuated wildly so Ruth went back to work, 'to get on top of the bills', despite believing that as a new mother she should stay home for the sake of her children. She chose to work as a cashier in a small neighbourhood store because the owner agreed she could keep her son with her throughout her shift. At first the boy could entertain himself watching television in the office while she took care of customers, but as he grew more boisterous this arrangement fell apart. She considered using day-care but financially this did not make sense. After quitting this job Ruth sought only retail employment where she could work shifts at night when Hank was home to mind the children.

Already stretched financially, Hank then suffered a shoulder injury for which he had no insurance protection and consequently had to wind up the business and look for less physically demanding regular employment. Previously when Hank was unemployed, the family had fallen back on personal savings and Hank usually found new work quite quickly. This time age and poor physical fitness stood against him and buying the house had used up their savings. Unable to get by on what Ruth earned at the supermarket they sought ways to generate income from the only other resource at their disposal, the house. A commercial tenancy would be out of the question with so unorthodox a sub-division, so as landlords the couple benefit from hard-up family members with insufficient credentials to secure mainstream rental accommodation. Today the Slater's live in less comfortable surround-ings than they previously enjoyed in their trailer, but they cling tena-ciously to the ideal of owning a piece of real estate. In this extreme case buying a house has come to signify far more than a physical shelter. While conditions of habitation for the Slater's are positively Dickensian, these 'deals on the house' demonstrate what can happen when state emphasis on self-reliance takes the place of a universal safety net.

Elsewhere we find the real 'winners' in circumstances where housing wealth can generate a home plus rental income. In Edinburgh, for instance, Mr and Mrs Egham, tell a typical story of two thirty-something professionals who when they met and married combined the property assets of two single-person households:

> We were lucky because we had two flats (between us) in the city centre and we'd sold mine and were able to move into (Mr Egham's) flat (while house-hunting) using (Mrs Egham's) equity as down-payment on a shared family home and getting tenants for (Mr Egham's) flat which pays its way. We've talked about numerous (plans) like, you know, if the kids end up going to university (the flat will pay their tuition) or it could be our pension nest egg. (Mrs Egham, Dual Career, Edinburgh – Craigmount.)

In these circumstances, UK home-owners in particular talk of their house as a source of pension security and they monitor every fluctuation in local house prices with avid interest. More prominent in the narratives of the better off US working family is concern with fluctuation in the stock market. Mrs Ford suggests the way her future plans (whether and when she and her husband might retire or cut back on working hours) are to some extent determined by the state of the US economy:

> Three years ago it was easy to be optimistic. We just expected the stock market to keep going up and we just expected our lifestyle to keep going up and that was going to take care of our retirement and it was easy to be passive. (Mrs Ford, Dual Career, San Francisco – East Bay, repeat interview in 2002.)

This suggests the way working families are compelled to be more actively self reliant, in situations where they have imperfect market information, thus taking bigger personal risks. Discussion now turns to this question of self reliance.

Self reliance

Structures of constraint in local housing and labour markets are always present in the biographies but so too are the local effects of state withdrawal from, or non-provision of, welfare services such as health and education. Here we find obvious cross national differences with respect to the way UK households benefit from a national health service whereas US households whose employment does not provide health insurance, or who have no insurance and are ineligible for the federally funded Medicaid,[8] can incur crippling debts in the event of an accident or chronic illness. In the book 'splintering urbanism', Steve Graham and Simon Marvin (2001: 5) highlight the paradox of cleaners in US hospitals unable to access the health services they serve to maintain (see also Jody Heymann's book 'Widening The Gap', 2000). Notwithstanding this fundamental difference, families in the UK too are feeling the effects of a 'postcode lottery' with respect to once universal health services. The classic example is very poor access to NHS dental services. The Citizens Advice Bureau report cases of patients having to travel hours to receive treatment, of others spending weeks in pain before getting an emergency appointment and of long queues forming outside new practices with people without any dental cover desperate to sign up. Those on low incomes and without their own transport have been the worst hit by the nationwide shortage, effectively excluding them from an ostensibly universal service (Moss 2005).

The research shows how the emphasis placed on a market-led system of healthcare disadvantages those such as Jim and Tammy Pound who have limited income and property entitlements. Jim earns only a modest income as a long-distance lorry driver and Tammy gave up paid work when she had her first child explaining that, restricted to low wage jobs, 'if I got a job all (my pay) would go to day care so what's the sense'. It has nevertheless been necessary for Tammy to earn additional income wherever possible because the family have repeatedly fallen behind on utility bills and have other accumulated debts. The largest debts relate to surgery Tammy received following a complicated pregnancy. The couple had no health insurance and are still paying off hospital bills five years after treatment. One strategy Tammy came up with to boost household funds, without leaving the children for outside employment, was to negotiate a discount on the cost of their Portland rented apartment. Tammy shows prospective tenants round the apartment block and cleans communal laundry facilities in exchange for reduced rent. Once again this illustrates how comparative advantage (and disadvantage) functions through housing, employment, health and financial security. In this case we also see that an unintended consequence of this imperative to be self-reliant is the reinforcement of traditional (persistently unequal) household gender divisions.

The biographies offer repeated evidence of unequal capacity to exploit housing as a resource, where social capital (including entrepreneurialism and risk-taking) are implicated alongside income and property as key characteristics of stratification. Some indication of the way material and social capital combine to exacerbate existing inequalities is evident in two contrasting examples of small-scale real estate specu-lation. In the first case, Mr and Mrs Skyla tell of a 20 year journey via dozens of rented apartments to a fixer-upper and ultimately self-build as the only viable route into affordable owner occupation. In the second case, Mr and Mrs Lonmore explain how having Mrs Lonmore run a small property venture from her kitchen table compensates for the loss of her salary as a lawyer when, to accommodate childcare, she switched into part-time 'mother-track' employment.

The day I met Brad and Becky Skyla they were celebrating having picked up the building permits on a property they intended to build: three weeks off 'digging the hole' they were understandably excited. In the course of a 20 year housing career they had lived together in dozens of rental properties, the length of stay, size and quality varying with income and employment status. While Becky had always brought home a regular pay check as a dental nurse, Brad experienced periodic unemployment as a carpenter. Between jobs he explains that he would: 'knock on doors and do this job for so and so, somebody that we know, or family, some of the times I would officially go on the unem-ployment and in some cases not'. During one period 'between jobs' in 1984, before the couple had their daughter, Brad took up the offer to contribute 'sweat equity' (skills and labour) in a business venture where his friend bought a run-down house in Renton, south of Seattle, which he then fixed up for re-sale. Misfortune for one family meant another took a small step up the housing ladder, as the couple explain:

> It had been an incredible purchase on the house, this guy (Brad's friend) was going through the foreclosure papers and he found it and the family needed to be out of the deal and they sold this house for 5,000 dollars or something, I mean it really was a fluke. We made good money on it. The house had just been trashed, just horrible, but it was fun (to fix it up). (Mrs Skyla, Flex Earner, Seattle – Kenmore.)
> This is a method where people purchase properties that are in dis-tress, someone who is, you know, not keeping up on mortgage pay-ments and we followed, there's publications where you can get some of that information – but we didn't come across another prop-erty that good again (because) by then (after 1986) values started to go up a lot. (Mr Skyla, Flex Earner, Seattle – Kenmore.)

Despite making money on the Renton fixer-upper it was never possible for Brad and Becky to enter owner occupation through conventional means. Prices in the Seattle area started to sky-rocket from the late 1980s. Even with two moderately good incomes they did not qualify for adequate loan finance. This lack of security troubled Brad's parents, who lived a few miles out of the city in Brier. They live in the same house they bought when Brad was two years old. Like many houses built on the fringe of the city in the 1950s it came with a generous plot of land. Wanting to see their grandchild securely housed in their life-time, they decided to give Brad a sub-division of their 'back yard' for a self-built home. This form of 'bungalow in my back yard' (BIMBY) development is endorsed by town planners on both sides of the Atlantic who want to see housing densities increase in peri-urban areas. In this case, sub-division represents a form of inter-generational exchange, similar to equity release. The fact that this story has a happy ending, against considerable odds, only serves to amplify the critical importance of resource entitlements (including extended family gen-erosity) as a passport to housing security in a highly competitive market-led economy. In such a climate, those with neither social *nor* material capital are truly disadvantaged.

While Mr and Mrs Skyla use sweat equity to inch their way onto the property market as first-time buyers, Steve and Cathy Lonmore benefit from cash equity accumulated over the course of previous transactions to expand their investment portfolio. Cathy explains that she started her London property venture in 1998 because she wanted to 'diversify sources of income' so she would have the option to drop out of full-time employment. She applies the vocab-ulary and business acumen acquired in her professional life to the way she manages family life. For instance, she views the wealth she generates dealing in buy-to-let property as a substitute for income lost shifting from full to part-time working, suggesting that it increases her say in household decisions. She also views her kitchen-table venture as part of a long-term plan to fund the private education she considers necessary for her son as an alternative to the poorly regarded inner London state school which he would oth-erwise attend. She also suggests that the decision to have a second child will depend on the success of this venture because they 'could not contemplate paying two lots of school fees' on Steve's salary alone. This is popularly known as the 'second child syndrome' whereby the financial costs and logistical constraints of a second child tip the balance of the dual earning household structure (Summerskill and Ryle 2001). Cathy looks for small terraced homes in traditionally working class neighbourhoods such as Leyton and

Camden Town and remodels them to meet the needs of her 'target tenants' who are 'people just starting out in the city, trainee accountants, trainee solicitors, people who want to rent somewhere respectable but not somewhere at silly prices, somewhere close to transport'. Her attitude to borrowing is that of the entrepreneur:

> I see it as, when you sit down and assess the risk, I actually consider the risk of doing this is a lot less than the risk of not doing this.
> Mrs Lonmore, Flex Career, London – Islington.

When it comes to providing the best for their son, Cathy and Steve fear being left behind.

The fear of 'being left behind' is widespread across the sample. Also in London, Mr and Mrs Lacey express this fear in relation to the access they have to affordable 'key worker' housing. Mr and Mrs Lacey live in a house owned by Mr Lacey's employer, the Metropolitan Police, on the edge of a very upmarket part of Islington. Mrs Lacey explains that the Police try to make affordable rented homes available 'to people with children because housing is so expensive'. But in a sense this way of solving the crisis serves to further perpetuate inequalities in retirement and with respect to inter-generational exchange. Now that the UK government actively encourages the release of housing equity to underwrite the cost of higher education, eldercare and the like, not being in a position to accumulate such a lump sum (few savings schemes appreciate to the extent that house prices have in recent years) puts the tenant at a disadvantage. This is certainly the way Mrs Lacey sees it. She refers to rent as 'dead money' and views owner occupation as a way to secure her children's future. The couple have consequently agreed to vacate their Islington key-working housing and relocate to where they can afford to buy a house in Welwyn Garden City, a one hour commute North.

> It will be a long journey for (husband) but we've got to balance out the schools and trying to buy a house. Obviously, we want to buy our own home because we've got to (get) back in the property market, I mean, it's easy to be cocooned in here and think we'll stay here (because) it's a good size and everything but when you retire you've got to get back into that market and you can't do that because you're bottom of the (ladder) so you're just paying dead money which is rent, it's just dead money, you're better to be in your own home (where) you can do what you want basically. (Mrs Lacey, Flex Earner, London – Islington.)

Dilemmas for the cab driver and his fare

Most of the working families in the sample appreciate that their perch in the city, though fraught with logistical difficulties, is relatively advantaged. Yet effort to achieve work/life balance is particularly difficult where the cost of housing is high. It often entails compromise – dropping out of accessible central locations, having one spouse sacrifice pay or promotion, working long hours or adopting more traditional gender roles than intended. This section traces the contrasting fortunes of two working families, neighbours in the same London district. Vignettes from these biographies are used to make connections between a host of resource attributes – housing, employment, childcare, transport and social capital – all implicated in a process of continual, incremental adjustment. Persistent inequalities underpin this process, notably with respect to 'chains' linking (and dividing) key workers and the professionals who rely on the services they provide. This is one way of addressing the need to broaden the scope of the work/life reconciliation policy agenda (Gross 2001).

A foothold in the city

Ed and Sonia Lewis share little in common with Harry and Kate Law except through the coincidence that Harry regularly travels to work as a passenger in Ed's taxi cab.[9] Ed and Sonia live in a social rented two-bedroom flat in the heart of fashionable Islington. Their flat is on the third floor of an attractive Edwardian terrace on a square with street parking arranged around a small communal garden. This is precisely the traditional neighbourhood design that the New Urbanism seeks to emulate (Ellis 2002). Despite living in a much sought after location their situation is far from ideal: their three children share one bedroom. This is crammed with bunk beds and a cot leaving no room for storage or space for the children to play. The only realistic way the family can move to a bigger property in the area is to take part in a mutual exchange, but scope to do so is limited by reduced social rented stock. When Ed and Sonia first moved in, many of their neighbours were buying their homes from the council under the 'right to buy' provisions of the 1980 Housing Act. Since then most have sold to incoming professionals in a classic illustration of state assisted gentrification. While Ed can 'earn a decent living' as a cab driver the only way he and Sonia could afford to buy a home of their own would be to move to a less expensive housing market outside London. But Ed insists that the living he earns involves long hours and the knowledge he can pick up work 'on his doorstep' as and when he needs. He explains:

> Because I'm a cab driver I can literally get in my cab and start work straight away. I can leave here at 8, half 8 in the morning and come home at 6 at night, like in the middle of both rush hours, but most taxi drivers tend to, when they earn good money, they move out, they can't do them hours, they have to come in at half 5 in the morning or start 2 o'clock in the afternoon, come in, like stagger it, the long shift, because they don't want to get stuck in the traffic. I do long enough hours as it is without getting stuck an hour and half in traffic both ends of the day just so we can have more room by moving out.

Being self-employed Ed is tempted to work very long hours. He routinely works a six day week and adds to this a Sunday shift if his takings for the week have been slow or the family face additional expenses such as a family holiday. His living is seasonal whereby 'January dies and I'll rob Peter to pay Paul, so February I'm playing catch up'. If he is sick and unable to drive he generates no income and like other independent contractors he must provide his own insurance or safety net against periodic loss of income. What he can earn putting in the same hours each week also varies, as he explains:

> I could leave here at 8 o'clock in the morning and I might not get a job for (a while), or I might get a stupid 2 or 3 quid job and then other days I can leave here and there might be a couple waiting on the corner wanting to go to Heathrow, it's just the luck of the day.

This lack of guaranteed income drives a regime of long working hours. Ed admits he will sometimes go out to work on a Sunday evening to 'get a head start on the week', anticipating poor earnings, but rarely reimbursing himself this time if takings turn out better than expected.

> I can just keep working and working and I can work as long as I want. It normally works out that I work Monday to Friday and that will cover the cab, tax and everything and the money for family life and then Saturdays tends to be for extras, if we've got stuff like we need to go shopping, clothes shopping, I call Saturday my Barclaycard Day, because that's what it covers! Then to pay for holidays I'll just try and work 3 or 4 hours every Sunday. It's the way

I like doing it, because I'll get the money that way, it's the perfect job because it's instant overtime but it does sometimes put a strain on your family life.

Time efficiency

Just as Ed Lewis defends living in central London in overcrowded accommodation in terms of the way it brings work to his door, so Harry Law, a successful investment banker, justifies his mode of transport by claiming it is more time efficient. Harry explains why he chooses to travel 20 minutes to Canary Wharf by cab each day:

I start work as soon as I step out the door. I'll have 15 voice mail messages and I deal with them on the way in. I work while I'm in the cab whereas if I take a bus or the underground I lose up to 45 minutes

But Harry and his wife Kate, a lawyer who is currently on maternity leave, demonstrate their strong attachment to a home in central London on the basis of quite different resource entitlements to Ed and Sonia. They recently bought a run-down terraced house in the London Fields area, which they identified as 'one of the last affordable bits of N1' because it met their taste in urban vitality. While they enjoy proximity to shops and restaurants they do not plan to send their son to the neighbourhood school. Once again this demonstrates the significance of unequal household resource distributions. Because of their superior resource entitlements (including inheritance and the perks of good employment) Harry and Kate can opt out of local neighbourhood disadvantage. Those without this escape route on the other hand are permanently excluded from opportunities of social (and spatial) mobility. By rejecting public transit in favour of a more private means of conveyance, Harry Law not only 'saves time' by speeding up the journey but also improves his capacity to conduct work on the move (buses are noisy and mobile phones do not work underground) (Nickols and Fox 1983; Jarvis et al. 2001: 2). Underwriting this perk, Harry's employer entitles him to 'jump the queue' in the competition for space on the roads (taxis use priority lanes and are exempt from inner London congestion charges). In effect the cab is a mobile workplace for both the cab-driver and his fare, but each experiences time as a resource in very different ways.

In this case we see how the time-squeeze compounds inequalities already existing within and between households whereby these pressures are met with different levels of resistance and resolved on the basis of unequal resource entitlements. This includes unequal access to time-saving technology and additional personnel (Silverstone 1993; Skinner 2003). We know from the previous chapter that time itself is a resource of unequal distribution. Daly (1996: 116–7) makes this point with respect to the 'speeding up' of family life:

> with the escalating sense of time scarcity, there are more conflicts – both within families and between families and the social order of which they are a part – about time control, allocation and entitlement. For families, this means examining time in light of increasing diversity and disorder in family structure and in relation to the accompanying ambivalences and indecision that exists with respect to relationships and gender arrangements.

Childcare shortage

Returning to Ed and Sonia's housing dilemma, it is apparent that this entails not only housing and income constraints but also gender divisions and parenting. The chain of connection mapped out above suggests that divisions *between* households also perpetuate inequalities *within* households. In order for Ed to be in a position to take his cab out at any time or day of the week to boost household income, Sonia has to restrict her job search to low paid local jobs in school hours. She experiences far less freedom to move about the city than Ed because of the hard (time-fixed) constraint of the school run and the soft constraint of bus routes and the time it takes to travel places on foot. This difference in gendered mobility is illustrated in Figure 5.1 as a stylised time-space prism. The difficulties of fitting any formal childcare arrangement around Ed's long and variable working hours has meant that Sonia has not worked for pay since her first child was born. Now, with two children in school, she is taking up a school office job. She chose this opening because it only requires her to work school hours. Nevertheless, childcare remains an issue for the youngest child (who has just turned one). Neither set of grandparents live sufficiently nearby to baby-sit and she could not afford the cost of a private nursery or childminder on her low wage. A subsidised place in a state nursery will only be made available when their son turns three. This means in the intervening period Ed will have to change his working hours to provide childcare during term-time when Sonia is at work. He can do this because he is self-employed but Sonia explains that this will reduce Ed's earnings more than the contribution she will make in

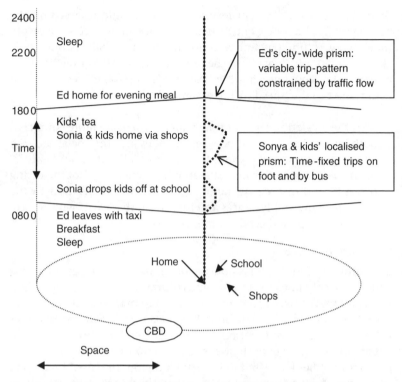

Figure 5.1   Stylised time-space prism for the Lewis family – showing gender difference associated with hard and soft mobility constraints

her new job. Having both of them work around the continuing demands of home-based childcare will not make them any better off. This is not then the solution to the housing problems they face ('trapped' in overcrowded social rented accommodation). While previously the financial 'logic' has been for Sonia to stay home to look after the children, the absence of any material benefit is not reason enough to keep her permanently out of the work force.

> we won't be any better off but what we said was if I could get this job that's going at the school, if I'm there now, if we can manage for a year and a half, once the baby's in at nursery then Ed could go back to work normal, you know, we wouldn't necessarily benefit from it (now) but I'd get my foot in the door to get the job because them jobs are hard to come by.

The problem of access to affordable childcare is well known. It is most severe for low wage households but shortages are also apparent for those who can afford private for-profit nurseries. This is reflected in the way mothers queue up for a nursery place long before they give birth and once this is secured they show great reluctance to switch facilities to suit a change in personal circumstance. The problem illustrates clearly the co-constitution of material and temporal constraint (housing and employment). Access to affordable childcare is not only limited by inadequate state provision: shortages occur in private-for-profit markets because wages paid to care-givers (the majority of them women) do not compete with more commercial activities.

Connection through division

Complicating the notion of a care-deficit (discussed in Chapter Four) and estimates of its likely scale is evidence that childcare is not limited geographically to the state-market-family mix of any one nation or region. In their book 'Global Woman: Nannies, Maids and Sex-workers', Barbara Ehrenreich and Arlie Hochschild (2003) generate the image of a 'global care chain'. They see the growing care deficit as the female underside to globalisation whereby:

> In the absence of help from male partners, many first world women have succeeded in tough 'male world' careers only by turning over the care of their children, elderly parents and home to women from the Third World (Ehrenreich and Hochschild 2003: 2).

Indeed there is growing concern for the way geo-politically uneven patterns of livelihood deliver desperate and indebted individuals as human links in a global chain of exploitative capital relations. In this way, Geraldine Pratt (2004: 32) claims that middle class women's participation in employment is bound up with the subjugation of migrant female labour, (re)producing middle class women 'in relation to their female counterpart, the racialised servant' (see also Bakker and Gill 2003).

This notion of a care chain is evident in the friendship struck between two London working families, each living half a mile from the other on the Hackney/Islington border. One family is the professional couple introduced above, Cathy and Steve Lonmore, both lawyers, living with their pre-school age son as owner occupiers with a string of investment in buy-to-let property. The other is a couple of similar age,

Madge and Pete Ling,[10] with two teenage children, who live in a maisonette allocated to them as public sector tenants 15 years ago, more recently bought under the right-to-buy scheme. While they anticipate their modest home is now worth considerably more than they paid for it six years ago, this new-found 'housing wealth' is illusory. They are in no position to move unless to an equivalent ex-council house in a less popular neighbourhood or leave the high-cost London housing market entirely.

When Madge had her son 14 years ago she gave up her job supervising an accounts office. She didn't question this at the time. Pete worked shifts at the Post Office and even if she had wanted to keep her job it would have been very difficult to arrange childcare. The only way she could earn income of her own was by taking on ad hoc cleaning jobs. For many years she cleaned for an elderly lady who in 1997 sold her home to Mr and Mrs Lonmore. Madge found herself effectively 'taken on with the house'. Friendship blossomed out of this unusual arrangement such that when Cathy was ready to return to work after maternity leave, it felt natural to ask Madge if she would take on the job of childminder. To the outsider the childcare arrangement the women negotiated might seem chaotic but in practice it mirrors the complex intertwining of their lives. Cathy explains:

> She's not a childminder in the sense that she only looks after (son), but she comes to collect him from us and takes him with her and then she or her husband brings him back. They have very flexible working arrangements and it fits in very well. She minds him from the morning until about 4 and then her husband comes home and he minds him from 4 until 6.30 and brings him home to me, so their family is kind of like ours. But neither she nor I want to work full-time so it suits us both perfectly.

Cathy admits she is heavily reliant upon Madge and Pete and has been discussing with them what to do when her son starts school. Madge has a lot of early evening activities such as Brownies which will make it difficult for her to make the school run on a regular basis and the private school Cathy has identified for her son is in the city within the zone of congestion charging. She thinks she has persuaded Pete to do the school run one day and Madge two days and wants to 'be there for (her son)' herself the remaining two days. Pete's involvement in the Lonmore's childcare routines has developed over time. Cathy prides herself that as an employer she offers more than a cash wage. When

Pete was unemployed recently Cathy employed him to work on her rental properties (described above) and found him other decorating jobs through her network of friends. By scaling back her professional career, Cathy has found time to build up a valuable network of contact. She claims:

> That's the difference between our lives and those of our friends really, that they haven't got the advantage of that informal network. Until you are at home yourself you don't dare accept any kind of school run arrangement or have someone mind your child as a favour because you can't reciprocate and you don't want to generate bad feeling over that fact. That's the difference, you have to have time to enter into these arrangements and money isn't sufficient on it's own – the time is more important.

Summary

The purpose of this chapter has been to probe the use working families in the five cities make of the resources at their disposal to compete for housing, employment, transport and childcare in tight market situations. The results show that households rely on multiple sources of income whether through having more than one job or wage-earner or by exploiting property income potential. While it is increasingly common to find both partners in couple families going out to work each day, the effort required to maintain this busy 'work-rich' lifestyle is at times overwhelming, as we saw in the case of the Poulter family in Chapter Four. Cross-national differences are apparent in these coping strategies but so too are generic dilemmas. It comes as no surprise to find that housing affordability, family welfare and childcare issues emerge as the greatest problems confronting working parents in all five featured cities. Entry barriers to owner occupation and lack of alternative forms of affordable housing, together with costs of caring for dependents, exacerbate underlying income inequality in these market-led economies. From the vantage of integrated biographic analysis the research demonstrates the interdependencies of these dilemmas in this respect. Of crucial significance is the evidence that working families with ostensibly similar assets and resources arrive at different solutions to these dilemmas. This advances the argument made previously that preference formation and decision making are culturally constituted and locally embedded rather than economically or structurally determined.

Where cross-national differences are most evident is with respect to the overall resource entitlements available to those in the sample on relatively low incomes. Key here is the suggestion that both the UK and USA demonstrate similarly extreme inequalities in absolute income but that UK working families on low incomes have greater public protection from the vicissitudes and risks of pure private market strategies. This is best illustrated with respect to national healthcare provision in the UK. The harrowing situation where Mr and Mrs Pound have for years been shackled to a mountain of child-birth, hospital, and prescription charge debts would be unthinkable in the UK. Health outcomes remain abysmally poor in the United States because an increasing proportion of poor families have inadequate access to medical care and are without any form of health insurance (Heymann 2000; OECD 2000b).

Turning to housing market strategies it is tempting to concede that less stringent planning and building regulation in the USA opens up more rungs at the lower end of the market, such as with the proliferation of low cost 'manufactured homes'. We saw this in the case of the Slater's whose first home was a trailer (caravan) and the Skyla's who are building their own home at the bottom of Mr Skyla's parent's garden. Families in the UK are generally denied these entrepreneurial routes to low cost owner occupation. Instead we find that social rented housing continues to play a significant role in protecting families unable to service a large mortgage, in some cases providing the safe and convenient stop-gap necessary to build up alternative assets and resources. We see this with Mr and Mrs Eagle. Their first home was a social rented flat in Leith where they lived for a number of years before combining a legacy they received from Mrs Eagle's mother with their accumulated savings as a deposit on an owner occupied maisonette. Both the Lewis and Ling families have benefited in the past from social rented housing allocated in central London neighbourhoods with good access to jobs and transport. The problem of overcrowding for the Lewis family stems from a lack of mobility in this diminishing sector. Of course the concern here is that this long-established source of protection is under siege. Looking to the future, it is likely that housing hardship will grow more acute a problem in the UK as the culmination of a long-term failure to supply sufficient new housing both in the private for profit and social rented sector in particular, as well as regulations prohibiting temporary or low cost self-built homes.

The coping strategies examined in this chapter represent those for working families comfortably sitting some way above the poverty threshold. These relatively advantaged households are nonetheless implicated in what is shown in secondary data analysis to be a rise in poverty and housing hardship among families with children. On the one hand the household narratives show that there are no guarantees that middle class families will not themselves fall on hard times, where employment is sometimes short-lived and high living costs militate against adequate personal safety nets. On the other hand the research illustrates how these households reproduce inequalities, by race, class and gender, in the solutions they arrive at to co-ordinate daily life. In a competitive climate where individual capability is emphasised in place of collective responsibility, middle class families unwittingly exploit those with weaker resource entitlements than their own. We saw this in the case of the London cab driver's family relative to his affluent passenger and the chains of exploitation linking the Lonmore and the Ling families. Madge Ling is paid to entertain and care for Cathy Lonmore's son but she was never in a position to have anyone do the same for her children. Moreover these chain link connections are ultimately global in extent with respect to the spatial divisions of labour which deliver economic migrants from overseas as nannies, cleaners, gardeners and dog-walkers. What might at first appear to be localised circuits of production and social reproduction ultimately contribute to the 'outrageous exploitation' Isabella Bakker identifies in the wake of hegemonic neo-liberalism and 'a globalization of the idea of self-help and possessive individualism' (Bakker and Gill 2003: 94; 14). This way, public failure to address fundamental (and growing) inequalities between households are exacerbated by the private struggles and coping strategies employed by busy working families who are packing more activities into each day. On the one hand, dual career couple conflicts over who does what are reduced by delegating unpopular tasks to paid domestic workers. On the other hand, those employed to help middle class families' co-ordinate daily life have fewer resources with which to reconcile their own pressures of work and the desire to improve their children's prospects.

With little offered in the way of public childcare parents in extreme market economies have to choose between help from friends and relatives and childcare purchased from nurseries and childminders. As we know from the previous chapter, such decisions are wrongly conceived as a straightforward trade-off made on the basis of income and the cost of childcare. The biographies show that the very definition of assets and resources from which to assemble routine co-ordination strategies resides in a local moral context: what is understood by the notion of a good parent or the compulsion to be true to oneself. Of course this is not to deny that it is not possible to define as preferable those assets and resources (or entitlements) which are not available. What individuals and households consider to be morally preferable in a given situation functions alongside Bourdieu's (1990) 'logic of the situation'. Thus we find that high rates of professional migration and scattered kin networks compel dual earning couples to make recourse to private childcare solutions (Mason 1999). Working parents in the UK who previously would have organised informal childcare with relatives, turn to private day-care in growing numbers, exceeding existing capacity. Even in the USA where the market for private day-care is more advanced there is widespread shortage. Part of the problem is that childcare is labour intensive and unsuited to the economies of scale of other mass-produced goods and services.

Childcare provision is unlike any other market. Pressure to keep costs down degrades the pay, status and skill of childcare workers such that many women working in this sector (for this is an intensely feminised sector) turn to better paid employment or drop out of the labour market entirely. Pre-schools often go out of business and staff turnover is extraordinary high (Blau 2001: 8). Although the working parents interviewed spend a large proportion of household income on day-care fees (typically more than they already have to set aside for monthly mortgage payments) this pays the nursery workers a paltry wage. Those who are themselves mothers typically rely on informal childcare solutions. Ultimately, then, the ability for middle class working mothers to go out to work each day rests with the unpaid grandmothers helping out their low-wage daughters and grandchildren. Reliance on individual women's unequal capacity to compete in the workplace exposes the fatal flaw in a system of partial economic accounting which disregards a significant proportion of the work which is the mainstay of affluent economies like those of the UK and USA. In this sense we see how the estimated £1 billion grandparents provide in unpaid childcare ultimately subsidises the marginal rate of productivity of affluent knowledge workers and the GDP. David Blau (2001: 8) looks in detail at the shortfall in childcare services in high cost cities in the US context. He finds that pressure to keep costs down to what working parents can bear in the private-for-profit sector degrades the pay, status and skill of childcare workers. This is evident in the UK too where the childcare workforce is the least well qualified in the EU, staff turnover is high and the average age of nursery workers is just 24 (Land 2002a). Reinforcing this message, Nancy Folbre and Julie Nelson (2000: 129) estimate that non-market (re)production childcare, eldercare and domestic labour account for upward of 60 per cent of the total value of US output, valued on the basis of time-use and labour inputs alone. Moreover, this assumes perfect substitutability between home-produced goods and commodities. In reality the working parents interviewed stress that there are no market substitutes for some labours of love.

The childcare shortage is made worse by the high cost of housing driving low-income families further out of metropolitan centres. To raise the deposit for a single family home (the majority aspiration), working families increasingly rely on inheritance, financial gifts from extended family, stock options and bonuses or equity from an earlier advantageous timing in the purchase of property as a single adult. This puts those without these resources at a huge disadvantage. We can see the sense in which home ownership has taken on elevated and manifold status in recent years by the emphasis the UK government now places on equity release as a source of welfare provision in old age. Of course while for the lucky ones the size of equity might appear large, there are only so many ways of slicing up this property pie before it is reduced to a plate of crumbs. A stark choice might exist in the future between helping adult children and funding the cost of medical care in old age. While this pattern of inequality is firmly established in the USA it crops up in the UK narratives as a more recent import. Yet this newly felt inequality has been increasing in the UK in recent decades (Atkinson 2002). Judging from the travails of relatively disadvantaged US working families presented in this chapter, it is not difficult to predict the future for those at the bottom of the heap in the UK if the trend towards rationing public services continues.

6
Sustainability

Energy use and time-squeeze

'Climate change is the most severe problem that we are facing today, more serious even than the threat of terrorism' Sir David King, chief scientific adviser to the British Government (Connor 2004).
The question remains 'whether high growth is sustainable, not only in conventional economic terms but also in terms of accompanying effects on our surroundings' (OECD 2000a: 5).
'Mobility is liberating and empowering, but it is possible to have too much of a good thing' (John Adams 1999: 1).

Claims that anthropogenic climate changes constitute a real and present danger are not new but they are more credible today than at any time in history. While Sir David King grabs the headlines above, the Intergovernmental Panel on Climate Change (IPCC)[1] reports worldwide scientific consensus that 'most of the warming observed over the last 50 years is attributable to human activities' (IPPC 2001: 5). Foremost among all human activity contributing to global warming is the tendency for rising numbers of people to adopt a high energy consuming, car-reliant lifestyle. The twin enemies of energy conservation are rising affluence and the speeding up of daily life. Many people take unlimited travel for granted, driving rather than walking short distances to enable them to pack more activities, more efficiently, more conveniently, into busy daily schedules; driving or flying sometimes vast distances – because rising affluence and transport innovation allows them to do so. Yet one legacy of the Iraq war is greater awareness among motorists, industry, and governments of the possibility of continued oil price volatility not unlike the shocks of the 1970s[2] (Roberts 2003). No longer is it radical or naïve to question the moral and economic justification of ever increasing living standards in the northern hemisphere: the United Nations Environment Programme and OECD raise this very concern in the documents cited above (Brown 1998; Black 1999).

Busy working parents in all five featured cities exhibit symptoms of time-squeeze: acceleration in the pace of life and addiction to time-saving innovation (mobile phones, hand-held computers, ready pre-pared meals). Yet emphasis in the literature on the 'speeding up' of daily life (particularly in relation to ICT) neglects the reality of all that slows people down a lot of the time (Jarvis 2005). Arguably, the stress of trying to reconcile activities of work with the rest of life is not just about hours in the day; it is also about getting from A to B and over-coming all the obstacles along the way. Mobility is unevenly dis-tributed, just like resources of income and property discussed in the previous chapter. Some people experience transport poverty and through this limited access to jobs, affordable homes, healthy food, social services and the like (Turner and Grieco 1998). In the UK, the Social Exclusion Unit view the high cost of running a car and the yet higher cost of public transit and its poor reliability as significant barri-ers to employment. Consequently they endorse a 'Wheels 2 Work' scheme (SEU 2003; Carter and Grieco 2000). This provides loan of a moped, sometimes a car, to low wage workers for six months to enable them to access employment and save towards the cost of their own vehicle at the end of the loan period. Also providing driving lessons, the scheme recognises that for some journeys and locations there is no realistic alternative to private motorised transport.

At the other extreme, a significant minority of well paid profession-als enjoy mobility in excess. Research by The Work Foundation (for-merly The Industrial Society) identifies mobility as a 'powerful new division in the world of work' creating a 'hyper-mobile' elite (Doyle and Nathan 2001: 43). Mobility is a way of life for the 'cosmocrat' whose office is the ubiquitous airport lounge and whose little used city loft apartment assumes the style of the more familiar boutique hotel. The working parents reported here are neither transport-deprived nor truly hyper-mobile (though two do not own a car and several are obliged to travel overseas regularly on business). Yet all have experienced a speeding up and growing complexity to the chore-ography of their daily movements and routines. Arguably an unin-tended outcome of this is an environmentally damaging increase in the use of motorised transport for short distances. This is coupled with the stress (sometimes leading to 'road rage') of more people following the same pattern of behaviour, adding to a high volume of traffic on the roads. This chapter tackles the problem of unintended consequences in the travel behaviour of the sample households. Particular attention is paid to the role of transport and mobility in common household dilemmas concerning school choice and gaps or failings in state planning for mass transport. The first part examines the problem of spatial mismatch. Evidence is compared for the UK and USA and across the five cities, looking at car ownership, modes of travel and local environmental cultures. The second part focuses on apparent dissonance between stated preference for compact urban living and the web of connections binding housing, employment, gender and environmental impact. This comparison draws on quasi-quantitative analysis of the household biographies. Finally it is argued that essential changes in travel behaviour are only possible if we question the conventional growth paradigm.

The problem of spatial mismatch

The spectre of a growing mismatch between job options and housing choice adding to a spatially fragmented lifestyle was first raised in Chapter One. Striking regional disparities are forged by population migration and uneven investment in business, transport and civic amenities. These factors directly influence patterns of settlement as well as localised segregation. Data recently released from the USA Census Bureau 2000 and the 2001 UK[3] Census of Population[4] show a widening gap between competitive and moribund cities and regions (Logan 2003). More than three quarters of the 32.7 million people added to the US population since 1990 settled within the South and West (Glaeser and Shapiro 2001: 9; Sohmer and Lang 2003). Equally, it is well established that the UK economy is heavily skewed toward London and the rest of the south-east (Jacobs 1992; Dunford and Fielding 1997). One third of the UK population reside in a region accounting for some 11 per cent of the total land area. Moreover, in the USA in particular, per capita land use and energy consumption is steep and rising faster than population. By way of example, population grew by less than 30 per cent in Kansas City between 1960 and 1990 while land devoted to housing and development rose by 110 per cent (Beatley and Manning 1997: 7). This rise in per capita consumption ripples out from land use to multiply the energy consumed in transport and waste disposal as we saw in comparative 'ecological footprint' data in Table 2.4. This way the USA accounts for 4.6 per cent of the world population yet it consumes more than 20 per cent of world energy resources while the UK accounts for 0.9 per cent of the world population and consumes a more modest two per cent of world energy resources (OECD 2000a: 6).

Implicit in the language of UK urban renaissance and US smart growth initiatives is belief that where an environmentally damaging jobs-housing mismatch exists this can be resolved in three ways. One course of action is to steer housing market activity towards new job opportunities and encourage more self-contained, integrated communities. The reverse steer is also popular among UK policy makers whereby John Prescott (Deputy Prime Minister) has made repeated claims that housing shortages in the South East of England could be solved by relocating whole departments of the civil service 'up North' where (as a caricature) whole streets of houses sit vacant and land is plentiful[5] (Brown 2003). A second approach is to move people more efficiently between jobs and homes, encouraging integrated transport and planning for new economic activity within designated transport corridors. This is illustrated, again in the UK context, by plans to build 200,000 new homes in the Thames Gateway (sites north and south of the Thames estuary east of London) (ODPM 2003). Third, proposals are to shift more information and telecommunications technology based employment into individual homes and residential neighbourhoods (Metro 1997). Whether initiatives focus on high density urban concentration or mixed use suburban settlement, the popular assumption is that local access to jobs, housing, shops and schools will reduce energy consumption (vehicle kilometre miles) and foster balanced communities through more localised living. It is constructive to consider each of these proposals in turn, from a household perspective, to critically examine this assumed correlation. Doing so helps explain why the challenge of radically changing Western consumer values and the growth paradigm has to be confronted – because technical planning solutions alone will not yield sustainable travel behaviour.

First, it is commonplace in international housing studies literature to report higher rates of residential mobility for US compared with European households (Strassmann 2001: 16–17). On aggregate, something like 18 per cent of US households live at a different address to that reported a year previous, compared with six per cent of British households (US Census Bureau 2000; ONS/LRC 2001). At the same time there is evidence to suggest that US households are less inclined than in the past to make voluntary short distance moves to accommodate residential, employment or transport adjust-ment (Fischer 2000: 5). Voluntary mobility is widely viewed as a pos-itive (if not equitable) manifestation of efficient housing markets. From this it follows that greater residential mobility serves to reduce jobs-housing mismatch. In practice, however, there is greater evi-dence of mismatch in US than European cities (Cervero 1986). Fischer (2000) notes that US skilled workers are more likely to migrate over long distances between states for the purposes of early career development, resulting in the common experience of middle class couples raising families far removed from networks of potential kin support. Once established in a strong metropolitan economy catering for two jobs or careers, these households are less likely to make any subsequent move. Of the one hundred couples inter-viewed for this project, twice as many US as UK working parents were migrants from another state or region.[6] The vast majority of parents ruled out any future move which would take them away from their current neighbourhood, claiming they would extend their journeys to work, travel further to maintain contact with family and friends or escort children to non-local schools if necessary, rather than move house.

Second, while housing debates appear to be stuck at the question 'where' jobs and housing should be steered, questions concerning 'how' we might live and work in the future are monopolised by transport and technology considerations. It is assumed that growth in long-distance commuting by rising numbers of suburban workers contributes the greatest volume of 'wasteful' journeys: hence emphasis on the goodness of fit between housing and labour markets (see for instance Com-munications Technologies 1987; and Cervero 1988 for the case of California's Silicon Valley; Downs 1992). Emphasis is also given to putting more work back into the home. Yet the relative location of jobs and housing, and the extent of business travel associated with individ-ual workers, at best partially explains the trend of increased and more dispersed movement. There is certainly evidence to support the idea that residents of compact, mixed-use neighbourhoods make more walk/bicycle trips than residents of lower-density suburban housing estates. Comparing shop trip-making, Handy (1993) found those living in compact neighbourhoods made 2–4 more walk/bicycle trips per week to neighbourhood stores than those living in nearby suburbs. Cervero and Radisch (1995) found that pedestrian-oriented designs exerted a strong influence on non-work trips for convenience shopping and leisure activities. Yet these studies concede that short walk trips neither replace car trips to regional shopping malls or single occupancy vehicle

(SOV) journeys to non-local schools or remote places of work. For instance, Kitamura et al. (1990) show that central city commuters engage in 'trip chaining' behaviour for the sake of time efficiency whereby individual trips are short but chained together they represent a lengthy journey and complex schedule. This point is further illustrated by data from the Nationwide Personal Transportation Survey (NPTS 1995). While the average journey to work distance has increased marginally in recent years, far more significant increase in proportion, quantity and length of household trips is attributed to 'shopping' and 'family or personal business'. These categories combined account for 46 per cent of all person trips and 34 per cent of all person miles travelled per household. Together with 'school/church' related trips these represent the majority of unpaid social reproduction work routinely required by the working family household. In Marin County in California, as much as 27 per cent of the traffic on the roads each morning is made of up parents driving their children to school (NCBW 2004). Associations have been made between this trend and an epidemic rise in obesity in children. A similar trend is seen in the UK where 30 per cent of all 5–16 year olds (up to 90 per cent of primary school children) are routinely driven to school by car, as compared with 12 per cent in 1975/76 (National Travel Survey 2003; see also www.transport2000.org.uk). Just to put this in perspective, following an exemplary national 'safe routes to schools' programme in the 1980s, 80 per cent of Danish children either cycle or walk to school each day (NCBW 2004). The effect of increased chaperoning by car is self-perpetuating: as more parents drive their children to school the roads appear less safe to those parents who would otherwise have allowed their children to walk or cycle so they too add to the race for space to drop off children at the school gates. Parking problems are also acute in residential areas where a number of state, independent and private schools compete for pupils from a wide geographic area.

Third, it is popularly believed that fast, global, networked Information and Communications Technology (ICT) eliminates the need to travel. Thus initiatives promoting 'flexible' working time arrangements (flexitime, the compressed week and staggered working) and telecommuting (information and communications technology installed in homes or local telecommuting centres) are favoured for environmental reasons (Handy and Mokhtarian 1995; Goelman 2004)). Belief that technology will overcome the compulsion to travel is arguably speculative, much the same way the proliferation of personal computers did not bring about the predicted paper-less office (Mokhtarian et al. 2004). Indeed as The Work Foundation research demonstrates, proliferation of ICT actually tends to increase energy consuming movement by the possibility of remaining 'always on', working while on the move (Doyle and Nathan 2001; see also English-Lueck 2002).[7] Teleworking is really only viable for a limited range of occupations (Peters et al. 2004). Consequently the proportion of US employees working from home was less than five per cent in 2000 (US Census Bureau 2000) and in the UK the proportion of the population working or studying at home in 2001 was 5.8 per cent in Edinburgh and 8.6 per cent in London (City of Edinburgh Council 2003). There are in addition serious psychological barriers to widespread home based employment (Allen and Wolkowitz 1987; Haddon and Silverstone 1993; Pliskin 1998). While there is greater scope for the expansion of more flexible working hours, it is questionable whether staggered working can sufficiently reduce peak hour traffic congestion. Indeed, a strong case can be made that individual 'flexible' labour market practices, when combined together in two wage households, are inflexible as we saw in Chapter Four.

Competing identifications

As noted in Chapter Two and above, there is a tendency for planners on both sides of the Atlantic to view the problem of mismatch as one of inadequate physical integration of land uses. It is popular to measure sustainable development by the ease with which local residents can walk to a corner shop for instance. But such a model fails to recognise that fragmented lifestyles are driven in part by growth in two-wage households and increasingly complex co-ordination behaviour (Cervero 1986; Jarvis 2001). Rarely does household decision-making represent a close-fitting reconciliation between home, job location and a minimum journey to work (Kwan 1999; Kwan and Weber 2003). This is reflected in the tendency noted elsewhere for dual-career households to consolidate a 'hub' residential location with access to one or several labour markets large enough to serve two careers over the long run (Jarvis 1999a). On the one hand, willingness to change jobs and commute extensively within a wide catchment area rules out a move for one spouse which would inflict a career sacrifice on the other through relocation. On the other hand, these compromises have negative social effects (greater energy consumption) and gender biases which, through daily commuting behaviour, reproduce a version of the 'wife's sacrifice' usually ascribed to household migration (Bonney and Love 1991; Cooke 2001; for evidence of shifting power balance in this regard see Smits et al. 2003).

This gender bias (and social cost) is noted in the case of Edinburgh. In eight out of the seventeen dual earning Edinburgh households (three are the male breadwinner type) the male spouse has in recent years commuted, or continues to commute long distance, usually for over an hour each way. These long distance commuting men are not employed in high level professions or earning top salaries. Rather this comes about through the city assuming the role of a dormitory 'hub' serving several far flung labour markets which are vetoed as places to buy a house or raise a family. This dual-earning household strategy heavily circumscribes opportunities for a dual-carer arrangement and thus gender equality. This is because it invariably requires that female spouse employment remains close to home, usually within walking distance or a short bus ride away. Mr and Mrs East describe how stressful and disruptive it was to have Mr East commute first to Glasgow and then to the Borders for 11 years. While both parents wished to be involved with childcare routines, the brunt of parenting fell to Mrs East because Mr East was away from the house from 7 am to 6.30 at night. One alternative would have been to move the whole family each time Mr East took up new employment, with Mrs East as the 'trailing spouse'. This was never seriously considered an option because the family felt a strong emotional attachment to Edinburgh (and a prejudice against moving to Glasgow in particular). Of course the question has to be asked whether the same solution would have been arrived at had it been Mrs East commuting long distance and Mr East picking up childcare responsibilities at both ends of the day. The data for this small sample certainly suggests that gendered patterns of mobility are remarkably persistent. This reinforces the claim that dual-earner mobility decisions (whether migration or immobility) are formed in the context of the 'linked lives' of the household and used to achieve desired (normatively gendered) home-work balances (Bailey et al. 2004: 1619, my emphasis in parentheses).

While this illustration suggests that local residential attachment is enduring it would be wrong to assume a fixed or simple trade-off on this basis. Instead the household biographies demonstrate that tastes and identities are contingent and mutable. Moreover, aspects of housing choice, environmental ethos, journey to work, gender division, and childcare provision are inextricably linked. Each decision is bound up in a web of competing identifications. In effect the households are 'torn between (these) identifications' in the coordination of their daily life (Pratt 1996: 26), in the preferences they form as individuals and decisions they negotiate as a household collective (Jarvis 2001: 253). This research shows that competing identifications mesh together in ways that are culturally constructed, embedded in local contexts (material, institutional, cultural) (see Chapter One; also Kristensen 1997) and largely detached from sites and arrangements over which planning and social policy have much influence (see for instance Hanson and Pratt 1995; Jarvis 1999a).

Environmental awareness in five cities, two nations

Just as the five featured cities are successful, so they also manifest signs of profound stress. Responding to the perceived threat to a treasured quality of life, civic leaders and planners are increasingly looking to the new urbanism for the solution to pressures of growth. This is demonstrated in the remarkable similarity in language, terms and references used in local and strategic planning documents across the five cities, as illustrated in Table 6.1. This shows how each city promotes urban living as the best way to reconcile economic development and environmental protection. A common aim is to steer development towards designated 'neighbourhoods', 'urban centres' and 'transit corridors' where transit provision is most concentrated. All emphasise higher densities, compact, mixed use and the reuse of 'brownfield', previously developed land (see Photo 6.1).

Running alongside a commonly adopted planning discourse are legacies associated with specific landscape, historic planning and local environmental cultures. In this way Portland and Edinburgh stand out as cities where issues of sustainable development and integrated transport

Photo 6.1   Portland – integrated transport

Table 6.1 The language of planning compared across the five featured cities

Portland
Future development of housing, transport, retail (and limited business activity) to be focused on the following: Central City; 9 Regional Centres (including City); new Station Communities; existing and new Town Centres 'with emphasis on compact development and good transit provision'; Main Streets supplying residential neighbourhoods with retail and service development served by transit; Corridors designed as high quality pedestrian environments adjacent to transit facilities with higher residential densities (e.g. 'row houses'); Employment Areas; Inner Neighbourhoods with housing on small lots; Outer Neighbourhoods zoned for 'residential neighbourhoods farther away from large employment centres with larger lot sizes and lower density housing' (Portland Metro 1995; 1997).

Seattle
Planning for the City of Seattle follows 'goals', 'rules' and 'regulations' set out in the Comprehensive Plan. The guiding principle of these as well as the tenor of the Vision 2020 Regional Plan are for greater urban containment, mixed development at higher density, investment in public transport focused on the following (mostly existing, some designated) neighbourhood types: 'Urban Centres', 'Hub Urban Villages', 'Transit Centres', 'Residential Urban Villages', and 'Neighbourhood Anchors' (enhanced main streets) (City of Seattle 1994; 1997).

San Francisco
Tax incentives for transit-based housing. Planning for City neighbourhoods stress eight elements: special character, being part of the whole, get around easily, walk to the shops, safe streets, gathering places, housing choice, city services.
    ABAG regional growth management typically enshrines 'New Urban' design principles, steering development toward: Central Cities, older suburbs, Transit Centres and Transit Corridors.
    Community design principles stress: clustering, connectivity, transit access, mixed-use, establishment of town centres, transit-oriented development and intensification, interconnected pedestrian and transit friendly neighbourhoods, bicycle networks and 'liveable urban communities' (ABAG 1995); (City and County of San Francisco 1995).

Edinburgh
Successful places have distinct identities and are easy to move around, especially on foot. They are sustainable (they) promote greener lifestyles, energy efficiency, mixed uses, biodiversity, transport and water quality (Scottish Executive 2001: 9). The consequences of energy consumption and pollution through dispersed land uses and car dependency could be lessened if existing or new towns and villages became more self-contained in terms of the balance between jobs and population (Lothian Region Structure Plan 1994: 16). A varied but balanced pattern of land use will help preserve a close relationship between residential areas and workplaces and assist in opposing the trend toward lengthy journeys to work (North East Edinburgh Local Plan 1998: 5).

Table 6.1   The language of planning compared across the five featured cities
– *continued*

London
The choice is to move away from policies of dispersal and accommodate the rapid growth (of London) (p. 3); promoting mixed use and mixed tenure housing at appropriate locations including housing in commercial developments to create sustainable communities; using public transport as the framework for new development; reducing congestion and encouraging use of alternatives to the private car (p. 7). The London Plan makes explicit that new development should be concentrated on existing town centres (of which there are 200 in London together with 1,500 small neighbourhood centres), 'urban villages' defined as 'large and underused brownfield sites which are made much more accessible by new and improved public transport services (...) seen as more comprehensively planned, high density developments, containing a mix of uses and a mixture of housing types and tenures' (GLA Towards the London Plan 2001: 13). The Mayor's Transport Strategy (2001) 'vigorously promotes walking (and) strongly supports the encouragement of cycling in London. The level of cycling is currently very low compared with many other European cities' (16).

Source: Authors content analysis of planning documents for the five featured cities.

have achieved a particularly high profile in recent years (Vuchic 1999). Portland was the first US city to adopt community design guidelines based on New Urbanism with the explicit intention of reducing car use by making public transit, walking and cycling attractive alternatives (Cervero and Radisch 1995: 1; Congress of the New Urbanism 1999). Adopting a strong Urban Growth Boundary in 1973 encouraged relatively high density development in a polycentric arrangement of satellite towns. This measure of containment has been strengthened more recently to redirect urban development around transit stops so that 85 per cent of all new growth is within five minutes walk of a designated transit stop (Newman 1999: 192). In the UK context, Edinburgh is widely recognised to have experienced an 'environmental renaissance' in recent years and the city attracts strong 'green' credentials for a number of innovative schemes (Mazza and Rydin 1997: 12). Edinburgh piloted co-operative car-ownership in 1999 (Edinburgh City Car Club; for a survey of car sharing travel behaviour see Katzev 2003) and approved a 1.4 hectare 'car-free', energy-efficient, Housing Association development. Dwellings on the Canmore estate are designed in keeping with traditional Edinburgh tenement blocks surrounding a shared courtyard, aiming to provide those choosing to live without a car a healthy environment to live in (Arlidge 1997; Beatley 2000: 148). While the remaining three cities enjoy a less explicitly 'green' transport planning reputation, they can each claim vociferous environmental move-ments. The Sierra Club and Audubon environmental groups record high rates of membership in the San Francisco region. Seattle is home to the original 'Voluntary Simplicity' movement which promotes energy con-servation through individual changes in consumer behaviour. Here cul-tures of deep ecology and high technology merge. Images of the 'great outdoors' are superimposed upon preference for low-density housing and auto-dependence. At odds with the visible effects of sprawl are pockets of resistance from environmental groups; Banners protest 'Traffic Jams Coming Soon to This Intersection' (Durning 1996); and a successful scheme for shared car-ownership (Flexcar.com) has been in business since 1999.

The obvious question to ask is how far these differences in urban containment and environmental ethos translate on the ground with respect to car-reliance. Comparable aggregate data on car availability by household and primary modes of transport are presented for the five cities in Table 6.2. This shows that Portland, while achieving international acclaim for transport and environmental planning, is only marginally less car-reliant than Seattle where each occupied housing unit has access to 1.63 cars on average. Emphasis on inte-grated land-use in Portland led to 4.6 per cent of the population

Table 6.2 Cars available and dominant modes of transport: UK and USA cities compared

City/County	Cars per household[UK] Cars per occupied housing unit[USA]	Mode of Travel to Work 2000/1 Percent of working age residents			
		SOV	Public	Walk	Cycle
Portland – Multnomah County	1.50	65.6%	11.1%	4.6%	–
Seattle – King County	1.63	68.7%	9.6%	3.6%	–
San Francisco County	1.08	40.5%	31.0%	9.4%	–
City of Edinburgh	0.80	36.1%	26.3%	20.8%	3.3%
Metropolitan London	0.86	33.5%	29.9%	8.4%	2.3%
(Inner London)	0.61	19.9%	42.1%	11.0%	3.5%

Note: SOV = Single Occupant Vehicle (car, truck or van); percentages do not add up to 100 because only key modes of interest included in this table. No separate data available on cycling in the US cities but the category 'other' ranges from 1.6 in Seattle to 3.6 in San Francisco.

Sources: US Census Bureau 2000 Gateway; City of Edinburgh Council (2003).

walking to work in 2000 compared with 3.6 per cent in Seattle. In San Francisco a resurgence in downtown living and the existence of a high density bus and rail network encourages 9.4 per cent of residents to walk to work and another 31 per cent to travel by public transit. This is close to treble the use made of public transit for journeys to work in Portland and Seattle. Moreover, rates of car ownership in San Francisco are close to parity with household numbers. Of course there are several ways to interpret this. Lower rates of car ownership in San Francisco could be the positive result of cost-effective and practical alternative modes of travel, or it could reflect high poverty levels. The proportion of households without access to private motorised transport in the three US cities in 2000 varies from 28.6 per cent in San Francisco through 12.7 per cent in Portland to 9.3 per cent in Seattle. Referring back to data presented in the previous chapter we find that the proportion of households in poverty (with less than 50 per cent median household income) follows the same rank order but differences are marginal (24 per cent in San Francisco compared with 22 per cent in Portland).

We know from the previous chapter that a used car or van is probably the last possession a poor American family will relinquish in times of hardship – it might even double up as a source of shelter in periods of temporary homelessness. In contrast the cost of owning and running even a used car is much higher in the UK.[8] Consequently, 39.5 per cent of Edinburgh households have no access to a motor vehicle, whether by choice or constraint, and in metropolitan London 37.5 per cent do not have a car available (with a far higher rate of 50.6 per cent recorded for Inner London). At the other extreme, nearly 18 per cent of Seattle households have three or more cars (14 per cent in Portland, nine per cent in San Francisco). In Edinburgh this category represents 2.4 per cent and in metropolitan London 3.7 per cent (Inner London 1.6 per cent). The data in Table 6.2 shows that in 2001 Edinburgh had the lowest ratio of cars per household at 0.80 and, associated with this, one in five residents walked to work. Inner London is an extreme case where less than one in five residents drove to work alone in 2001 (pre-dating imposition of a £5-a-day 'congestion charge' to drive into central London. Clark and Muir 2003). Public transport use in Edinburgh is by bus, whereas in London a majority is by underground rail.

If discussion were limited to this aggregate scale of analysis the conclusion might be that car reliance (or scope for reduction) is indeed determined by settlement design such as land-use integration and infrastructure density. Overall we find greater car-reliance in the US cities, with close to double the ratio of cars to housing units. Super-ficially at least, compact and high density settlement patterns like those of Edinburgh, Inner London and downtown San Francisco do appear to reduce private motorised transport and encourage walking and use of public transit instead. Working families living in central urban neighbourhoods of all five cities would pass the corner shop liveability test. Those living in the outer urban neighbourhoods would not. The San Francisco study areas are particularly well served by restaurants and ethnic 'Mom and Pop' shops. Portland's more compact arrangement achieves some environmental saving compared with Seattle but nothing like the achievements of Edinburgh. Yet we see in research which critically examines the 'popsicle test' that journeys on foot do not necessarily replace the rising volume of car journeys in traditional (walkable) US neighbourhoods (Bartlett 2003). Of course, the geographic units being compared here are not directly commensu-rable: Portland's Multnomah County covers a larger area and includes more suburban neighbourhoods than the City of Edinburgh. More importantly though, if analysis turns to the scale of individual travel behaviour, it is clear that variation occurs *within* each city on the basis of socio-economic factors rather than spatial arrangement. To under-stand what drives energy consuming movement it is crucial to scruti-nise processes of preference formation and decision-making from a household perspective.

At one level, working families differ in their personal politics, the extent to which they feel comfortable with risk, are endlessly on the go, or prefer to consume less. Chapter Four introduced this idea with respect to five meta-narratives representing sub-sets of all one hundred households interviewed. The groupings reflect common ways in which the households co-ordinate daily life, including their attitudes towards mobility and travel. As might be expected, *resist the treadmill* house-holds are most explicit in their environmental awareness and efforts to reduce energy consuming movement. By way of example, Mr and Mrs Eagle walk to work and encourage their daughters to walk every-where too. The family do not own a car because it seems a luxury they can manage without. They make a virtue of walking and the way they have adapted their life to suit a slower pace of life compared with many of their neighbours. Mrs Eagle explains that they plan their day to 'make the time it takes to walk' by neither of them 'working excessive hours'. She explains:

> I'm a wee bit against cars because I feel there's too many, I feel a lot of kids that I see in the school where I work, they don't walk

whereas (my two daughters) would walk for miles and miles. (Eldest daughter) is probably responsible enough to walk to school (it takes 25 minutes) but I just feel, well, I'm going that way, I quite enjoy walking with them because we have a wee chat. (Mrs Eagle, dual earner, Edinburgh – Leith.)

In Seattle Mr Stevens similarly explains why he and his wife choose not to drive their son to the usual round of after-school activities. They resist the treadmill more successfully in this respect than they do in their business lives:

Traffic is a big consideration, after a day of doing errands and driving around for meetings for our business, getting in the car again is not much fun for our kid, he hates getting in the car, so we try not to, it's expensive, it's risky, I mean the danger on the roads has gone up tremendously. (Mr Stevens, Dual Career, outer Seattle.)

In contrast, Mrs Philpott values the 'car time' she spends with her daughters, driving them to school each day on the way to her workplace. From a *career egalitarian* perspective, taking the car on the school run is time-efficient and it doubles up as family-time:

Car time is so important. Car time with my daughters, I just find the discussions we have about friends and such, it's amazing. (Mrs Philpott, dual career, central Portland.)

Of course, it is one thing to identify working families that hold with ideals of simplifying their lives and reducing energy consuming movement. It is quite another for them to exercise control over competing spheres of activities (and colliding interests) such as school choice and job prospects. As Mrs Eaton observes, there are practical limits to everyday co-ordination such as those as mundane as the timing and location of events, as defined in Chapter One:

There are times when it would be nice just to have one car, partly from a 'green' point of view, but because of child-care timing there is just no way (husband) could drop off a child, get on a bus, get to work, get back on the bus in time. (Mrs Eaton, dual career, Edinburgh – Craigmount.)

At another level then, ideal-type attitudes toward energy conservation, recycling, reduced consumption and slower pace of life are disrupted by changes in the nature of work, including longer working hours, families with two parents working, emphasis on competition in education and healthcare and rising affluence (Hinchliffe 1996). From this it can be argued that growing convergence between UK and US cultures of work and long working hours usher in the prospect of increased reliance on private motorised transport, with limited scope for planning policy intervention. There is no denying that the urban village concept is extremely popular as a way of selling new homes. People like the aesthetic variety of homes oriented around a pocket park or shops in which to browse at the weekends. But we have to ask whether preference for compact, self-contained neighbourhoods translate into environmentally friendly decisions about where and how to live in practice.

Dispelling the myth that preference makes practice

The empirical analysis which follows employs the lens of preference formation and decision-making to capture the impact of intra-household negotiation and compromise on residential location and travel behaviour. The aim is to explain seemingly perverse behaviour 'revealed' in market decisions (such as consumption of 'wasteful' journeys for non-local services). Arguably, if working families are to be encouraged to co-ordinate their lives in less environmentally damaging ways, we need to understand the constraints preventing them from responding 'rationally' to the assumed benefits of land-use integration. It is important to study what might be termed the action prequel of decision-making because individual preferences may be shelved through conflict or transformed by compromise in order to meet group goals. Conflict can arise between individuals balancing the demands of competing careers or between mutually exclusive tastes and identities. For instance, we find households professing strong green credentials concerning house insulation choosing to live, work and educate children in such a way as to travel frequently between scattered activities because it is not deemed possible to maintain lifestyle, career and parenting goals within a single locale (Jarvis 2001: 240).

Evidence of dissonance is captured by an exercise involving detailed analysis of one hundred household biographies across the five cities, 20 in each city, combining individual employment biographies, maps and diaries of individual and household spheres of activity, together with narratives of the decisions made by couples[9] across all spheres of daily life. Together these generate a time-space portrait of each household. The analysis is in two discrete stages, one identifying stated preference for features of 'liveability', the other establishing the extent to which these preferences are 'lived' in practice. These preferences are then compared with data recording revealed behaviour. The result is a high degree of dissonance. This emerges as a consequence of mutually exclusive individual and group goals, tastes and identities – what Geraldine Pratt (1998) describes as the plight of being 'torn between identifications'. A classic illustration of this is provided in the case of one San Francisco couple living in the central Mission district, where property prices have been rising rapidly, yet the inner city 'grunge factor' (as this couple put it) remains.

Mr and Mrs Florin choose to live within the city limits to escape what they view as the Bay Area 'freeway mayhem'. Superficially, they are the quintessential urban pioneers depicted in the gentrification literature. They shop for groceries on the Internet to escape car-park and trolley rage. They patronise local restaurants and wax lyrical about the diversity and vitality of city life. Yet they find themselves running two cars, driving to two different childcare and kindergarten facilities and have both taken new jobs, neither of which is at all convenient to public transit. They only have off-street parking for one car so they expend considerable effort shifting the second car from street to street, dodging parking restrictions and street cleaning days. Mr Florin explains:

> this past year we both got (new) jobs, neither one of which was at all convenient to public transit and we have two children who have to be dropped off and picked up everyday from two different daycare facilities, it just wasn't possible to do this by public transit, so now we have two cars, it's like, we just look at each other and say, hey, we live and work in the city so we're not dependent on the automobile and yet here we are, you know, and we only have parking for one of them so every day we're driving around looking for parking, avoiding the road cleaning days! (Mr Florin, dual career, central San Francisco.)

This narrative is by no means unique. A common source of dissonance occurs through identification with central city living at the same time as attempting to meet the norms of the 'good parent' in terms of children's education and cultural capital. Urban dwellers are effectively torn between identifying with urban cultural cachet and middle class parenting characteristic of racially segregated suburbs. This tension drives consumption of 'wasteful' journeys whereby families effectively straddle multiple place-bound identities.

Identifying preference for compact neighbourhood design

Qualitative research software was first used to 'mine' the data for evidence of expressed values concerning aspects of urban living. Popularly promoted features of 'liveability', such as pedestrian friendly environments, convivial streets, cultural diversity and convenient, safe, accessible integrated transport, provide the basic frame of analysis. Word and string (phrase) searches were undertaken to assign values for each feature, yielding descriptive statistics for each city (Gahan and Hannibal 1998). For example, households volunteering information that they like being able to walk to the corner shop or explore neighbourhood parks on foot contribute a positive 'walkable' value to their respective city assessment. If no mention was made of this feature, no score is recorded. Households contribute only once to the positive recognition of each feature of liveability, regardless of the number of times this feature is mentioned by either spouse in the course of the interview. Thus a 100 per cent 'walkable' score would mean all 20 households commented positively on their ability to walk to local amenities. The results of this layer of analysis are presented in Table 6.3.

Table 6.3 Household preference for compact neighbourhood design: five cities compared (100 per cent = 20 households volunteer preference for this element of 'liveability')

'Walkable'
Portland: 20%
'we wanted to live where we could walk and cycle to places' (Poulter, dual career, central)

Seattle: 20%
'we wanted more of a neighbourhood rather than kind of a urban sprawl, out at our old house you couldn't walk to a playground without feeling like you were going to be hit by a car' (Scully, dual career, central)

San Francisco: 60%
'we do things in the city, we have friends (who) live in the city and we walk around a lot (...) we don't so much use public transit but we do walk a lot' (Fraser, dual career, central)

Edinburgh: 75%
'it's nice to live where you can walk places' (Edwards, flex career, central)

London: 25%
'it's all the stuff that's available within walking distance, it's close to where we both work' (Law, traditional, central)

'Convenience'
Portland: 0
Seattle: 15%

Table 6.3   Household preference for compact neighbourhood design: five cities compared (100 per cent = 20 households volunteer preference for this element of 'liveability') – *continued*

San Francisco: 10%
'there's something to be said for the convenience of when you have a densely popu-lated area and I guess there's going to be a lot of Mom and Pop shops on the corners, and more restaurants and stuff (...) but the Mom and Pop shops are relatively small and limited in their selection' (Floyd, dual career, central)

Edinburgh: 30%
London: 15%
'there would be something very nice about just, if you have a dinner party on a Saturday, walking up the road to a butcher, but we've never had it and we knew that wasn't here, we'd never have expected it' (Locke, dual career, central)

'Urban density/cultural diversity'

	Urban	Restaurants	Museums/Galleries/Theatre
Portland:	15%	0	0
Seattle:	30%	10%	5%
San Francisco:	40%	55%	30%
Edinburgh:	0	10%	5%
London:	30%	25%	10%

'we like the community, we (get) much more diversity, you know, you see, you see many African American children, a lot more gay population here, just a lot more diversity than the West side, they are ivory white graduation classes you don't, you don't see any people of colour or, so for me being in human resources that's really important to me to have my children raised around that' (Philpott, dual career, central)
'I mean, we do have traffic noise from the freeway, but we'd rather have the conve-nience of living here where there's, it's more of a diverse mix of people, other than our old neighbourhood which was white, blue collar worker' (Scully, dual career, central)
'It very much suits our politics, um, we like the diversity of people here' (Florin, dual career, central)
'it's kind of fun not to have everybody like you and to just pass through the crowds and not to understand the languages (...) the variety, we don't like to overhear conversations of boring white people!' (French, flex career, outer).
'It's a funny mixture of old dears and young types, because we've got these gardens but at the same time it's dead urban here, really close to town' (Lord, dual career, central).

'House with a yard/garden'
Portland: 35%
(All but two households interviewed live in a single family dwelling with a yard – viewed as the norm)

Seattle: 40%
(All but one household interviewed live in a single family dwelling with a yard – many lived in apartments in early family formation)

San Francisco: 40%

Table 6.3   Household preference for compact neighbourhood design: five cities compared (100 per cent = 20 households volunteer preference for this element of 'liveability') – *continued*

(8 out of 20 households interviewed live in apartments or lofts – most had private or shared access to a small yard but idealisation of a bigger/private yard was commonly expressed)

Edinburgh: 70%
(Most set great store by the hard-to-find house with garden because they started out in one of the tenement buildings typical to the city of Edinburgh, with shared entry and no private garden)

London: 35%
(wanting access to a bigger house or private garden typically differentiates outer from Central London families)

Source: authors interviews with one hundred working family households across five cities, twenty per city.

The expectation is that Portland and Edinburgh households cite preference for walkable, convenient, village-like communities more frequently than households in Seattle. This is because their residential location more closely resembles this settlement type and households voluntarily moving to a house and locale typically voice a high level of residential satisfaction (Saunders 1990: 94–5). In turn, it is anticipated that San Francisco and London households comment more frequently on urban cultural attributes. The results largely confirm these expectations. Portland households do speak more frequently of the virtues of village-like, small-town communities and a sense of rurality in the city (this preference was unique to the US cities, cited by 30 per cent of Portland interviewees) and 20 per cent choose to live where they can 'walk places'. Yet Edinburgh households were three times as likely to voice preference for walkable neighbourhoods, with 75 per cent boasting the ability to walk to local amenities. Seattle households more frequently mention having a house with a yard (garden) as being particularly important (40 per cent of Seattle households mentioned this in relation to previous or future residential location decisions). This reflects the dominance of low density housing in this metropolitan area (see Photo 6.2). Frequent mention of a 'house with a garden' as a preference in Edinburgh (70 per cent mentioned this feature of residential choice) largely reflects the scarcity value of this idealised family accommodation in a city where tenement apartments are the norm. San Francisco residents make particular reference to specifically urban qualities such as access to restaurants and museums. The way that Mr and Mrs French favour access to numerous ethnic cuisines is widely repeated across the San Francisco sample. Similarly in London, residents of inner urban neighbourhoods credit theirs as a distinctly urban lifestyle by, as Mrs Liddell puts it, the fact they have 'Vietnamese and Turkish restaurants at the end of (the) street'.

While the anticipated hierarchy of compact to world city status is largely borne out in the data, some of the results are surprising and there are notable differences *between* households *within* each case study. While it is appealing to view urban living as the antithesis of suburban living, individuals and households rarely construct their lives according to single, fixed or coherent identities in this regard. Evidence from the biographic analysis suggests an evolving and contingent slippage whereby it is more realistic to conceive of metropolitan areas offering a matrix of lifestyle opportunities. This way, committed 'urbanites' can find themselves living in quiet neighbourhoods with a suburban aesthetic through their pursuit of competing tastes or aspirations: good schools; or affordable, more spacious family housing. Presenting the findings of a recent residential preference study, Seattle planners acknowledge that higher-density compact living will appeal most to people who already live in central urban neighbourhoods (City of Seattle 1994). This may yet overstate the possibility of steering population back to the city as a means to locally reconcile home, work and family life. Extending the notion of the matrix we find those households living in central neighbourhoods no more likely than those living in low density suburbs to limit and contain their daily movement within a discrete area (Jarvis 2001, p. 247).

Photo 6.2   Seattle suburbs – large homes for small families

It is in San Francisco rather than Portland that positive mention is made of neighbourhood 'walkability' but this does not contribute to a sense of convenience. Indeed, the attribute of 'convenience' rarely gets a mention outside of the Edinburgh sample. Mrs Fraser's positive description of San Francisco's walkability in Table 6.3 contrasts with her experience of this as a difficult place to raise a family. She explains: 'it is actually not an easy place to raise children because you need to have so much money to buy a house that's appropriate for having a family, that's got room for a family'. The Fraser's currently live in an owner occupied two-bedroom live-work loft apartment. They have a three year old daughter and another baby on the way. They suggest a desire to live in a house with a yard but a tension exists between this 'suburban' preference and their strong identification with central urban living where there are few single family dwellings and fewer still priced within their reach. Nevertheless, the descriptive statistics in Table 6.3 clearly demonstrate strong contrasts *between* city samples. The suggestion is that preferences associated with environmental ethos and everyday co-ordination, as well as parenting norms, are locally constructed (Jarvis 2003).

Conflict between stated preferences and revealed practices

In the second stage of analysis, map, diary and interview data are re-examined, this time searching for evidence of reported (observed) movements associated with home, work, shopping, childcare, school and recreation. For each city sample, a portrait is built up charting the quantity, duration and spatial reach of daily movement. Table 6.4 provides a summary of observed practices pertaining to each of the features introduced in the previous table. The selected snapshots of household daily life describe a common trend of dissonance between stated preferences and revealed behaviour. This suggests that 'where' people live rarely matches their preferences for living, their opportunities for working and their goals for parenting. Dissonance is more pronounced across the US than UK sample. Perhaps not surprisingly, one significant source of dissonance is attributed to parental concern to find that elusive 'good school'. This is frequently identified some distance from the preferred 'hub' residential location. Schools are so universally cited as a quality of life factor that it was unnecessary to include them in the previous analysis. Every working parent interviewed volunteered the same concern. Increasingly, rather than moving house to 'purchase' entry to a preferred school, housing and school choice are effectively de-coupled through purchase of private

Table 6.4   Observed household practices co-ordinating home, work and daily life (for comparison with preferences stated in Table 6.3)

'Walkable'
The Edwards':
One car; Mr Edwards commutes long distances but family would never relocate, 'Edinburgh's a nice place to come home to'.

The Poulter's:
Two cars; both parents drive to work; they opted for a non-local childcare facility which is in the opposite direction to both places of work.

The Scully's:
Two cars; one parent drives and one travels by bus to work; both cars required for non-local childcare/shopping after work.

The Fraser's:
Two cars; neither parent has ever worked in the city; both commute to different work sites on the Peninsula (30–50 minutes drive each way); local city life consumed at weekends.

The Law's:
Mr Law journeys to work each day by taxi; neither parent wishes son to attend local school.

'Convenience'
The Floyd's:
One car and use of public transit; no local social or kin attachments; few activities undertaken in the immediate neighbourhood except use of restaurants. Drive south to larger supermarkets and shopping malls for wider selection of produce/for easy parking.

The Locke's:
Both parents drive in separate cars to work in the same street because they each drop off children attending different non-local schools.

'Urban density/cultural diversity'
The Scully's:
Quality of local schools never entered the equation of residential choice because both parents felt living anywhere in Seattle they would 'need a private school' for their son.

The French's:
Two cars; worked hard to secure a public (state) tax supported school place for their daughter 'where the rich kids live', because they were 'morally very opposed to the modern trend of putting your kids in private schools' and accepted instead that this arrangement meant Mrs French would have to drive 'clear across town' morning and afternoon, limiting the hours she can work from home freelance.

Lord: 'there are negatives, the quality of the air, the schools are appalling. We don't know if we will stay in London forever'.

Source: authors interviews with sixty working family households in three cities.

education or the practice of transporting offspring daily to non-local schools. This trend is evident in Britain as well as the US (Jarvis et al. 2001: 65–66).

There are other points of tension between household preferences and daily practices which emerge when Tables 6.2 and 6.3 are compared. Take for example the Fraser's who were introduced above as advocates of San Francisco's 'walkability'. The Frasers identify themselves strongly with urban living yet they spend little time in the city during the working week. Walking in San Francisco provides weekend recreation rather than a practical component of everyday co-ordination. This is because neither spouse has ever worked within the city limits, each commuting to Silicon Valley jobs in separate cars, taking turns to drop off and pick up their daughter from childcare.

Neither does living in a compact city such as Portland overcome tensions between environmentalism and work-life reconciliation in the successful city. The Poulter's voice a strong preference for central city living and situate this within an anti-car ethos, yet both currently require a car each to go about their daily work routine. Furthermore, they have changed the location of both employment and childcare in ways which increase their need to travel. In Edinburgh too, Mr and Mrs Edwards make a virtue of owning just one car and walking a great deal but they enjoy their home so much they would never consider relocating, though this means Mr Edwards has to commute long distance. Mr Edwards regularly travels away from home on business and it is in this context he idealises scope to walk about in Edinburgh from the perspective of somewhere to return to at weekends.

Co-ordination dilemmas

The question was asked above whether co-ordination of daily life is less environmentally damaging for two-wage households living in compact urban neighbourhoods compared with more dispersed forms. The results are mixed. While Portland residents, particularly those who are migrants from California, articulate a strong preference for the city because of its 'relaxed pace' and 'convenience', there is little evidence of reduced auto-dependence in practice. The volume and reach of movement are similar for busy working parents in both urban forms. While there is greater evidence of localised living in Edinburgh, this reflects persistent gender inequalities. Here, the school run and domestic routines are managed labour intensively by mothers who sacrifice career opportunities for local and short-hours employment. This is expressed in difference between time spent travelling to and from work, with fathers travelling for 32 minutes each way on average compared with a 22 minute trip each way on average for mothers.[10] In contrast, London mothers actually spend longer commuting than fathers. This is explained by mode of travel rather then distance. A higher proportion of mothers in London travel to work by public transit rather than by private car, extending their journey time for short distances. This is reflected in the proportion of London households owning one car as compared with the San Francisco two-car norm. Nevertheless only one London family in the sample considers it possible to get by without access to a car at all. Indeed, Mr and Mrs Lynsted argue that because car crime is so high and parking so difficult where they live, owning a car is a liability. Mr Lynsted explains that selling the family car was a practical rather than ideological decision:

> It wasn't really (ideological), although neither of us like cars, you know, in the sense that it's a pain to have them in the city, it's silly, but we had two (cars) for a while and then just one...one was stolen, vandalised, one died eventually (but the main thing is) parking is ridiculous, you can park round the corner where there's a high level of crime, you know, car theft. But also with our jobs, we are in such a way that it wasn't convenient for me to go to Wimbledon, a car is no quicker than (public transport) and (wife) can't park at all in Islington. (Mr Lynsted, dual career, London – Hackney.)

Elsewhere in London, despite the availability of bus and rail transport at relatively high density, working families claim to rely on access to at least one car. Major obstacles to going car-free are the timing, location and multi-destination trips associated with childcare and the school run. The extent to which parents feel compelled to drive their children to school (often en route to their place of work) has increased in recent years, along with the frenzy of competition associated with securing a place in a school which performs well in the annually published league table of exam results. Remarkably few of the London parents send their children to the neighbourhood school. Indeed, of the sixteen families with school age children (the other four had infants) twelve paid to educate their children privately. A survey of parents in the city of Edinburgh reveals one in four pay for private education (Puttick 2001). In some cases the cost of private school fees and the 'hassle factor' of transporting children to non-local schools is justified on the basis that parents took advantage of affordable family housing in 'less desirable' neighbourhoods. In others the trade-off was between this and a long commute to a home outside the city where it was deemed the state schools would be acceptable. Similar explanations accompany high rates of private education in the central San Francisco sample.

School choice

Both UK and US education authorities are experimenting with widening school choice in various forms. Again we see an active flow of policy ideas between the USA and UK with both favouring voucher schemes and subject-specialist 'foundation' or 'charter schools' (for the US debate over school choice see Chubb and Moe 1990; for proposed changes to English state education see DfE 2004). Yet the shift in the 'right to choose' is likely to exacerbate the problems of mismatch between where families live and where they choose to send their children to school. It is widely reported that identifying a suitable school and getting to grips with locally variable admissions procedures is frustrating and time-consuming for parents (BBC 2004). One argument for abandoning the assumption that children should attend the school nearest to where they live is the widespread practice of post-code (zip-code) selection. This gives those families who can afford to pay the premium it costs to buy a house in proximity of a good school a comparative advantage. In the UK context it has been estimated that houses in good school districts exchange for 10 to 15 per cent more than equivalent houses outside the catchment area (Cheshire and Sheppard 2002; see also Leech and Campos 2003). Equally it can be argued that unless tax-payers meet the cost of transporting children to non-local schools, widening choice will not help low-income families achieve equal access to the same quality of education middle class parents can obtain by mobilising entitlement to cars and nannies. Far from recognising that mobility and time are scarce and unequally distributed resources, the latest School Transport Bill proposes that local authorities charge for bus services that are currently free (PA News 2004). This is further example of the lack of joined up thinking and confused logic of pure market solutions. The 'choice' debate in education is countered by the idea of the right to be able to choose to have a good local school. It is meaningless to talk about choice outside the context of unequal access to transport and the like. Real choice would be to guarantee all children good quality education in their own neighbourhood.

Arguably there is a conflict of interests between promotion of open markets in childcare and education and efforts in transport policy to reduce congestion. Prompted by concerns at levels of congestion caused by the school run, local authorities are drawing up school run 'travel plans' with the intention of persuading parents who chaperone children to school to abandon their cars in favour of 'soft modes' (such as walking and cycling), either by extolling the health benefits of regular exercise, or by restricting parking around schools to make car travel less appealing (see Jarvis et al. 2001: 6). The Walking Bus scheme mentioned in Chapter One is part of this initiative. While such pro-posals assume the language of environmental quality and sustainable communities enshrined in the Urban White Paper, it is questionable whether they will achieve their ultimate objective.

Typical of the growing emphasis on school choice in the US is the case of Sam and Sally Philpott who have chosen not to send their children to the neighbourhood school but instead drive them across town to where Sally's mother was formerly a teacher and has inside knowl-edge of how the school is managed. Sam acknowledges that extending the school run can be 'inconvenient' especially with respect to the knock-on effect of this on travel-time for kids' parties and to 'soccer programmes or basket ball programmes' but the couple 'just deal with it' because they view this effort necessary to secure the right education for their children.

Similarly, Mrs Stevens stresses that she dislikes the location where she and her family live but picked this house for the school district, for her son. This highlights a common dilemma for the working families interviewed: how to reconcile home and work considerations with competing family goals. In this case, preference for an urban lifestyle has been compromised to achieve access to a school with a good repu-tation. As a consequence of living where she feels she does not truly belong, Mrs Stevens admits she and her husband drive to other neigh-bourhoods closer to the city centre to do their grocery shopping, to eat out and visit friends:

> This doesn't match our personality, we don't patronise, for example, most of the restaurants here, they serve unhealthy food, we're health nuts, so we eat (elsewhere)... you know, I travel 20 minutes one way to a grocery store (to the Green Lake area) for good bread.

Mr and Mrs Saunders also live a dislocated lifestyle though they live in central Greenwood and espouse a distinctly urban identity. While they always anticipated a 'move to the suburbs', particularly once they started a family, they have grown to appreciate 'being able to walk places, to be able to bike (and) having sidewalks'. Moving out of the city remained a consideration for many years. One factor was time spent travelling to work. Both separately commute to an industrial park in Bothell, at the far city limits. Thoughts concerning their children's education also played a part. But as they invested more time and energy in remodelling their home of 12 years, the anticipated benefits of moving diminished. Despite strongly articulated preferences for urban living, however, urban tastes do not translate into routine co-ordination. Primarily as a consequence of school choice, the family accepts a series of spatially fragmented attachments. Mrs Saunders explains:

> We didn't pick our neighbourhood school, we picked a school further away that was closer to our day care person's house, so that he can drive (daughter) and pick her up on certain days of the week.... for our life it (was) a better choice for us in terms of keeping our eldest daughter's after school day care with our younger one, so the sisters can be together..... for us it was just the quality of the child care was worth it....so that costs us half an hour each way, morning and evening, to do that, and what's funny is (that neighbourhood, Blue Ridge) has kind of become our community even though we live over here (in Greenwood).

In the case of the Locke family, both parents drive in separate cars to work in the same street because they each drop off children attending different schools. This narrative begins with the conscious decision this couple made, both working full-time as partners in the same entrepreneurial business, to live and work in central London so as to create a time-efficient, distinctly urban, non-commuting lifestyle. Mr Locke explains:

> What we've created is a business close to our home, which is a 10 minute drive away, where our business revolves around Hackney, Clerkenwell and Islington. So we're neither of us commuters. We've created that lifestyle for ourselves.

Then Mrs Locke goes on to explain how, searching for schools they felt were suitable for each of their four children, they abandoned this local way of living.

> Now our commuting is all family related, not work related. It's all about the kids, the school run and all that. Because our two youngest children go to school in Knightsbridge and you can't get much further than that.

With two children attending school in Knightsbridge, a third near Regents Park and a fourth in the City of London itself, each parent drives for over an hour before finally reaching their place of work located just three miles from the family home. Moreover, as their business has prospered and the effort of living at the heart of a congested city has increased, they have invested in a holiday home 'in the middle of the Norfolk countryside' where they 'have a separate lifestyle' 'when (they) need to escape'. Thus, what started out as a justification of city living on the basis of time efficiency soon became a narrative of time-squeeze.

Contrast this strategy with that employed by Lois and Steve French. Lois and Steve always wanted to live in San Francisco. They explain their strong attachment to city life as a reaction to having both grown up in 'fringey, semi-suburban rurality, burnt fields and ditches' in the Midwest. Describing themselves as frugal and risk-averse they chose to buy a modest home in working-class Excelsior so they would not panic about the size of the mortgage, rather than to stretch themselves to gain access to a more desirable neighbourhood. They were adamant on political grounds that their daughter should attend a state school but were aware that those in their neighbourhood had a poor reputation. That they managed to secure a place in 'an excellent public tax supported school' 'clear across town where the rich kids live' is the result of the couple's social capital, their ability to research the system of selection and, critically, generate unpaid domestic labour through recourse to traditional gender roles. Steve designs computer games and admits his industry is renown for a macho culture of very long working hours. He describes the decision to separate out earning and parenting roles as the need to eliminate the 'extra tension, the issue of co-ordinating it all, the stress'. Nevertheless, adopting this gender segregated *path of least resistance* strategy does not overcome all the stresses of daily co-ordination. Tensions between competing goals and identities still persist. As Lois explains, it would not be possible to secure this quality of education for her daughter if she had chosen to pursue her career or if the household relied on a second income:

> I was raised on the idea of frugality, you clip the coupon out of the newspaper, I could really stretch a dollar on a lot of things, we wouldn't be so darned frugal if it wasn't fun to go to yard sales, goofing around on a bit of a treasure hunt, but it also lets us live very cheaply, so we don't panic about losing a job for a few years....so one of the reasons I don't have a full time job is so I can

drive (daughter) to school and back everyday clear across town.....It took a lot of research, you (have to) fight and elbow your way in (to the popular schools), they have a lottery system with a complex formula.

Both families gain comparative advantage from the resource entitlements at their disposal: the Locke's have access to sufficient income to buy their children a private education and pay the additional personnel and transport costs required to perform a complex school run; Mr and Mrs French benefit from Lois staying home and forfeiting financial independence so as to invest the time and energy required to 'work' the state education system to their advantage. Both families tax themselves heavily to ensure their children are well educated, yet they do not bear the full cost of their actions. Both strategies incur social costs to the environment and Lois recognises that school choice precludes her daughter participating in energy efficient car-pool arrangements because none of the neighbouring children attend the same school. These complex, integrated compromises bear some similarity to the household patterns found by Fagnani and Brun (1994) in their study of Paris. They found that middle class couples who expressed strong attachment to an urban lifestyle and a dislike of commuting were far less concerned about housing choice. The same could be said for concern with neighbourhood amenities. In this research, the quality of a child's education is increasingly viewed by middle class parents as an amenity to be purchased or shopped around for in its own right rather than something which comes as part of a package deal – such as with a house and garden in the suburbs.

Transport failure

What is striking about the household analysis is the range of solutions ostensibly similar working families arrive at to address these generic dilemmas. As we saw in the case of housing dilemmas, school choice is not adequately understood outside the web of connections binding parenting values with gender relations, residential location, working hours and consumer status. Issues of time and space conjointly underpin the where and how of living in the city. By way of example, Chapter Four introduced an unusually close melding of working times and spatial arrangements in one *resist the treadmill* family whereby Mr and Mrs Smith each works reduced hours (30 hours per week) as part of a job-share (equivalent to a 1.5 full-time income structure overall). By working alternate days they manage to share earning and parenting roles as well as use of a single family car. They explain the 'luxury' of being able to travel to work by bus (sharing the same bus pass), made possible by the fact they do not have to combine the journey to work with childcare, the school run or shopping trips. Choosing where to live they took close account of major bus routes, recognising that all Seattle neighbourhoods were not equally accessible. Mr Smith explains:

> We wanted to bus commute, for a variety of reasons, and the north end (Kenmore and beyond) you can't, it's very difficult to get a bus ride down under an hour, you have to transfer, you have to walk some of the way, and, so it was very hard to do that, you could do it just barely...so that was one of the criteria, the desire to get closer to commute and then, this did it for us, because we thought, a bus arrangement that's good enough that we sold our second car, whoever is home has the car, the bus (journey takes) 45 minutes to an hour now including some walking but, you know, I think now we see the walking as a positive thing, well, that might be the only exercise I get in any given day.

Scope for environmentally friendly travel behaviour rests with the infrastructure of daily life as identified in Chapter One. This not only entails the moral rationalities of parents, making what they see as the best choices for their children (purchasing private education, cocooning their children in fortified vehicles), it also reflects what alternatives are available by location, cost and reliability. Take for example the case of Mr and Mrs Loxton, both full-time lawyers living in central London. They can afford to pay a day nanny to look after their two children (aged six and eight) after school as well as employ a cleaner once a week. Living where they do in Islington, in walking distance of a North London Line station (east-west fixed rail), they hoped to run only one car and otherwise take advantage of London's high density bus and rail networks. It was Mr Loxton's intention to take the children to school by train each day on his way to work in the city. This arrangement fell apart because severe overcrowding made it impossible to predict journey times:

> We tried to use the train but it was absolutely hopeless. You couldn't get on the train it was so full when it arrived. Then of course you are really in trouble, because you are stuck at a station, they are only every 15 minutes, you can't get on the train, what you end up doing, you come back here, get the car and drive, you know.

Now the Loxton's run two cars so Mr Loxton can drive one to his central London office each day and the nanny they employ can use the other for the school-run. Mrs Loxton alone uses public transit, travelling to work each day by bus. The fact that this family can afford to run two cars and employ a nanny and enjoy a home in an accessible central location is not the point. Co-ordinating daily life in this fragmented way is labour (time) intensive and energy inefficient. We see here how private solutions to overcome infrastructure failure impose heavy social costs (more private cars on the roads contributing pollution, congestion and hazards to pedestrians and cyclists).

In the current climate of neoliberalsim it is alarming to witness an obstinate faith in technical fixes and pure market solutions to serious environmental hazards. In the USA this reflects a growing shift away from regulation, including refusal to sign the Kyoto protocol on the reduction of carbon dioxide emissions. Moreover, market solutions can be ambiguous. A good illustration of this is the confusing range of both taxes and fiscal incentives applied to the new hybrid gasoline/electric cars. For London motorists who do not wish to swap the luxury of private motorised transport for crowded underground trains there is the option of purchasing one of the new generation of fuel efficient hybrid cars and receiving a 100 per cent discount on the £5-a-day congestion charge to enter the city. Owners of hybrids also pay less road tax. Given the UK commitment to reduce greenhouse gas emissions by five per cent by 2010 it is consistent to differentiate between gas-guzzling, fuel efficient and low emission vehicles. Perplexing here is the fact that this unique tax on motorists in London is a *congestion* charge, not a pollution charge: hybrid cars still occupy space on the road. The message is clear: price signals encourage greater efficiency in the status quo rather than to change travel behaviour by investing in viable alternatives. Oregon appears similarly inconsistent in its approach. This is one US state with sophisticated environmental legislation yet it justifies charging owners of hybrids double the vehicle registration fee and higher road taxes than owners of ordinary combustion engines on the basis they generate less revenue from fuel taxes (because of their efficiency) while continuing to 'create wear on the highways' (Pryne 2004). The cynic would argue this shows greater concern for lost revenue and economic growth than costs to the environment of ever increasing expectations of individual mobility.

At the other extreme, Oregon is proposing to introduce a mileage tax (which the UK government is studying with interest) as an even-handed approach to the negative environmental impact of all private motorised travel. A mileage tax recognises that the challenge is to reduce wasteful journeys as a way to both ease congestion *and* reduce pollution. While there are compelling arguments in favour of mileage and road user charges (see Oswald 2000 for a good non-technical summary) current policy proposals provide too blunt an instrument. So far, little attempt has been made to differentiate between essential and excessive travel, or ability to pay.

Summary

Emerging from this analysis is the paradox that popular and economically 'successful' cities, where a strong public (and private) anti-growth and anti-car sentiment exists in the forms of regeneration initiatives and environmental social movements, coincide with growing reliance on private motorised transport which ultimately threatens the 'liveability' attracting relatively advantaged working families in the first place. There is a powerful sense in which routine household practices shape the urban environment at the same time that environmental conditions and qualities enter the crucible of household decision-making. Spheres of human behaviour and environmental change are mutually reinforcing. As Colin Clark wrote in 1957, transport shapes city development but city form shapes travel choices (Clark 1957). Arguably, the impact of sprawling growth, congestion and car-oriented shopping and leisure are particularly visible in US metropolitan areas. At the same time, many European metropolitan regions (notably South East England) face a similar malaise.

The question was asked whether compact urban forms are synonymous with energy conserving localised living. The answer appears to be they do not. Household residential location and travel behaviour are more significantly influenced by the ease with which aspects of daily life come together in a practical sense, a matter of space-time co-ordination which is at best partially determined by material integration of residential, commercial and transport development. Competing preferences and identities associated with children's education, local social networks and moral cultures cross-cut those of housing choice, journey to work and personal environmental ethos. This matrix of dis-location is made worse by the actions of state institutions and the inexorable shift toward market solutions and emphasis on individual capability and self-reliance.

This is not to say we should abandon this environmental goal. We need instead to understand why in Portland, in many ways the paragon of integrated environmental and transport planning, efforts to design 'traditional' 'village-like' compact communities are being undermined by compromises made within households of growing internal complexity. Significantly this reflects the way workers' daily lives, their working schedules and patterns and activities of social reproduction are getting more complex and fragmented. Consequently, essential connections need to be made between spheres of housing, transport, technology, work, employment and family life before it is possible for us to positively influence the social-environment interface.

If planners and policy makers are ever to influence residential location and travel behaviour, to bring about sustainable human settlement and movement, the very real tensions underpinning individual and household decision-making have first to be understood. By focusing attention on the physical arrangement of land use, the danger is that regeneration will remain a two-dimensional blue-print rather than a coherent lived experience. The importance of architecture, planning and landscape to the renaissance of cities is undeniable. Cities have to be attractive places in which to live, work, socialise and raise families. Yet it is misleading to promote this 're-packaging' exercise as the solution to serious environmental problems. The danger is that widespread belief that designing compact 'village-like' neighbourhoods will significantly reduce car-use, congestion, pollution and sprawl will draw attention away from arguments for more fundamental changes in cultural values and transport behaviour. As a crucial first step the future of cities has to be understood alongside the future of work, employment and everyday life.

7
A View From the Bridge

Dysfunction

View from a bridge – Seattle

The view from the bridge is grim. A red thread of brake lights signal stop-and-go congestion on the highway below. The engine drone and acrid exhaust would irritate motorists if they were not cut off from the world in private air-conditioned bubbles of preoccupation. Out of view beneath the bridge is a cardboard city for migrant labour. Each day the gang-master pulls up in a mini-bus, selecting the fittest men for casual labour. Several enterprising Mexican youths (who would be East Europeans in another setting) venture into the smog, sponge and squeegee in hand, seizing the opportunity to earn a few dollars cleaning fresh grime off powerful new people-carriers. No-one wants this service but they pay what is pocket-change anyway, alarmed and self-conscious at having to confront poverty close up. The clock is ticking and appointments will surely be missed; a stressed out executive talks urgently to her childminder by car-phone; an engineer scrolls down the calendar of his palm-pilot, reorganising projects to make time for his daughter's school play. The dream for all is to have choices: a home of ones own; a car in the garage; children at college. These are signs of a booming urban economy. Yet as Thorns (2002: 228) observes 'the world of the global urban condition is one of paradoxes'. Captured in this snap-shot (which could be drawn from any one of the cities featured in this book) is the paradox of growing divisions in the successful city; between rich and poor, between head-hunted knowledge workers and those with undervalued skills who serve them; between men and women.

A feature of 'new' economies which distinguish 'successful' from moribund industrial cities is that they rely on pools of creative and entrepreneurial talent. To succeed, the post-industrial city has to attract skilled labour and venture capital. Indeed, Peter Hall (2000) goes so far as to claim that growth of culture industries provides the 'magic substitute' for lost factories and warehouses. The perceived advantage of this high value employment, combined with traditional 'liveable' urban neighbourhoods, is today the universal weapon of choice to combat sprawl (Henton and Walesh 1998; Sommers et al. 2000). The UK government and many US metropolitan authorities share similar concern to accommodate urban growth in 'smart' ways where cities are magnets for international and domestic migration (American Urban Land Institute 1996; Litman 2003; Frey 2003). This challenge invariably focuses on the question *'where* will the new households forming live?' and *'where* will the people work?' (Breheny 1999; CPRE 1997). Similarly in the US, planners in the San Francisco Bay Area ask the question *'where* will we live and work?' (ABAG 1999: see also Hall 1990). Yet, as Chapters Two, Three and Six clearly demonstrate, any approach which confines discussion to the question *where* new housing and settlements are to be located, assuming that the density and integration of land uses alone determines car dependence, travel behaviour, balanced communities, and the vitality of social interaction (Newman and Kenworthy 1999; Crane 2000; Rose and Silas 2001) must be vigorously resisted (De Roo and Miller 2000). Just as important to future sustainability is the question *how* people will manage their daily lives, given unequal household resource distribution and uneven development (Jarvis 2001; 2003).

This takes us back to the popular association of improved urban competitiveness with a high tech future. Arguably there is a tendency to eulogise the economic benefits and gloss over the negative social and environmental externalities of this formula for success. True, California's Silicon Valley is a phenomenal success story, the envy of the competitive world, but top jobs in high-profile silicon industries are few compared to the numbers employed in more mundane occupations on modest and minimum wages. More importantly, the featured cities are not island economies. They rely fundamentally on links with surrounding suburbs and the wider region. San Francisco and London arguably function as part of what Diane Perrons (2004) identifies as 'superstar regions'. In this context it is questionable whether the indicators normally used to measure quality of life are steering development in an appropriate direction. As the household research shows, economic measures such as GDP per capita, unemployment or employment rates, or stocks of vacant or derelict land (Begg 2002: 312) promote a model of growth which is at odds with the reality of daily life.

Existing scholarship in urban studies usually highlights the many ways that US and UK cities differ. The 'urban problems' most associated with US cities, such as minority ethnic ghetto's, citadel gated communities, and fiscal divisions between cities and suburbs, do not register as such pressing issues for UK cities (Perrons 2004: 226; Suarez 1999: 252; Burchell et al. 1997). Moreover differences in land-use planning and urban politics influence the shape and growth of settlement patterns. Mark Pennington (2000: 141) contrasts the practice of zoning in the USA, which is generally sympathetic to a growth-oriented agenda, with the way the planning system in Britain allows the anti-growth lobby greater influence in the planning process. Yet major changes introduced in England and Wales in 2003 to speed up the process of bringing land forward for development alter this presumption. Likewise, a pro-growth agenda arguably underpins the London Plan where future development can be summed up as 'go east', 'raise densities' and bring back high-rise construction (Buck et al. 2002: 388; Hamnett 2003: 231). Consequently urban conditions in these two extreme market-led economies are not as different today as they once were.

This book looks beyond the postcard promise of the five featured cities to examine how everyday life is organised for ordinary working families. It recognises that the middle class two-parent household is a dwindling minority in most urban areas. In part this is because of changing demographics whereby more people are living alone for longer at the beginning and end of their lives, with couples postponing or choosing not to have children and relationships breaking down.

Historically too, family formation is associated with relocation to low density suburbs with green spaces and good schools. In this context the urban families interviewed are tenacious pioneers. But it is also true that cities offer few incentives for families to remain. They are hostile places for the very old and the very young. Visit any of the new up-market waterfront developments and it is patently clear children do not feature in the marketing strategy (Marshall 2001: 40). Cities are also difficult places for anyone juggling multiple caring and earning roles, where neo-liberal emphasis on self-reliance combines with ruthless competition for scarce amenities. But just as cultural diversity is increasingly viewed as a prime asset to attract knowledge workers, so dynamic cities must embrace a balanced population of breadwinners, carers and dependents.

No-one appears to gain from this divided and unequal society. The once popular bumper-sticker '(s)he who dies with the most toys wins' is at odds with survey evidence that 'happiness' is at some point inversely proportionate to wealth accumulation. Research by David Blanchflower and Andrew Oswald (2004) compares data from the US General Social Survey with that for Britain from the Eurobarometer Survey. The resulting analysis confirms the Easterlin hypothesis – that growth does not raise wellbeing. According to the data 34 per cent of those interviewed in the US in 1972 described themselves as 'very happy' while in the same year 33 per cent of Britons reported being 'very satisfied' with life. By the late 1990s the proportion of 'very happy' Americans had declined to 30 per cent while in Britain the proportion remained unchanged. This distinction reflects greater inequality in the USA. The understanding is that in a very unequal society, where some people get a lot richer than others, those left behind feel relatively worse off, even if better off in absolute terms. In contrast, more people have got better off *together* in Britain and consequently fail to recognise any improvement in their wellbeing. This is not to say that UK families experience anything like the benefits of income redistribution characteristic of European social democratic welfare regimes (Harkness and Waldfogel 1999). Indeed, comparing these two extreme liberal market economies pushes home the understanding that the UK does not represent a 'third way' between US flexibility and European fairness (harking back to Gordon Brown's speech referred to in Chapter One) (see Giddens 1998 on the 'third way'). With evidence of increasingly grotesque levels of inequality, the UK looks remarkably like the USA. Which way the UK government should instead look for policy inspiration is clear from the wider European welfare context presented in Chapter Two. As Joan Tronto (2004) observes, the dominant neo-liberal paradigm is a bad model to roll out across the advanced industrial world. To Pierre Bourdieu it represents a 'utopia of endless exploitation', 'destroying all collective structures which may impede the pure market logic' (Bourdieu 1998: 1).

The most striking finding of the well-being research is the significant extent to which non-financial variables influence human welfare (Blanchflower and Oswald 2004: 11). According to Richard Layard (2003: 20) if we are to escape the miseries of a Me-First mentality the aim of a social democracy has to be the greatest happiness for all – each person counting for one. What is encouraging about this body of research is that economists are starting to scrutinise the quest for work/life balance and speaking out in greater numbers against the conventional growth paradigm (Layard 2002; see also Kay 2003).

Back to the main themes

Arguably, we will not achieve balanced lives and sustainable cities if we do not first tackle inequalities within cities and uneven development between dynamic and disadvantaged areas. Here the metaphor of the bridge is useful once again. The bridge both enables and constrains the flow of people and capital: it connects two points but is at the same time a barrier to movement. We see this in the claim then Mayor Paul Schell made in 1977 that bridges were Seattle's enemy, a catalyst for urban decay (Bennett 2000). Similarly Mr and Mrs Smith chose not to set up home a mile south of the Ship Canal because they feared their family, who all live in North Seattle, would never visit them because the bridge presented a huge psychological barrier. This highlights the way the research approach adopted here differs from that applied elsewhere to questions of segregation and inequality in urban studies and social policy. Findings are *not* presented for the most visible social and economic divisions, those representing life on the wrong side of the bridge so to speak. Instead the research emphasises connections between housing, employment, transport and childcare, and the integrated nature of people's daily life from the perspective of within-class variation in relatively advantaged middle class neighbourhoods. Wider social and environmental consequences are then identified through the cumulative effect of unequal resource distributions within and between households. This is illustrated most potently with respect to housing ladders and care chains.

The late 1990s saw a booming economy in the USA. Though economic growth was enjoyed nationally, development was highly uneven: local factors played a part too. In Seattle, for instance, there was the 'Microsoft factor'. Microsoft employees continue to have access to in excess of $1 billion in company stock options and cash windfalls despite the 2001 downturn in the electronics industry. With Microsoft employees heavily concentrated on the Eastside and to the North of downtown Seattle this phenomenal infusion of wealth has had a significant impact on local housing markets. In 2000 one Eastside real estate agent was quoted as saying that Microsoft millionaires (dubbed Baby Bills) had single-handedly defined a new price tier for 'monster mansions' (Rhodes 2000). Chuck Darrah and Jim Freeman describe the similar proliferation of 'trophy homes' in Silicon Valley and the San Francisco Bay Area (Darrah and Freeman 2002 personal communication).

Employees on good incomes who receive huge cash windfalls (stock options, dividends, bonuses) typically use these to buy bigger homes and new automobiles (sales of gas-guzzling Sports Utility Vehicles soared in the late 1990s) (US Department of Commerce 1999). This exacerbates problems of housing affordability for those without this comparative advantage. Unsurprisingly, interviewees who felt the booming economy had left them behind looked to a major correction, even a disaster, to level the playing field so they could maintain their perch in the city. For example, when I interviewed Mr and Mrs Fox in September 2000 they were packing up to leave San Francisco. They were reluctantly moving with their son to Sacramento where they hoped to be able to trade up out of a cramped one bedroom apartment. Mrs Fox explained:

> We have to leave the city, there's no housing. We can't pay 22 hundred dollars a month, so staying in the city isn't an option unless something happens with the market that it suddenly plummeted, like we need another earthquake or something.

Of course, a year later the economy did indeed falter as a consequence of both the 2001 dot-com collapse and in the wake of terrorist attacks in New York and Washington. But even had Mr and Mrs Fox waited for this 'correction' it is unlikely they would have found housing any more affordable. Mark Horner (2004: 170) notes that in hindsight the downturn failed to alleviate local housing shortages or ease travel demand and the practice of excess commuting.

Though working families in both UK and US dynamic cities face similar problems securing an affordable home in a location where they want to live, the nature of the housing crisis is rather different in the two countries. In the UK, especially the South-east of England, a housing supply shortfall combines with a gap in affordability. This is highlighted in the government commissioned Review of Housing Supply produced by economist Kate Barker (2004). Nevertheless, while a shortfall in new construction is well documented, simply increasing the supply of housing appears not to be the solution, especially if attempts are made to 'steer' housing supply to deprived areas where demand is currently low. In the USA the problem of affordability is one of spatial and product mismatch rather than a shortfall in new construction. Here by far the most serious problem is the increasing distances individuals and families have to travel to find a home they can afford which meets their preferences.

Problems of access and affordability are made worse in both national contexts by the expectation that housing provide a source of capital accumulation to finance private responsibility for welfare functions (in education, health and retirement) which in social democratic regimes would be matters of social protection. Various forms of equity release are growing in popularity on both sides of the Atlantic (Council of Mortgage Lenders 2004). Moreover, in many parts of the UK the bottom rung of the housing ladder, usually the preserve of first-time buyers, is entirely dominated by investors in buy-to-let property. These rarely meet the needs of those who would once have been housed by the local authority. Chapter Five provided evidence that UK and US housing market conditions percolate through household biographies and coping strategies to produce different forms of inequality. Housing hardship in the UK is associated with state abandonment of a good quality social rented sector and failure to replace this source of protection with viable alternatives. In the US those in greatest hardship (aside from the homeless) occupy unregulated rungs at the very bottom of the housing ladder, markets associated with disproportionate personal risk (in terms of finance and health). There is a strong argument in both these extreme liberal market contexts to return to a situation where adequate housing is recognised as a basic human right.

The tyranny of small decisions

In 1966 ecologist Alfred Kahn observed that individuals make consumption decisions which appear trivial in isolation – such as driving a child to school because of concerns for road safety – but which cumulatively degrade the environment (see also Hillman 1983; 1993). There are parallels here with Garret Hardin's (1968) 'tragedy of the commons' thesis and to what is recognised in environmental economics as the 'free-rider' problem of unrestricted and uncoordinated access to common goods. Arguably on the basis of the household research presented here we are also witnessing the *tyranny of interdependence*. Traditionally families have constructed clear boundaries around 'work-work' and 'home-work' through the differential meaning attached to the work week and weekend, family time and vacations – but these are increasingly difficult to maintain (Gottlieb et al. 1998). A mundane example of this tyranny of interdependence is offered in the explanation Mrs Fox gives for her change in shopping habits:

> We used to go to the grocery stores a lot more and walk, you know, I used to have bags that I would carry with me, but now it's just too much, it's the time element, our time is really different now, my job takes up a lot more time, plus we have a child now, so our time is really precious.

The escalating volume of car journeys found across the sample is not explained by reasons of time efficiency alone. Fear for road safety, the value attached to comfort, convenience and privacy and use of the family car as a metaphorical extension of the kitchen table, as a space for parents and children to catch up on events are also prevalent in the narratives. The evidence reinforces the concern raised elsewhere that children who are chaperoned everywhere by car never gain road safety awareness or experience essential independent mobility (Hillman et al. 1990; see also Nabhan and Trimble 1994). They also miss out on fresh air and exercise. This book exposes the tyranny of small decisions by identifying the structures of constraint underpinning everyday routines. The consequence of interdependent and competing household preferences is that it is becoming harder for individuals to resist the treadmill of increased production and consumption. It is no coincidence that in the wake of the terrorist attacks of September 11 2001, when the US economy teetered on the brink of recession, Americans were instructed to 'go out and shop for their country'.

The research demonstrates that the process of household decision-making does not represent a utility maximising 'trade-off' such as in the model favoured by orthodox economic theory. Decisions are entirely 'rational' from the perspective of the individuals and families concerned, given their moral values and selective processing of information, though they often appear sub-optimal or perverse to the outside observer. This is illustrated by an observation from my interview with the Eastcott family. Shortly before I arrived to interview them, Mr and Mrs Eastcott had been discussing where they would send their son to school to ensure he received specialist help for his dyslexia. Out on the table in front of them was a sketch map of the city and surrounding region. On it they had circled the location of various schools they had visited as well as their work-places, their daughter's school and their home. They considered the impact each school would have on their journeys to work and daily co-ordination. They also considered the possibility of moving house. They laughed to acknowledge that the exercise had served no real purpose: in the end they had gone with their 'gut instinct' on the school and could not bring themselves to move house. They would simply 'put the blinders on' about the extra travelling and tricky co-ordination. Of course this family had choices open to them that others would not. This family consists of two parents, each with their own car, so it is feasible that they chaperone one child each to schools in opposite directions before journeying on to their separate places of work. This also demonstrates how neo-liberal emphasis on the parent's right (moral duty) to choose the best school for their child contributes to both 'wasteful' journeys (to distant schools) and increased inequality, by establishing an unfair contest between households with unequal access to resources of income, time, transport and personnel. In this competitive climate it is rational for this family to consume the maximum public services their resource entitlement and schedule will allow (for further evidence of parental sacrifice and spending on children see Middleton et al. 1997). Moreover, the social costs of increased pollution, energy consumption and social segregation have no bearing on this private 'small decision'. As argued in the previous chapter, a far more equitable and less environmentally damaging system would have all neighbourhood schools provide education and amenities to the same high standard, thus preventing implicit rationing, whether by postcode, social capital or access to transport.

This case also reinforces the argument that the UK government (ODPM) and US local authorities (under the auspices of Smart Growth) are wrong to assume that the design solutions of the new urbanism can deliver solutions to serious social and environmental problems. Time and energy wasted in excess commuting is not environmentally determined. Thus the more compact cities of Portland and Edinburgh and mixed-use 'urban village' style neighbourhood renewal in San Francisco, London and Seattle do not alone overcome the tendency for households to move between increasingly scattered activities. Dislocation instead flows from the private solutions to common dilemmas or 'problems of living' (Rose 1996: 37) – most reflecting state abandonment or privatisation of once public or collective responsibilities (Rose 1999). The design solutions of the new urbanism will not alone solve routine co-ordination problems because the problem is not simply one of spatial arrangement but also concerns time (use, timing, availability) and questions of sovereignty and dominant cultural values. A sense of the transformation that might be brought about once social, cultural and environmental concerns are viewed holistically is glimpsed in the radical shift in values instilled in the Italian 'Slow Cities' movement, as well as local time use policies deployed through the Modena 'time in the city' project.

The essence of small and slow

The notion of the Slow City grew from Slow Food, at first a playful protest at plans to locate a McDonalds fast-food outlet at the foot of the famous Spanish Steps in Rome in the 1980s. Out of this single protest emerged a cultural movement which has widespread public appeal in Italy today. The underlying philosophy rejects heavily trans-ported mass-produced imports on ecological grounds and instead pro-motes local food production.[1] Appreciation of wholesome cooking traditions and conviviality is encouraged by insistence on the leisurely lunch, thus linking it with work-time reduction initiatives. It was logical then to extend this idealisation of 'good living' to redress the negative effects on the urban environment of a frenetic pace of life (Slow Cities 2004). Slow Cities thus take a number of distinctly European values, such as efforts to reduce working time, emphasis on environmental stewardship, civic pride and belief in social democracy, and converts them into a coherent social movement. These same values are also found in a series of 'time in the city' projects rolled out across 200 Italian towns and cities in recent years. These projects seek to make practical connections between working time initiatives (in co-operation with trades unions) and city time scheduling (bus time-tables, shop and school opening hours) as well as raise the profile of caring work, voluntary sector activity and environmental conservation. One the earliest examples, Modena, for instance, developed new prac-tices in working time alongside a network of state supported child and eldercare (Pillinger 2001; TUC 2002). Crucial to appreciating the success of '*i tempi della città*' is the strength of state sector collaboration with public commitment to collective responsibility. The combined forces of grassroots enthusiasm and state support contrast starkly with 'business case' family friendly policies favoured in the UK and USA where flexibility and innovation rely on individual agreements to modify the status quo.

Though predominantly Italian, the Slow Cities network has international aspirations and more than 33 member towns currently display the 'Slow Cities' logo – a snail crawling past two building, one ancient, the other modern (CNN 2000). Detractors seize on this logo as evidence this is a backward-looking anti-globalisation gimmick. Less easily dismissed are serious goals including locally sourced organic school meals, controls of air quality, improvements in public transport and alternative sources of energy. It is telling that so far the only British members of the Slow Cities network are small market towns, such as Ludlow in Shropshire, where environmental regulation is bound up with heritage preservation and economic growth from tourism can be seen to benefit from the attractions of a compact, car-free setting. By contrast, larger cities struggle with a more profound tension between environmental quality and economic vitality. Moreover, it is harder to justify slow-growth initiatives in situations of inequality and deprivation. It is in this context that Slow Cities are accused of elitism in the same way that urban village settlements discussed in Chapter Two escape collective responsibility for inner city problems, rationing access to a particular quality of life to a minority who can afford high house prices and the cost of private security.

European Slow Cities promote values which are antithetical to US pro-growth neo-liberalism. This distinction crystallises the brink on which the vision of future UK planning and social policy teeters. In stark contrast with US withdrawal from the 1997 Kyoto accord the current UK government expresses firm commitment to the defeat of climate change. Yet it is far behind Continental Europe in adopting solar and wind energy and investing in the density of mass-transit necessary to lure drivers of single occupant vehicles off the roads. The railway network has been abandoned to the market and consequently provides a far inferior and costly service to passengers. Reluctance to intervene in everyday travel decisions corresponds with reluctance to reduce long working hours. A dominant 'business-case' politics in the UK is profoundly at odds with European concerns for social and environmental sustainability. This is illustrated by Ruth Lea, Director of the Centre for Policy Studies and former head of policy at the Institute of Directors, in a scathing attack on European 'short hours' culture and the 'social engineering' of work/life campaigners. She claims that unfavourable comparisons between Britain's workaholic long hours culture and European work-time reduction promotes the wrong economic model. She argues instead that Britain should follow the example of 'economies that have a better track record, including the US where hours worked are significantly longer' (Lea 2004).

At the heart of this statement is the choice, very rarely articulated in public debates, between what Anders Hayden (1999: 3) identifies as two alternative responses to the problem of over-consumption: the path of 'sufficiency' versus the path of 'efficiency'. Sufficiency focuses on 'how much is enough' and has been favoured by much of the green movement and co-incidentally by European work-time reduction initiatives. At the extreme it presents a 'wholesale critique of Western civilization's concept of progress' underpinning the conventional growth paradigm (Hayden 1999: 3). We know from the happiness research above that once basic needs are met, curbing excess consumption does not lead to misery or a lower quality of life. The path of efficiency, by contrast, promotes the use of technology to moderate some of the most damaging environmental impacts of human activity 'without abandoning the pursuit of unlimited economic growth' (Hayden 1999: 3). Distinctions between sufficiency and efficiency can be illustrated with respect to alternative approaches to travel behaviour. An efficiency approach is seen in the promotion of more energy-efficient automobiles, such as the hybrid car. This reduces the amount of energy consumed per vehicle kilometre travelled, without tackling associated problems of car dependence such as congestion, parking, land-use, and the cultural factors stimulating increased trips and distances travelled. A sufficiency approach would question the need to consume excess travel and seek to change behaviour. There are arguments for combining both greater efficiency and restraint in material ambitions such that 'quality of life' is redefined in the advanced North. This would recognise the non-financial assets which are currently neither measured or valued (principle of which is women's unpaid caring work) and reduce environmental impact, redirecting per capita growth to the impoverished South (Schor 1995: 71; Hayden 1999: 30).

Lessons from comparative research

A striking feature of the household research is evidence of within-class variation in coping strategies. The implication is that conventional class analysis neglects the crucial role of non-financial time-use and knowledge resources relating to social capital and access to unpaid family personnel. This is particularly true in the US where most if not all of the sample would agree with the claim 'we are all middle class now' (but see also Butler and Robson 2003: 185 on London). An appreciation of the 'whole economy' of the household allows scope to identify patterns and processes of stratification relating to unequal household resource distribution and the quality as well as quantity of employment. In this latter respect it is not sufficient to consider income as the primary determinant of household coping strategies. This is why Amartya Sen's concept of entitlement has such resonance for this project. It sheds light, for instance, on the significance of gifts or inheritance from relatives which serve to boost housing market entry or ladder assent for a fortunate minority.

Another stark finding of the household analysis is the limited extent to which individual households actively resist the speeding up and intensification of daily life. The question has to be asked why less than ten per cent of the working families interviewed opt for a slower pace of life with respect to working hours, consumer expectations and standards of parenting and home comfort. We learn that *resist the treadmill* strategies are most evident in Seattle and Edinburgh but as the outcome of quite different socio-cultural narratives. In Seattle they are an expression of counter-cultural personal politics where resistance is to conspicuous consumption. This expression is limited to those families endowed with sufficient resources (capital and personnel) to combat the urge to work more to accumulate more. Moreover, the cynic will point to equally conspicuous forms of ethical consumption witnessed in the proliferation of pricey urban farmers markets; boutique health-food stores; and a dozen different grain types in a single loaf of bread. In Edinburgh, on the other hand, resistance is more a feature of making-do with less where less is available than it is a statement of lifestyle preference. The Eagle and Eden families are good examples of this. Crucially though, making do with less is *only possible* as a function of everyday infrastructural endowments; including good public transport, local shops and neighbourhood schools and regular contact with social and kin networks of reciprocity and exchange.

If we are to encourage a culture of 'sufficiency' by reducing the compulsion to travel as part of a frenetic life and this way generate positive externalities of social cohesion and less degraded environments, lessons need to be learned from Seattle and Edinburgh. We need to cultivate restraint in consumer aspiration at the same time as investing in institutions and material environments which allow people to do this without undue hardship. Basic infrastructures are vital because they determine what services and amenities are actually available, given access and affordability constraints. This was illustrated in Chapter Five in relation to transport access to jobs and in Chapter Six with respect to school choice. The former is a bottom-up process bubbling up through new social movements to promote environmental awareness and social justice. Here state intervention might take the form of greater regulation of advertising for instance. By contrast, the latter requires a wholesale shift in public commitment to universal wellbeing rather than growth for the sake of accumulation.

A related observation is that *path of least resistance* strategies are disproportionately found in the UK sample. This indicates that local cultures of parenting and gender roles continue to exert a powerful influence. This household strategy accompanies persistently high levels of female part-time employment as identified in Chapter Four. The implications are that strategies to reconcile work with the rest of life more frequently reinforce gender role asymmetry in the UK. This results in a larger wage gap and greater occupational sex segregation and gendered resource disadvantages which typically extend into old age. In contrast, the minority of UK working families which pursue *career egalitarian* strategies look very like US working families. Here global influence is dominant with respect to work-place cultures insinuated through multi-national corporations and globally competitive markets for innovation and knowledge. This way, career egalitarian households engaged in cultural industries in London (such as digital artists and designers) share more in common with households similarly occupied in San Francisco than they do with their own neighbours who experience a different set of occupational constraints. Yet here too the strain of a work-centred culture takes its toll. A large part of the problem is not the length or timing of the working day (though long hours and business travel are common to this group). Instead pressure comes from the emphasis on self-reliance and the added effort required to secure suitable education, healthcare and pension provision.

In this respect it is important to acknowledge that household biographies are fluid. Over the four years taken to gather and analyse the data introduced in this volume I learned of many alterations to personal circumstances. Shortly before completing the draft manuscript, I received a touching letter from one of the dual-career couples I interviewed in San Francisco. When I met Guy and Greta Florin in 2000 they lived in the heart of the Mission district. They wrote to tell me that a year after the interview they were forced to abandon the 'beautiful city' to set up home in the small university town of Davis. Greta had been struck by a debilitating illness and her health insurance was inadequate to cover the cost of treatment and time off work. Reduced to one salary for several months they could no longer afford the rent on their small apartment or the private school fees they felt necessary to ensure their sons received adequate education. For this couple and their two children the 'tipping points' were several: costs of living which called for two 'good salaries' and perfect health or, failing that, costly medical and unemployment insurance; lack of affordable housing; and run-down state schools fuelling the sense that extra money had to be found from the household budget to compensate for perceived shortcomings in public services. Davis, coincidentally an early product of New Urbanism, offered Guy a commute to work by bicycle and a place each in good local state schools for the two boys.

Collective responsibility

Reflecting on the happiness findings above, Richard Layard (2003) reflects on what it would take for society to be psychically better off. Besides unemployment, he identifies the intense pace of production and workplace insecurity as reducing wellbeing. He cites research by Landers et al. (1996) claiming that US lawyers work harder than they used to and would prefer to work shorter hours for less pay. But to do this would require a change in *culture* brought about through collective action (including legislation). Employees are prevented from individually resist-ing the pressure to work long hours as they risk castigation (Layard 2003: 6). This explains why it is wrong to rely on business-case family friendly initiatives alone to deliver greater work/life balance. These rely on the individual risking isolation by negotiating flexible ways of working. We know from survey findings that working fathers in particular are unwill-ing to take up opportunities for work-time reduction and family leave which are rightfully theirs for this very reason (Land 2002). To allow individuals who value something other than work to pursue a less work-centred life requires a radical shift in dominant cultural values. Moreover, collective action is required to redress imbalances between the value placed on production (the business case) relative to unpaid social benefits (the family-community case).

The household research clearly demonstrates the limits to individual scope for resistance. This is not to say people are dupes or rats in a maze of events over which they have no control. Instead it is to concur with claims made by sociologist Zygmunt Baumann (2001), introduced in Chapter One, that cultural values and ethics based on collective social responsibility have been progressively eroded by a consumption-driven individualism. This is illustrated in the way the working parents interviewed see time moving differently from place to place. This is particularly true of families migrating from the San Francisco Bay Area to Portland in search of a 'more manageable place and slower pace of life'. Families making this move do not readily fit the usual profile of 'down-shifters'. On paper, Portland and Edinburgh families work no fewer hours nor travel any less than do families in London and San Francisco or indeed Seattle. So the difference is not between 'fast' versus 'slow' cities. Instead, those fleeing London and San Francisco express deep frustration at all that slows them down and hampers their ideal of shared parenting and egalitarian careers. Again this suggests that it is not sufficient to regenerate cities like London, Seattle and San Francisco to look more like the polycentric and compact forms of Portland and Edinburgh, where neighbourhoods emulate traditional village congregations. Without a fundamental shift in what is valued by states and citizens, these technical, engineering and design solutions are destined to remain a two-dimensional blue-print the true vision of which is unlikely ever to be realised.

This takes us back to the plea of 1970s feminists that the personal *is* political. It is with respect to everyday co-ordination that feminised social reproduction work is most undervalued. The result of not having a monetary value attached to it is that a large part of the economy is rendered invisible, as 'informal', private, and taken-for-granted. This invisibility explains why the crucial functions of everyday co-ordination receive little if any attention in the practices of urban planning and social policy. This inspires me to reflect on the raw feminism I practiced 20 years ago, marching to Westminster on International Women's Day, demanding 'wages for housework'[2] (see also Palm and Pred 1974). Though often considered narrow and elitist, had this social movement not fallen on deaf ears, women's unpaid contributions to social welfare might receive proper recognition today. Afterall, they are estimated by Nancy Folbre and Julie Nelson (2000: 129) to account for upward of 60 per cent of US GDP.[3] Yet, the research demonstrates the solution is not simply to throw money at the challenge of reconciling 'work' and 'life'. When a child is ill or unhappy at school it is entirely natural for a mother or father to choose to personally intervene, even at high cost to themselves. Rather than be seen as an aberrant disruption to production these socially reproductive services need to be properly valued as the bedrock of a civilised and caring society (Brandt 1995).

Concluding remarks

This book set out to engage students of urban studies and social policy in an unfamiliar but essential debate; one where human and ecological wellbeing collide. A cursory glance through the list of references that follows on from this conclusion highlights the signal lack of such a debate at present. Adopting an integrated analysis has required that literature be drawn from disciplines and policy agendas which stand in splendid isolation of each other. One reason why so few attempts have been made to connect housing, employment, transport and childcare, or to highlight city-family interdependencies, is that the conclusions are disheartening. An anticipated criticism of this book is that it offers no straightforward solutions or a blue-print for better cities and happy families. Quite so: it is instead vital to stress the risks planners and policy-makers take in *believing* there are discrete technical fixes confined within the ambit of each discipline or government department. The danger is that cosmetic solutions will distract attention away from the urgent need for more radical changes in labour relations, consumer behaviour and urban management. Instead the conclusion appears banal – that to properly realise a viable and sustainable future, genuine commitment is required to academic interdisciplinarity and cross-departmental 'joined up' thinking.

What then are the prospects for a radical shake-up in thinking? What about those people who *do* value something other than productivity and growth? In the UK context this question inevitably falls to the position it currently holds, somewhere between wholesale US style neo-liberalism and the possibility of a more social democratic model of welfare. There is a wealth of literature across the disciplines to show what a social democratic future *could* look like for the family and the urban environment. The purpose of this book has been to raise awareness of the private and social costs of *not* taking this preferred route. What is worrying at this crucial turning point is that an opportunity for holistic understanding of the problems has been recently squandered in the very narrow remit of a newly established Academy for Sustainable Communities (ASC). Rather than tackle social and environmental sustainability as flip-sides of the same coin, the signs are this skills initiative is about constructing new town developments like those of the new urbanism in Seaside, Florida, so admired by Deputy Prime Minister John Prescott (discussed in Chapter Two).

The future looks bleaker still for those in the US who want to resist the time-squeeze treadmill. Here the best hope is for grass-roots dissent. Crucially, the seeds of change lie in collective endeavour rather than what is currently fashionable with respect to private actions on an individual scale through Voluntary Simplicity and NIMBY-style slow-growth initiatives. As critics point out, these represent essentially elitist middle class actions to protect property values, and the kind of lifestyle down-shifting only possible for those who have sufficient surplus to relinquish in the first place. Instead a glimpse of public opinion turning against a profits before people ethos was witnessed in strike action by the United Food and Commercial Workers (UFCW) union in Santa Monica in 2003. Of significance was the fact that shoppers boycotted supermarkets in support of shop workers threatened with cuts to health and pensions benefit (Campbell 2003). What is encouraging about this living wage protest is the speed with which shoppers realised the power they could wield – by not shopping. There are other inspiring examples of collective action in recent history, those mobilised by Rachel Carson's assault on the pesticide industry being a case in point (as discussed in Chapter Two). Today the challenge is to move beyond single issue protests towards a more coherent opposition to fetishised productivity and growth. Just because there are no quick fixes does not mean we should avoid difficult debates about prevailing cultural values.

Appendix A   Sampling Frame Specifications

The intensive household research required two discrete stages of preparation. In the first stage, a cluster analysis of Census of Population data was generated for each city, ranking all wards/postal districts according to key social, economic and demographic variables. On the basis of this exercise it was possible to select central and outer urban/suburban neighbourhoods, all similarly positioned within a matrix where 'family' and two-income household structures together with high levels of owner occupation were a dominant feature.

In the second stage, access to the target population was gained through a postal questionnaire distributed to 150 households in each neighbourhood which, from register of voters data, appeared to be young family households (two opposite sex adults, living with no other adults, born in the period 1957 to 1970). The postal survey was used to refine selection of 20 households per city sub-population for tape-recorded interviews (i.e. to ensure all were couples with one or more dependent child with at least one partner economically active). This was not a scientific sample. Instead the research incorporated a high degree of specificity to ensure that common household practices and patterns of behaviour could be clearly extracted from the largely idiosyncratic stories emerging from in-depth qualitative research. If the project were to have allowed greater variation in terms of class and ethnicity, further cross-cutting cleavages would have emerged and fewer shared experiences made visible overall. This way the project isolated sources of tension pertaining to a particular household structure and localised contexts of urban restructuring. Households selected according to pre-determined criteria effectively provide 'reference points or "peepholes" from which to get information about a culture and a way of life. (Indeed) the total population studied is far larger than the reference (households). Together these make up the basis of the generalisations in the study' (Gullestad 1984: 46). It was imperative to identify households expressing a willingness to be interviewed. This is because households are required to invest a considerable amount of time and effort in recalling biographic detail. In these circumstances Sandra Wallman (1984: 47) suggests that 'willingness to co-operate (is) sufficient grounds for selection'.

Use of register of voter information provides a useful means by which to generate a database which represents the closest possible fit with the target population for this research. Presence of children cannot be determined from either British or US register of voter data and only in the USA are information fields for date of birth, years at this address and place of origin available. With the US data it is possible to use date of birth as well as household membership data to eliminate single person, extended, 'non-standard' and non-family households as well as retired couples.

A number of 'traditional' male breadwinner families were included in each sample to reflect the inherent fluidity of household employment whereby, at any moment in time, 'traditional' male breadwinner households might exist as temporarily shelved dual-earning households, while dual-earning households may verge on abandoning attempts to sustain two jobs or careers.

The 100 household interviews included individual employment biographies, maps and diaries of individual and household spheres of activity together with narratives of the decisions made by couples concerning residential location, spatial mobility, all forms of work undertaken and networks of informal support making up daily routines. In-depth interviews, each lasting at least one hour, were conducted along similar lines to the well-established method of 'biographic' research (Wallman 1984; Campanelli and Thomas 1994; Halfacree and Boyle 1993; Jarvis 1999). Couples were interviewed together so as to engage directly with issues of spouse negotiation in the joint telling of both everyday routines and milestone events. While it is likely that male and female partners offer different, perhaps more personal responses to questions relating to domestic relations when interviewed alone, much can be learned about the processes of negotiation which go to make up the co-ordination of daily life when interviewing partners together (Valentine 1998). An example is where one partner frequently contradicts the other. It is also possible for the interviewer to gain some insight, as a participant observer, into domestic practices and arrangements (such as who answers the door, makes tea, attends to the baby etc.). From a practical point of view too it is difficult to contrive interviews in a home setting with each partner individually. It would mean banishing one partner to another room of the house, something likely to reduce levels of co-operation and exposition. Each interview followed a topic guide structured around the four substantive themes of home (housing and journey to work); employment (and unpaid work); family (childcare and support networks) and relationship (negotiation of roles, points of tension in current practices and arrangements). To probe the process of decision-making further, couples were presented with a number of hypothetical scenarios. The answers to these revealed the extent to which couples either discussed issues openly or took particular patterns of behaviour for granted.

Analysis of the interview transcripts (each interview typically generating thirty pages of narrative) was both formal and intuitive. Use was made of QSR NUD*IST computer software to code dialogue and narrative according to frequency and correspondence of thematic occurrence (Gahan and Hannibal 1998). Detailed thematic interpretation followed the themes of the topic guide, thus grounding interpretation in the theoretical design of the research project (Miles and Huberman 1984; Strauss and Corbin 1998).

Appendix B   The UK and USA Systems of Planning in Outline

With its strong executive powers the UK government has adopted a course of liberal-intervention (as opposed to non-intervention) in the housing market and maintained from 1947 a comprehensive system of town and country planning which ensures a high degree of consistency in the planning policy framework (White and Allmendinger 2003: 954; Allmendinger 2001). Notwithstanding the devolution of many government functions to Scotland, Wales and Northern Ireland, the UK planning system remains highly centralised and hierarchical with Westminster policy guidance intended to 'trickle-down' through regional planning to local development plans. Major changes to the planning system in England came into effect from September 2003 following the Planning Policy Statement, *Sustainable Communities – Delivering Through Planning*. Now based on two tiers (eliminating former county structure plans) the changes are intended to speed up the planning application process and strengthen strategic plan making. Regional Spatial Strategies (RSS) are now prepared in consultation with the Regional Development Agencies (RDAs) and used as guidance to local authorities in the preparation of new Local Development Frameworks (LDF) (ODPM 2002). The relationship between the RSS and other strategies (such as on air quality, climate change, etc.) is intended to be two-way but RSS have statutory status. These changes are intended to address the criticism that high costs and lengthy delays contribute to the growing shortfall in the development of new homes (Pennington 2002: 46, 106). Others argue that because the UK planning system does not employ the sort of prescriptive zoning found in Continental Europe and the USA it delivers greater flexibility. Local authorities are free to interpret regional guidance (now RSS) to suit local conditions when making decisions on individual proposals or applications (White and Allmendinger 2003: 954). This encourages systematic engagement with environmental sustainability initiatives (Rydin 2003: 4). Nevertheless, a major difference between the US and UK systems is the limited scope UK local authorities have to specify spending priorities. This is because 75 per cent of funding comes from national block grants calculated to redistribute tax revenue according to relative need. (See also Tewdwr-Jones 1996.)

In contrast, the US federal system of government and public attitude to property reflects powerful resistance to any prescriptive approach or top-down control. It is the role of individual states, not federal government, to define policy objectives. Individual states and cities are able to raise funds through sales tax, business rates and local income tax. Locally autonomous spending tends to reinforce divisions between affluent and disadvantaged populations where opportunities for urban development reflect the size of the tax base. When the Regional Planning Association of America was established in 1923 it attempted, unsuccessfully, to lobby for a comprehensive regional planning system. The organisation proceeded through the influence of architect-planners such as Lewis Mumford to stage periodic utopian revivals of self-contained communities originally inspired by the British Garden City movement (Cullingworth 1997: 50). There is evidence of such resurgence in popular arguments for greater land-use regulation and better environmental protection in the US today. This is evident in relation to the Congress of New Urbanism discussed in Chapter Two. Promotion of 'smart growth' suggests growing public concern for the restriction of urban sprawl (Teitz 1990; 1996). Notwithstanding renewed emphasis on the compact city, land-use planning in the USA remains a local matter, varying from place to place (see Diamond and Noonan 1996). The degree of local variation is evident in the cities examined in this book, discussed in Chapter Six.

Appendix C   Spouse Labour Market Combinations in Four Cities

Economic sphere/ contract type	Mode of work/ drivers of long hours working		Obstacles to two-wage Work-life balance
'New economy': knowledge-based, high-technology, multimedia, ICT, research and development			

1. Freelance:
– 1a. contractor
– 1b. home-based
2. Employee:
– 2a. temp/contract
– 2b. standard
London (L) = 3
Edinburgh (E) = 4
San Francisco (F) = 5
Seattle (S) = 5
Portland (P) = 3
	Freelance:
	e.g. computer analyst
	fluctuating income
	and periodic tight
	deadlines; welfare/
	benefits limited by
	ability to pay.
	• Financial
	  incentive
	• Enthusiasm for
	  the work
	Employee:
	e.g. biotech researcher;
	'dot-comer'
	frequent/intense
	deadlines; creative
	collaboration pre-
	cludes tele-working.
	• Enthusiasm for
	  the work
	• Tight deadlines
	• Portfolio worker
	  survival
		LORD (Dual) 2b + 4b
		LIDDELL (Dual)
		1a + 5b
		LAND (Dual) 2b + 5b
		EVANS (Trad) 2b
		EDWARDS (Flex)
		1a + 5b
		EATON (Dual) 1b + 5b
		EMBER (Dual) 4b + 5b
		SAYER (Flex) 2b + 5b
		STEVENS (Dual)
		1b + 1b
		SAGE (Dual) 2b + 7a
		SPRING (Dual) 1b + 5b
		SHEARER (Dual)
		1b + 5b
		PIKE (Trad) 4b
		PRIEST (Flex) 2a + 2a
		PARR (Flex) 2b + 5b
			Difficult to sustain two careers of this nature without significant recourse to marketised forms of social repro-duction. Dual career households in particu-lar experience extreme intensification of working hours together with potentially com-peting demands for out of hours 'networking', business travel, 'hyper-mobility' and/or 'fugue-like' work practices.

'Established professional': legal, financial, organisational and administrative service delivery			
3. Self employed/ entrepreneurial: 4. Private sector: – 4a. temp/con-tract/shift – 4b. standard 5. Public sector – 5a. temp/con-tract/shift	Entrepreneurial: *e.g. inventor/* *consultant* Typically associated with high levels of risk and personal commitment; fluc-tuating income. • Financial incentive	LAW (Trad) 4b LAZER (Flex) 4b + 6 LEXINGTON (Flex) 5b + 5b LEMON (Flex) 4b + 5a LONMORE (Flex) 4b + 5b LOXTON (Dual) 4b + 4b	Difficult to sustain two ('equal') full time) careers of this nature. Spouse employment is liable to be sacrificed if frequent job relocation is required to secure promotion/specialist post ('trailing spouse').

Economic sphere/ contract type	Mode of work/ drivers of long hours working		Obstacles to two-wage Work-life balance
– 5b. standard London (L) = 10 Edinburgh (E) = 12 San Francisco (F) = 7 Seattle (S) = 9 Portland (P) = 13	• 'Macho' goal-oriented • Demand-led Employee (standard contract): *e.g investment banker; medic* Significant 'face-time' component precludes home-working; 'out of hours'/'on-call' work invades home; early career development often requires relocation. • Demand-led • 'Macho' goal-oriented • Moral obligation • Presenteeism Employee (non-standard/shift-work): *e.g. fire captain; nurse* Variable/rotating shifts; physically/ emotionally de-manding work; compulsory compe-titive tendering im-pacts on many job terms and condi-tions. • Moral obligation	LINKLATER (Dual) 5b + 5b LYMINGTON (Dual) 5b + 5b LOCKE (Dual) 3 + 3 LYNSTED (Dual) 3/ 5b + 5b ELLIS (Trad) 4b ENDEL (Trad) 4b EASINGTON (Flex) 4b + 4b EYWOOD (Flex) 5b + 5a EAST (Flex) 5b + 5b EWELL (Flex) 7b + 4b ECCLES (Flex) 5b + 5a EIDER (Dual) 5b + 5b EASTCOTT (Dual) 5b + 5b EGHAM (Dual) 5b + 5b EDGELEY (Dual) 4b + 5b EARNLEY (Dual) 3 + 3 STAMP (Trad) 4b SNAITH (Flex) 2a + 7c SARGENT (Flex) 5a + 5a SHAW (Flex) 4a + 5b SHAYLER (Flex) 5a + 4b SAUNDERS (Dual) 3 + 3 STRONG (Dual) 4b + 5b SCULLY (Dual) 4a + 5b SMITH (Dual) 5b + 5b POYNTER (Flex) 4b + 7c PLATT (Flex) 5b + 5a PARIS (Flex) 5b + 5b PARKER (Flex) 5b + 5b	While a high degree of autonomy is possible, this is often circum-scribed by face-to-face meetings that cannot be rescheduled and business travel. Public sector salaries trail private sector salaries for comparable occupa-tions. Historically public sector emp-loyees gained greater job security and occu-pational benefits in recompense for lower salaries. This 'trade-off' is weakened today by cultures of long hours working in both public and private sectors albeit reflecting differ-ent drivers and impe-ratives.

Economic sphere/ contract type	Mode of work/ drivers of long hours working		Obstacles to two-wage Work-life balance
		PALMER (Flex) 3 + 4b	
		POST (Flex) 5b + 3	
		PAYNE (Dual) 4b + 4b	
		POLLY (Dual) 4b + 5b	
		PUGH (Dual) 4b = 5b	
		POULTER (Dual) 4b + 5b	
		PACEY (Dual) 5b + 4b	
		PHILPOTT (Dual) 4b + 4b	
		PINK (Dual) 3 + 4b	

'Modern': production (craft) and personal services

6. Self employed:	Self employed:	LEWIS (Trad) 6	Real wages trail those
7. Private sector:	*e.g. cab driver;*	LEE (Trad) 6	of more globally inte-
– 7a. standard/	*plumber*	LACEY (Flex) 8b + 7b	grated/high-perfor-
salary	Fluctuating income;	LIVINGSTONE (Flex)	mance occupations;
– 7b. hourly paid/	personal financial	6 + 8a	irregular and/or shift
shift	risk; irregular/sea-	LIVELY (Flex) 7b +7a	ing male spouse hours
– 7c. temp/irregular	sonal workload.	LANGHAM (Flex)	of work consign
8. Public sector:	• Financial	LITTLE (Dual) 7a + 8b	female spouse to low
– 8a. standard/	incentive	EARL (Flex) 7a + 8c	status/part-time
salary	• Demand-led	EAGLE (Flex) 8a + 8b	employment; evening
– 8b. hourly paid/	(seasonal)	EDEN (Flex) 6 + 7c	and weekend work
shift	Employee (stan-	EASTER (Dual) 8a + 8a	requires access to
– 8c. temp/irregular	dard contract):	SUMMER (Trad) 7b	child-care out of
London (L) = 7	*e.g. auto mechanic;*	SLATER (Flex) 6 + 7b	normal hours.
Edinburgh (E) = 4	*bank clerk*	STONE (Flex) 8b + 8c	
San Francisco (F) = 8	Increasing influence	SLOCUM (Dual)	
Seattle (S) = 6	of 24/7 service prov-	8b + 7b	
Portland (P) = 4	ision/expectations.	SAND (Dual) 6 + 7a	
	• Demand-led	SKYLA (Dual) 7b + 8b	
	• Presenteeism	PLACE (Trad) 7a	
	Employee (non-	POUND (Flex) 7b	
	standard/shift-work)	PEET (Flex) 8b + 7b	
	e.g. merchant mariner;	PINDER (Flex) 7a + 7b	
	janitor; cab driver		
	Shift-work can entail		
	extended periods		
	working away from		
	home, irregular, sea-		
	sonal or anti-social		
	hours.		
	• Moral obligation		
	• Demand led		

(*Note*: equivalent San Francisco data is presented in Table 3.3)
Source: author's survey of working family households.

Appendix D   Potted Biography for Sharon and Jamie Fuller – Intersections of Housing, Employment, Gender and Generation

Sharon Fuller grew up in Alameda, California, in the same house her mother still owns, where she and Jamie now live with their four year old daughter. After graduating from Berkeley, Sharon moved to New York, first to pursue a career in publishing, then to attend law school. By the time she met Jamie, six years later, she was a practising attorney, working to pay off student loans of some fifty thousand dollars. Jamie had always lived on the East Coast, shuttling between various small towns, working ten years to pay his way through college before moving to Manhattan to pursue a career in photography. Setting up home together in the northern end of Manhattan, both in their early 30s, they reached the decision they were 'finished with New York'. They disliked having to commute for an hour by train each way to work, standing most of the way – 'it was horrible'. Talking about more manageable places to live, Jamie dreamed of settling in small town Upstate New York while Sharon favoured city life and said she missed her family in California. Sharon admitted 'pushing (Jamie) a little bit' and presenting the Bay Area as the ideal compromise. Jamie was prepared to move anywhere within reason so long as it was 'near a coastline'. The benefit of moving to the Bay Area was they could live rent-free with Sharon's mother in Alameda while Sharon studied for the Bar exams she needed to pass in order to practice law in California. Jamie also recognised the advantage of having a major market for freelance photography on his doorstep in San Francisco.

The ten years that followed Sharon and Jamie's 'big move' in 1988 illustrates clearly the co-constitution of housing and labour market opportunities as well as the role of such negotiated traits as relative acquisitiveness, the propensity to take risks and moral rationalities (cultural norms) concerning family life. After living a year in Alameda Sharon found work with a law firm in San Francisco. The couple moved to a private rented apartment in Bernal Heights, an easy commute by public transit to the financial district. Feeling settled at last, they married. Four years later they felt ready to buy their first home together. They were a week away from exchanging contracts on a town house in Berkeley when Sharon was made redundant. Because she was the primary breadwinner they feared being unable to make the mortgage payments and reluctantly backed out of the deal at the last minute. Having given up their rented apartment in San Francisco they had little option but to move back with Sharon's mother in

Alameda. This time it took four months for Sharon to find a new job and declare she 'could not live with her husband and mother under the same roof'. Not feeling sure enough of their income to enter owner occupation they rented an apartment in an area of Oakland they had 'discovered' on frequent car journeys between San Francisco and Alameda.

A year later and now with a young daughter, the family faced eviction from their Oakland apartment and were alarmed at the level of rent they would have to pay for a similar home. Sharon had no taste for the 'big bucks' legal work and was still struggling to pay off her student debts. Even with two incomes they found it hard to find a home they could afford. The option of living with Sharon's mother seemed attractive once again. This time the move 'back home' was permanent. To justify this apparent capitulation, Sharon presented the move as one of mutual benefit whereby her mother 'helps somewhat with childcare when we get in a pinch' and she is helped in turn by them '(taking) her shopping and to her doctors appointments' because she is barred from driving on medical grounds.

Notes

Chapter One: The Personal *is* Political

1. The term 'portfolio worker' refers to the varied set of skills a worker must invest in to ensure they are selected for competitive short-term contracts. Accompanying the loss of a 'job for life' is the proliferation of project-based freelance working where workers need to reskill constantly to adjust to changes in technology and niche market demands. Consequently workers in the new economy tend to move between firms and locations in such a way that it is no longer the firm that ensures the worker has up to date and relevant skills but the worker investing in their own 'portfolio' (see for instance Platman 2004; Cohen and Mallon 1999; Aronwitz and DiFazio 1994).
2. This was before proliferation of the palm-pilot.
3. Ed Soja describes a similar situation as the basis of the 'Justice for Janitors' struggle for access to affordable housing and living wages in Los Angeles throughout 1999/2000. The struggle was for a 'spatial justice' or distributive justice to recognise the rights of workers to live within acceptable commuting distance of the jobs available (see for instance Soja 2000; Harvey 1996).
4. The universal worker model is epitomised by Tony Blair's introduction to the UK document on welfare reform: 'work for those who can, security for those who cannot'. In this way the male breadwinner system of welfare is considered 'out of date' in economic rather than social terms (Lewis 2002: 52).
5. Will Hutton, Director of The Work Foundation, identified the '30/30/40 society' from labour force data in the mid-1990s which indicated a new segmentation based on the quality as well as the quantity of employment. He identified 30 per cent of the working age population as disadvantaged through economic inactivity, unemployment and government training schemes; a further 30 per cent were 'newly insecure' on the basis they were on temporary, part-time, newly self-employed or in low waged employment. At the top of the heap he recognised 40 per cent of the working age population as privileged by virtue of full-time, well paid employment and established self-employment (Badcock 2002: 140). This model takes no account of household structure as it focuses only on individual level labour force data.
6. It was recently reported in the UK that parents clock up an average of 5,000 miles a year driving their children to school, parties and leisure activities, the majority organised by mothers (Marston 2005). In Denmark, by contrast, 90 per cent of secondary school children walk or cycle to school without parental escort.
7. As early as 1988 reference was make in Scotland to the emergence of an industrial cluster taking advantage of non-union labour traditions in the Silicon Glen new town developments to the west of Edinburgh (Harvey 1988: 101–34).
8. This allusion to the 1970s British sit-com 'The Good Life' is fitting (the series was one of the first to poke fun at acquisitiveness, featuring a comic lifestyle

of 'simplicity' and self-sufficiency) but of course it is a caricature. More generally the reference is to renewed emphasis on wellbeing which is not confined to the individual but oriented toward social justice.

Chapter Two: Cities and Families

1. These original 'new towns' were as physically removed from industrial inner cities as they were morally bound to civil obedience, commissioned as they were by puritan philanthropists such as Robert Owen (New Lanark in Scotland 1800), Titus Salt (Saltaire in Bradford 1853), George Cadbury (Bourneville village in Birmingham 1879). William Heskith Lever (Port Sunlight in Birkenhead 1888) and Joseph Rowntree (New Earswick in York 1902) (Rudlin and Falk 1999: 29). As recently as 2003 a residents survey voted Bourneville 'one of the nicest places to live in Britain' because it is 'neighbourly' and peaceful – much like an old-fashioned village. Unusually today, Bourneville successfully blends social rented and owner-occupied housing – a social mix which differentiates this from market-led suburban estates (Casciani 2003).
2. By tragic coincidence Rachel Carson herself died of breast cancer at the age of 57.
3. While the community functions independently, with its own system of regulating property and behaviour, this separate existence is now under threat. Rising urban land values have triggered renewed interest in state redevelopment of the site and, as a consequence, heightened police surveillance aimed at driving out illegal or anti-establishment activities and with them residents of this community.
4. The derogatory term 'snout house' is popularly applied to a style of house which has a prominent garage and blank facade as the feature pedestrians see when walking through the neighbourhood. In 1999 the Portland City Council banned the construction of new houses with snouts on the basis that they discouraged neighbourliness.
5. Source: 2001 Census; Key Statistics. Census output is Crown copyright and is reproduced with the permission of the Controller of HMSO and the Queen's Printer for Scotland.

Chapter Three: Living and Working

1. In 1976, Steve Jobs and Steve Wozniak hand-assembled the first Apple computers in a Silicon Valley garage. Within a decade, Apple, now a Fortune 500 corporation, introduced the far more sophisticated Macintosh assembled on an industrial scale (Hayes 1989: 86).
2. It is *de-rigeur* for specifications to boast 'high ceilings, hardwood floors, open-plan space' (Matteucei 1998).
3. Mayor Willie Brown's Proposition K only achieved 39.2 per cent for a Yes vote while the Proposition L grassroots initiative achieved 49.8 per cent. Neither gained sufficient majority to pass into law.
4. Pseudonym/anonymised address.
5. It was estimated that Californian dot-com closures occurred at a rate of 20 per month through 2000. This rate accelerated markedly in the months

following the Nasdaq 'dive' (San Francisco Chronicle 2000). Another report recorded a loss of 12,828 US dot-com related jobs in January 2001 alone and a total of 610 dot-com closures in the period December 1999 to January 2001 (Saracevic 2001).

6. IPO – Initial Public Offering: the sale of equity in a company, generally in the form of shares through an investment bank to be traded on a stock market such as Nasdaq. Start-up companies have to demonstrate the potential to develop into a profitable company before selling equity – though achieving IPO status does not protect them from economic shocks.

7. This belief is enigmatically captured in the Hollywood film 'Pirates of Silicon Valley' about the growth of the personal computer industry.

8. Many of the direct action advocacy groups had acronyms aimed for battle: AARGG! (All Against Ruthless Greedy Gentrification), PODER (People Organised to Demand Environmental and Economic Rights) and alluding to the products of technology MAC (Mission Anti-Displacement Coalition) (Whitting 2000). A banner on the streets at this time echoes the popular demand for 'Room to Breathe'.

Chapter Four: Flexibility

1. It is important to note that a 'necessary household wage' is contingent on many factors. Necessity relates to that which households aspire to, as well as what is essential to facilitate their 'getting by'. Of course, this is totally subjective but that is the important point to note. People choose to compromise on some issues to achieve other ends. The iron laws of economics are thus exposed to be far more malleable than typically conceived.

2. UK workers have generally been protected against working excessive hours by implementation of the European Working Time Directive in 1998 as part of the Social Chapter (S.I. 1998/1833). This puts a ceiling of 48 hours on the maximum average working week and a limit on night work of an average 8 hours in every 24. The regulations are extremely complex with many employees exempt from this protection. According to 2002 Labour Forces Data around one million workers were exempt in sectors excluded from the WTD such as transport, police, armed forces, doctors in training. New measures to extend the WTD came into effect on August 1st 2003. These are likely cover around 770,000 previously exempt workers. It remains the case that employees whose working time is not predetermined (such as managers) are only partially covered where individuals effectively opt out of the regulation (whether voluntarily or by compulsion) (TUC Briefing http://www.aasa.org.uk/wtd.html) viewed on-line August 6 2003 (see also Neathey 2001).

Chapter Five: Equity

1. Though originally named the 'Young Men's Christian Association' few facilities are sex-segregated today. Instead the acronym stands for 'members' who are no longer exclusively young, male or Christian. I was once employed by the Embarcadero (San Francisco) YMCA to hand out freshly laundered towels to executives working-out as members of the private gym there. Both as a former employee and as a temporary resident I experienced

a Janus-faced institution, one which mirrors in no small measure social divisions evident in urban neighbourhoods across the USA.

2. Barbara Ehrenreich (2001) could find no statistics on the number of employed people living in cars or vans though it is estimated that nearly one-fifth of all homeless people in the USA are in paid employment (p. 26). Anecdotal evidence suggests that a car often provides refuge during periods of temporary homelessness and this is a notable cultural (logistical) difference between the USA and UK. A used car which is relatively cheap to run is possibly the most valuable asset anyone can have 'to get by' in the USA and consequently the last asset to be relinquished when facing hard times. The opposite is true in the UK where running a car is prohibitively expensive for low-wage workers. UK homeless workers also lack access to the sort of non-traditional housing options common in the USA, where less stringent regulations encourage a market for rented trailers (caravans), mobile and manufactured homes and adapted out-buildings. In contrast, it is estimated that the number of family households staying in bed and breakfast accommodation (as a form of local authority provision in situations of homelessness) increased three-fold in London between 1997 and 2002 as a consequence of housing shortage and high cost of living (National Statistics Online 2004)

3. This extreme does exist of course. Just because the UK and USA have enjoyed low national unemployment since the mid 1990s does not detract from the fact that where unemployment exists it is heavily concentrated in particular locations.

4. Reference to entitlements here is distinct from the narrow definition of means-tested or other official entitlement to state welfare benefits, where the latter is the subject of critique in the Communitarian belief in 'no rights without responsibilities' (see Mead 1986).

5. A living wage is not the same as the minimum wage. It relates to the cost of living by region. Collective strike action took place in London in 2002/3 between teachers, postal workers and refuse collectors all pressing for a rise in the London cost-of-living allowance, effectively to raise earnings to a 'living wage'. Many local authorities argue that public sector wages are not low because the lowest wages in the private sector are far lower still.

6. According to the report 'Your Place, Not Mine' co-published by the homeless charity Crisis and the Countryside Agency, most of the 380,000 hidden homeless stay with family and friends because their only alternative would be to sleep rough (Prasad 2003).

7. One scheme offers 'key workers' such as NHS staff, teachers and others loans of up to £50,000 which can be used to buy a home on the open market or a Housing Association property. The loan is re-paid when the property is sold or the worker leaves their employment. The scheme is limited to workers with a total income of below £60,000 and the homes must be 'suitable to their needs' (Starkey 2004: 25).

8. Medicaid is a strictly rationed health insurance for low-income families, limited to families with *total* assets below $20,000.

9. In fact the coincidence is that one household biography features a cab driver and the other an executive who travels by cab each day to work. To illustrate the 'chains' linking and dividing key workers and the profession-

als who rely on the services they provide, I have employed the technique of 'fictional composite' of events though not of characters or narrative (see for instance English-Lueck 2002: 42).

10. Mr and Mrs Ling did not form part of the original sample of working families, their biography was built up through that of Mr and Mrs Lonmore as a way of following up all relevant aspects of their daily life, including social and kin contacts.

Chapter Six: Sustainability

1. Not only is the IPCC open to all members of the United Nations Environment Programme and the World Meteorological Office, many hundreds of scientists contribute in the process of knowledge assessment through peer reviewed publications.
2. Oil prices reached a 13 year high of $45 a barrel in May 2004. Nearly 60 per cent of oil the US uses is imported from the Middle East and elsewhere (Pimental and Giampieto 1995; Beatley and Manning 1997). A fuel protest by UK road hauliers in 2000 disrupted the supply of petrol at the pumps.
3. Constitutionally the UK is composed of four nations (England, Wales, Scotland and Northern Ireland). The empirical study draws on observations from two of these (England and Scotland); most secondary data relates to the three which make up Great Britain while parliamentary papers typically refer to the UK in its entirety. In global economic terms it is appropriate (and useful as a shorthand) to generally refer to the UK as a general rule.
4. Administered in parallel by the Office for National Statistics in England and Wales, the General Register Office in Scotland and the Northern Ireland Statistics and Research Agency, these bodies work closely together and use very similar methods, although they do not produce collated data for the UK for all topics (Tunstall 2004: 8).
5. In his budget speech of March 2004, Chancellor Gordon Brown accepted the recommendations of Sir Michael Lyons for 20,000 civil servants to move out of London and the South East and for pay rates in the new locations to be aligned with the 'going rates' in those areas. Running alongside proposals for decentralisation are job cuts resulting from Sir Peter Gershon's July 2004 efficiency review. Both the Lyons and Gershon reviews form part of Prime Minister Tony Blair's reformation of the civil service. The policy anticipates that re-locating middle ranking posts to areas of cheaper accommodation, combined with lower salary costs, will deliver savings to the public purse and also help alleviate pressure for affordable housing in the South East (Brown 2003a).
6. A survey of biographic data reveals that 15 out of 80 UK working parents originate in a different region (or come from another country) compared with 50 out of 120 US parents.
7. The potential conflicts facing compact city and decentralised telecommuting initiatives are widely reported elsewhere (Breheny 1992; Gillespie 1992; Graham 1997).
8. Based on May 2004 average fuel prices, a litre of unleaded petrol/gasoline cost on average 79 pence a litre in Britain and 27 pence in the USA. Petrol

prices in the UK are second in expense only to the Netherlands when average pump prices are compared across Europe.

9. Interviews were conducted with partners together so as to engage directly with issues of spouse negotiation in the joint telling of both everyday routines and milestone events (see Valentine 1998 for a discussion of the benefits and limitations of interviewing partners together).

10. This data compares with an average of 24 minutes for all economically active residents of Scotland as a whole, varying by mode from a 'walk' mean time of 12 minutes to a 'rail' mean time of 52 minutes and a 'bus' mean time of 32 minutes (Scottish Executive STS 2001a).

Chapter Seven: A View From the Bridge

1. The Slow Cities vision in many ways echoes the 'small is beautiful' philosophy developed in 1974 by E.F. Schumacher and kept alive through publications by the E.F. Schumacher Society. Moreover, the language of 'less is more' is employed by the growing Voluntary Simplicity movement popular in the US Pacific North-West.

2. From the late 1960s the women's movement set out to challenge women's 'double day' which consisted of rising contributions of paid work but no parallel decline in unpaid domestic labour which was 'naturalised' as women's burden. A socialist-feminist coalition emerged in 1972 in the form of the International Wages for Housework Campaign. This actively sought recognition for housework as a capitalist struggle alongside that of the male factory worker, publishing pamphlets, organising marches and lobbying politicians. One of the founders was Selma James, wife of the Trinidadian revolutionary socialist CLR James. Born in New York, but later a resident of London's bohemian Hampstead neighbourhood, Selma's first political pamphlet 'A Women's Place' formed the basis of the Wages for Housework Campaign. More than 30 years later it is still based at the Crossroads Women's Centre in Kentish Town, North London (other branches continue to thrive in North America, the Caribbean and across Europe. The campaign web site (http://www.allwomencount.net/) continues to demand recognition and payment for all the unwaged work women and girls do, claiming that at least 2/3 of the world's work is done by women and girls, mostly unwaged, the rest for low wages. On March 8th 2000 the Campaign organised the Women's Global Strike in support of these aims. While considerable support has been achieved for a more holistic system of accounting, to value women's social and economic contribution, women still earn less than men and are under represented in top jobs, fundamentally as a consequence of their double day.

3. This valuation is based on time-use and labour inputs alone as a proportion of the total value of US output and is likely to significantly underestimate the true value of non-market (re)production.

Bibliography

ABAG (1995) *Smart Growth Strategy: Shaping the Future of the Nine-County Bay Area*. Internet: http://www.abag.org/ San Francisco: Association of Bay Area Government.

ABAG (1999) *Bay Area Futures: Where Will We Live and Work. Projections '98*. San Francisco: Association of Bay Area Government.

Abbott, C. (1994) 'The Oregon Planning Style'. In *Planning the Oregon Way: a Twenty Year Evaluation* (eds) C. Abbott, D. Howe and S. Adler. Corvallis: Oregon State University Press.

Abrams, F. (2002) *Below the Breadline: Living on the Minimum Wage*. London: Profile Books.

Ackroyd, P. (2001) *London the Biography*. London: Verso.

Adams, J. (1999) 'The social implications of hypermobility'. Conference proceedings of The Economic and Social Implications of Sustainable Transportation, Ottawa Workshop; working party on pollution prevention, working group on transport. Paris: OECD. (Env/epoc/eppc/t(99)3/Final/Rev1): 99–133.

Agree, E., B. Bissett and M.S. Rendall (2003) 'Simultaneous care for parents and care for children among mid-life British women and men'. *Population Trends* **112**, 29–35.

Aitken, S. (2000) 'Mothers, communities and the scale of difference'. *Social and Cultural Geography* **1**, 65–82.

Aldous, T. (1992) *Urban Villages: A Concept for Creating Mixed Use – Urban Developments on a Sustainable Scale*. London: Urban Villages Forum.

Allatt, P. (1996) 'Consuming schooling: choice, commodity, gift and systems of exchange'. In Consumption Matters: *The Production and Experience of Consumption* (eds) S. Edgell, K. Hetherington, and A. Warde. Oxford: Blackwell.

Allen, D. (1987) *Oregon Workforce 2000*. Salem: Oregon Employment Division.

Allen, J. and C. Hamnett (eds) (1991) *Housing and Labour Markets: Building the Connections*. London: Unwin Hyman.

Allen, S. and C. Wolkowitz (1987) *Homeworking: Myths and Realities*. London: Macmillan.

Allmendinger, P. (2001) 'The head and the heart: national identity and urban planning in a devolved Scotland'. *International Planning Studies* **6.1**, 33–54.

American Urban Land Institute (1996) Internet: www.demographia.com/db-adb-uli-htm, accessed August 10 2003.

Anderson, B. (1993) *Britain's Secret Slaves: an Investigation into the Plight of Overseas Domestic Workers*. London: Anti-Slavery International and Kalayaan.

Arlidge, J. (1997) 'Green homes for people without cars'. *The Guardian Weekly*. April 27 1997: 30.

Aronwitz, S. and W. DiFazio (1994) *The Jobless Future: Sci-tech and the Dogma of Work*. Minneapolis: University of Minnesota.

Astone, N.M. and S. McLanahan (1991) 'Family structure, parental practice and high school completion'. *American Sociological Review* **56**, 309–320.

Atkinson, J. (1987) 'Flexibility or fragmentation? The United Kingdom labour market in the eighties'. *Labour and Society.* **12**, 87–105.

Atkinson, T. (2002) 'Is rising income inequality inevitable? A critique of the 'Transatlantic Consensus'', in *World Poverty: New Policies to Defeat an Old Enemy* (eds) P. Townsend and D. Gordon. London: Polity Press.

Atkinson, J. and N. Meager (1986) *New Forms of Work Organisation.* Lewes, Sussex: Institute for Employment Studies.

Badcock, B. (2002) *Making Sense of Cities: a Geographical Survey.* London: Arnold.

Badshah, A.A. (1996) *Our Urban Future: New Paradigms for Equity and Sustainability.* London and New Jersey: Zed Books, 1–7.

Bailey, A.J., M.K. Blake and T.J. Cooke (2004) 'Migration, care and the linked lives of dual-earner households'. *Environment and Planning A* **36**, 1617–1632.

Bakker, I. and S. Gill (eds) (2003) *Power, Production and Social Reproduction: Human In/Security in the Global Political Economy.* Basingstoke: Palgrave.

Barker, K. (2004) *Delivering Stability: Securing our Future Housing Needs. Review of Housing Supply. Final Report – Recommendations.* London: ODPM/HM Treasury.

Baron, S., J. Field and T. Schuller (eds) (2000) *Social Capital: Critical Perspectives.* Oxford: Oxford University Press.

Barry, A., T. Osborne and N. Rose (1996) *Foucault and Political Reason: Liberalism, Neoliberalism and Rationalities of Government.* London and New York: Routledge.

Bartlett, R. (2003) 'Testing the 'popsicle test': realities of retail shopping in new 'traditional neighbourhood developments''. *Urban Studies* **40.8**, 1471–1485.

Bauman, Z. (1997) 'No Way Back to Bliss'. *Times Literary Supplement.* January 24th, 4–5.

Bauman, Z. (1998) *Globalization: the Human Consequences.* Cambridge: Polity Press.

Bauman, Z. (2001) *The Individualized Society.* Cambridge: Polity Press.

BBC (2004) 'Parents urged to stop school run'. Internet: http://newsvote.bbc.co.uk/mpapps/pagetools/pring/news.bbc.co.uk/ accessed 23.02.2004.

Beatley, T. (2000) *Green Urbanism: Learning From European Cities.* Washington DC: Island Press.

Beatley, T. and K. Manning (1997) *The Ecology of Place: Planning for Environment, Economy and Community.* Washington DC: Island Press.

Beck, U. (2000) *The Brave New World of Work.* Oxford: Polity.

Beck, U. and E. Beck-Gernsheim (2002) *Individualization.* London: Sage.

Becker, G. (1976) *The Economic Approach to Human Behaviour.* Chicago: University of Chicago Press.

Begg, I. (ed.) (2002) *Urban Competitiveness: Policies for Dynamic Cities.* Bristol: The Policy Press.

Bennett, S. (2000) 'Two mayors review city's past'. *Seattle Daily Journal of Commerce,* May 22 2000.

Berger, P. (ed.) (1998) *The Limits to Social Cohesion: Conflict and Mediation in Pluralist Societies.* Boulder, Co.: Westview Press.

Bianchi, S.M. and J. Robinson (1997) '"What did you do today?': Children's use of time, family composition and the acquisition of cultural capital'. *Journal of Marriage and the Family* **59**, 332–344.

Biddulph, M., M. Tait and B. Franklin (2001) 'Urban villages: an obituary'. *Urban Design Quarterly* **81**, 39–40.

Bielby, W. and D. Bielby (1989) 'Family ties: balancing commitments to work and family in dual earner households'. *American Sociological Review* **54**, 776–789.

Black, D., G. Gates, S. Sanders and L. Taylor (2000) 'Demographics of the gay and lesbian population in the United States: evidence from available systematic data sources'. *Demography* **37.2**, 139–154.

Black, I. (1999) 'Paradise seeks a barrier against the rising tide', *Guardian*, Monday, September 27 1999, 18.

Blair, S.L. and D.T. Lichter (1991) 'Measuring the division of household labour: gender segregation of housework among American couples'. *Journal of Family Issues* **12.1**, 91–113.

Blanchflower, D. and A. Oswald (2004) 'Well-being over time in Britain and the USA'. *Journal of Public Economics* **88**, 1359–1386.

Blau, D.M. (2001) *The Child Care Problem: an Economic Analysis*. New York: Russell Sage Foundation.

Blood, R.O. and D.M. Wolfe (1960) *Husbands and Wives: the Dynamics of Married Living*. Illinois: The Free Press of Glencoe.

Blower, A. (1993) 'Environmental policy: the quest for sustainable development'. *Urban Studies* **30.4**, 775–96.

Bookchin, M. (1991) *The Limits to the City*, 2*nd* edn. Buffalo: Black Rose Books.

Bondi, L. (1991) 'Gender divisions and gentrification: a critique'. *Transactions of the Institute of British Geographers NS* **16**, 190–98.

Bondi, L. and H. Christie (2000) 'The best of times for some and the worst of times for others? Gender and class divisions in urban Britain today'. *Geoforum* **31.3**, 324–343.

Bondi, L., S. McEwan, S. Smith, H. Christie and M. Munro (2000) 'The anatomy of a housing boom'. End of grant report to the ESRC. Edinburgh: University of Edinburgh/Edinburgh College of Art/Heriot Watt University.

Bondi, L. and D. Rose (2003) 'Constructing gender, constructing the urban: a review of Anglo-American feminist urban geography'. *Gender, Place and Culture* **10.3**, 229–245.

Bonney, N. and J. Love (1991) 'Gender and migration: geographical mobility and the wife's sacrifice'. *Sociological Review* **39**, 335–348.

Borger, J. and D. Teather (2003) 'America still in the dark over power disaster'. *The Guardian*. August 16 2003, 4–5.

Bosch, G. (2004) 'Towards a new standard employment relationship in Western Europe?' *British Journal of Industrial Relations* **42.4**, 617–636.

Bott, E. (1957) *Family and Social Network: Roles, Norms and External Relationships in Ordinary Urban Families*, 2*nd* edn. London: Tavistock.

Boulin, J.Y. and U. Mückenberger (1999) 'Time in the city and quality of life'. BEST; European Studies in Time. European Founding for the Improvement of Living and Working Conditions.

Bourdieu, P. (1977) *Outline of the Theory of Practice* (translated by R. Nice). Cambridge: Cambridge University Press.

Bourdieu, P. (1990) *The Logic of Practice*. Stanford, CA.: Stanford University Press.

Bourdieu, P. (1998) 'The essence of neoliberalism: utopia of endless exploitation'. *Le Monde Diplomatique*, December 1998, Translated by Jeremy J. Shapiro. Available on-line: http://www.homme-moderne.org/societe/socio/bourdieu/varia/essneoUK.html

Boyle, P., T. Cooke, K. Halfacree and D. Smith (1999) 'Gender inequality in employment status following family migration in GB and the US: the effect of relative occupational status'. *International Journal of Sociology and Social Policy* **19**, 109–42.

Brandt, B. (1995) *Whole Life Economics: Revaluing Daily Life*. Philadelphia: New Society Publishers.

Brannen, J. and P. Moss (1991) *Managing Mothers: Dual Earner Households After Maternity Leave*. London: Unwin Hyman.

Brechin, G. (1998) 'Pecuniary emulation: the role of tycoons in imperial city-building'. In *Reclaiming San Francisco: History, Politics, Culture* (eds) J. Brook, C. Carlson and N.J. Peters. San Francisco: City Lights.

Breheny, M. (ed.) (1992) *Sustainable Development and Urban Form*. London: Pion. 1–24 and 138–160.

Breheny, M. (ed.) (1999) *The People: Where Will They Work?* London: Town and Country Planning Association.

Brenner, J. (1993) 'The best of times, the worst of times: US feminism today'. *New Left Review* **200** (July/August).

Brewer, A.M. (2000) 'Work design for flexible work scheduling: barriers and gender implications'. *Gender, Work and Organization* **7.1**, 33–44.

Bronson, P. (1999) *The Nudist on the Late Shift and Other Tales of Silicon Valley*. London: Secker and Warburg.

Brooks, D. (2000) *Bobos in Paradise: the New Upper Class and How They Got There*. New York: Touchstone.

Brookings Institution (2003) *Living Cities: The National Community Development Initiative. Portland in Focus: A Profile from Census 2000*. Washington DC: The Brookings Insitutions, Center for Urban and Metropolitan Policy.

Brown, G. (2003) The Budget Speech in Full. Internet: http://www.guardian.co.uk/budget/2003/story/.

Brown, P. (1998) 'Climate change analysis: adapt, and they might survive'. *The Guardian*. Friday October 30, 25.

Brown, P. (2003a) 'Plan to send ministers to the regions – permanently'. The Guardian. Wednesday September 3. Internet: http://www.guardian.co.uk/northsouth/article/0,2763,1034334,00.html

Buck, N., I. Gordon, P. Hall, M. Harloe and M. Kleinman (2002) *Working Capital: Life and Labour in Contemporary London*. London: Routledge.

Budd, L. and S. Whimster (1992) *Global Finance and Urban Living: Study of Metropolitan Change*. London and New York: Routledge.

Burchell, R.W., D. Listokin and W.R. Dolphin (1997) *The Development Impact Assessment Handbook*. Washington: Urban Land Institute.

Burdett, R. (2000) 'The coolest city'. In *Metropolis Now!* (ed.) R.K. Biswas. New York: Springer Wien.

Burgoyne, C.B. (1990) 'Money in marriage: how patterns of allocation both reflect and conceal power'. *Sociological Review* **38**, 634–65.

Butler, T. (1997) *Gentrification and the Middle Classes*. Aldershot: Ashgate.

Butler, T. and C. Hamnett (1994) 'Gentrification class and gender some comments on Warde's 'gentrification of consumption''. *Environment and Planning D: Society and Space* 12, 477–93.

Butler, T. and G. Robson (2003) *London Calling: The Middle Classes and the Re-making of Inner London*. London: Berg.

Calfornia Government Datamart (2000) San Francisco Bay Area County-County Commuters 1960–2020. Internet: http://www.mtc.ca.gov/datamart/stats/cntycomm.htm

Callahan, D. and S.B. Heintz (eds) (2000) *Quality of Life 2000: The New Politics of Work, Family and Community. A Briefing Book*. New York: Demos. also available on the Internet: http://www.demos-usa.org/publications/QOL2000/

Calthorpe, P. (1993) *The Next American Metropolis: Ecology, Community and the American Dream*. Princeton: Princeton University Press.

Calvan, B.C. (2003) 'Homeless are key issue in San Francisco race'. *Boston Globe*. June 14.

Campanelli, P. and R. Thomas (1994) *Working Lives Development Research – Issues Surrounding the Collection of Work-Life Histories*. London: DoE/Joint Centre for Survey Methods.

Campbell, D. (2003) 'US shoppers join counter revolution'. *The Guardian*, 29 November, International news, p. 23.

Camstra, R. (1996) 'Commuting and gender in a lifestyle perspective'. *Urban Studies* **33.2**, 283–300.

Carlson, D., C. Haugen, J. Looney, J. McIntire, B.J. Narver and S. Reder (1999) *Housing Affordability Study: University of Washington Faculty and Staff*. Institute for Public Policy and Management, Daniel J. Evans School of Public Affairs. Seattle: University of Washington.

Carson, R. (1963) *Silent Spring*. London: Penguin.

Carter, C. and M. Grieco (2000) 'New deals, no wheels: social exclusion, tele-options and electronic ontology'. *Urban Studies* **37.10**, 1735–1748.

Casciani, D. (2003) 'Is this the nicest place to live in Britain?' BBC news online, accessed 10/07/03 http://news.bbc.co.uk/2/low/uk_news.

Casey, B., H. Metcalf and N. Milward (1997) *Employers' Use of Flexible Labour*. London: Policy Studies Institute.

Cervero, R. (1986) *Jobs-Housing Imbalance as a Transportation Problem*. UC Berkeley. Institute of Transportation Studies.

Cervero, R. (1988) *America's Suburban Centers: a Study of the Land-Use-Transportation Link*. Prepared for the Office of Policy and Budget, Urban Mass Transportation Administration and Rice Center, Joint Office for Mobility Research. Washington: Department of Transportation.

Cervero, R. (1996) *Suburban Grid-Lock*. New Brunswick, New Jersey. Center for Urban Policy Research. The State University of New Jersey.

Cervero, R. and Kang-Li Wu (1995) 'Polycentrism, community and residential location in the San Francisco Bay Area'. *Institute of Urban and Regional Development Working Paper* **640**. Berkeley: University of California at Berkeley.

Cervero, R. and Kang-Li Wu (1998) 'Sub-centring and commuting: evidence from the San Francisco Bay Area, 1980–90'. *Urban Studies* **35.7**, 1059–1076.

Cervero, R. and C. Radisch (1995) 'Travel choices in pedestrian versus automobile oriented neighbourhoods'. *Institute of Urban and Regional Development Working Paper* **644**. Berkeley: University of California at Berkeley.

Champion, A.G. (1989) *Counterurbanization: The Changing Pace and Nature of Population*. London: Edward Arnold.

Champion, A., D. Atkins, M. Coombes and S. Fotheringham (1998) *Urban Exodus*. London. Council for the Protection of Rural England.

Chant, S. and C. McIlwaine (1998) *Three Generations, Two Genders, One World: Women and Men in a Changing Century*. London: Zed Books.

Cherlin, A. (ed.) (1988) *The Changing American Family and Public Policy*. Washington DC: Urban Institute Press.

Cheshire, P. and S. Sheppard (2002) 'Capitalizing the value of free schools: the impact of land supply constraints'. *Lincoln Institute of Land Policy Conference Paper CP02A08*. Cambridge, MA: Paper presented at Lincoln Institute Conference on the Analysis of Urban Land Markets and the Impact of Land Market Regulation.

Chubb, J. and T. Moe (1990) *Politics, Markets and American Schools*. Washington: Brookings Institute.

City of Edinburgh Council (2003) *Edinburgh's Census 2001. City Comparisons: Comparisons between Edinburgh and Selected Other UK Cities*, available on-line: http://download.edinburgh.gov.uk/Census_2001_City_Comparison/City_Comparisons_Census.pdf

City and County of San Francisco (1995) General Plan of the City and County of San Francisco. San Francisco: San Francisco City and County Planning Department.

City of Seattle (1994) *Seattle's Comprehensive Plan: Toward a Sustainable Seattle, a Plan for Managing Growth 1994–2014*. Seattle: City of Seattle Strategic Planning Office.

City of Seattle (1997) *Seattle's Comprehensive Plan: Toward a Sustainable Seattle, a Plan for Managing Growth 1994–2014, Appendices*. Seattle: City of Seattle Strategic Planning Office.

Clark, C. (1957) 'Transport: maker and breaker of cities'. *Town Planning Review* **28**, 237–50.

Clark, A. and H. Muir (2003) 'Congestion charge speeds up traffic but burdens tube'. *The Guardian*, Saturday May 17 2003: 2.

Clark, A. and H. Muir (2004) 'Backlash at £2 fare for one-stop tube journey'. *The Guardian*, January 20 2004.

Clark, D. (1982) *Urban Geography*. London: Croom Helm.

Clark, D. (1996) *Urban world/ Global city*. London and New York: Routledge.

Clearinghouse on International Developments in Child, Youth and Family Policies at Columbia University (2004): http://www.childpolicyintl.org/countries/

Clement, W. (2004) 'Revealing the class-gender connection: social policy, labour markets and households', *Just Labour* **4** (summer 2004), 42–52.

CNN (2000) 'Farewell fast lane: Italy inaugurates 'slow cities''. July 20 2000. Internet: http://www.cnn.com/2000/WORLD/europe/07/20/italy.slowcities.ap/

Cochrane, A. and J. Clark (eds) (1993) *Comparing Welfare States: Britain in International Context*. London: Sage/Open University.

Cohen, L. and N. Mallon (1999) 'The transition from organizational employment to portfolio working: perceptions of 'boundarylessness''. *Work, Employment and Society* **13.2**, 329–352.

Cole, H.S.D. (1973) *Thinking about the Future: a Critique of the Limits to Growth*. University of Sussex Science Policy Research Unit. London: Chatto and Windus for Sussex University Press.

Communications Technologies (1987) 'The commuting behaviour of employees of Santa Clara County's Golden Triangle'. San Francisco: Report Prepared for the Golden Triangle Task Force.

Congress of the New Urbanism (1999) *Charter of the New Urbanism*. New York: McGraw Hill.

Connor, S. (2004) 'US climate policy bigger threat to world than terrorism'. *The Independent*. January 9, 2004.

Cooke, T.J. (2001) "Trailing wife' or 'trailing mother'? The effect of parental status on the relationship between family migration and the labour-market participation of married women'. *Environment and Planning A* 33, 419–430.

Coser, L.A. (1974) *Greedy Institutions: Patterns of Undivided Commitment*. New York: The Free Press.

Council of Mortgage Lenders (CML) (2004) 'Property wealth will grow for 'golden generation''. Council of Mortgage Lenders News & Views Newsletter. London: CML, www.cml.org.uk.

Coupland, D. (1995) *Microserfs*. London: Flamingo.

Cox, R. (2000) 'Exploring the growth of paid domestic labour: a case study of London'. *Geography* 85.3, 241–251.

Cox, R. and P. Watt (2002) 'Globalization, polarization and the informal sector: the case of paid domestic workers in London'. *Area* 34.1, 39–48.

CPAG (2004) *Poverty the Facts (summary)*. London: CPAG.

CPRE (1997) *Household Growth: Where Shall We Live? A response by CPRE to the Government's Green Paper*. London: Council for the Protection of Rural England.

Crane, R. (2000) 'The influence of urban form on travel: an interpretive review'. *Journal of Planning Literature* 15.1, 3–23.

Creighton, C. and C.K. Omari (eds) (1995) *Gender, Family and Household in Tanzania*. Aldershot: Avebury.

Crookson, M., P. Clarke and J. Averley (1996) 'The compact city and the quality of life'. In *The Compact City: A Sustainable Urban Form?* (eds) M. Jenks, E. Burton and K. Williams. London: E & F Spon.

Crompton, R. (1996) 'Paid employment and the changing system of gender relations: a cross-national comparison'. *Sociology* 30.3, 427–45.

Crompton, R. (1998) 'Women's employment and state policies'. *Innovation* 11.2, 129–145.

Cullingworth, B. (1997) *Planning in the USA: Policies, Issues and Process*. London and New York: Routledge.

Daly, K.J. (1996) *Families and Time: Keeping Pace in a Hurried Culture*. Thousand Oaks, Ca.: Sage.

Darrah, C. and J. Freeman (2002) personal communication, face to face meeting, August 28 2002. Mountain View, Ca.

Darrah, C.N., J.A. English-Lueck and J.M. Freeman (2000) 'Living in the eye of the storm: controlling the maelstrom in Silicon Valley. *Draft working paper presented at the Centre for Working Families*. University of California at Berkeley, September 2000.

Davis, J.A. (1996) 'Patterns of attitude change in the USA 1972–1994'. In *Understanding Change in Social Attitudes* (eds) B. Taylor and K. Thomson. Aldershot: Dartmouth. 151–84.

Davies, K. (2001) 'Responsibility and daily life: reflections over timespace'. In *Timespace: Geographies of Temporality* (eds) J. May and N. Thrift. London: Routledge.

De Grove, J.M. (1994) 'Following in Oregon's footsteps: the impact of Oregon's growth management strategy on other states'. In *Planning the Oregon Way: a*

Twenty Year Evaluation (eds) C. Abbott, D. Howe and S. Adler. Corvallis, Oregon: Oregon State University Press.

De Roo, G. and D. Miller (eds) (2000) *Compact Cities and Sustainable Development: a Critical Assessment of Policies and Plans from an International Perspective.* Aldershot: Ashgate.

Dear, M. (2000) *The Postmodern Urban Condition.* Oxford: Blackwell.

Department for Education (DfE) (2004) *Five Year Plan for Education in England.* London: Department for Education.

Department of Trade and Industry (DTI) (2004) Employment Relations – Work and Parents. Internet: http://www.dti.gov.uk/er/individual/workparents_feature.htm

Devine, F. (2003) *Class Practices: How Parents Help Their Children Get Good Jobs.* Cambridge: Cambridge University Press.

Dex, S. and L. Shaw (1986) *British and American Women at Work.* Basingstoke: Macmillan.

Diamond, H.L. and P.F. Noonan (eds) (1996) *Land Use in America.* Washington DC: Island Press.

Dicken, S.N. and E.F. Dicken (1982) *Oregon Divided: A Regional Geography.* Portland: Oregon Historical Society.

Dolowitz, D.P. (1998) *Learning From America: Policy Transfer and the Development of the British Workfare State.* Brighton: Sussex Academic press.

Dowie, M. (1995) *Losing Ground: American Environmentalism at the Close of the Twentieth Century.* Cambridge, Mass.: MIT Press.

Downs, A. (1989) *High Home Prices: a Worldwide Problem.* Bond Market Research Report, Real Estate. New York: Salomon Brothers.

Downs, A. (1992) *Stuck in Traffic: Coping with Peak-hour Traffic Congestion.* Washington DC: Brookings Institute.

Doyle, J. and M. Nathan (2001) *Wherever Next: Work in a Mobile World.* London: The Industrial Society.

Doyle, J. and R. Reeves (2001) *Time Out: The Case for Time Sovereignty.* London: Industrial Society.

Duany, A. and E. Plater-Zyberk (1991) *Towns and Townmaking Principles.* New York: Rizzoli.

Duesenberry, J.S. (1960) 'Comment on Becker's 'An Economic Analysis of Fertility''. In *Demographic and Economic Change in Developed Countries,* a Conference of the Universities-National Bureau Committee for Economic Research, 231–34.

Duncan, S.S. (1991) 'Gender divisions of labour'. In *London: a new metropolitan geography* (eds) D. Green and K. Hoggart. London: Unwin Hyman.

Duncan, S.S. (1991a) 'The geography of gender divisions of labour in Britain'. *Transactions of the Institute of British Geographers, New Series* **16**, 420–439.

Duncan, S.S. (1995) 'Theorizing European gender systems'. *Journal of European Social Policy* **5.4**, 263–84.

Duncan, S.S. (2003) 'Mothers, care and employment: values and theories'. *CAVA Working Paper.* Bradford: CAVA and University of Bradford.

Duncan, S.S. (2005) 'Mothering, class and rationality'. *Sociological Review* **53.2** forthcoming.

Duncan, S.S. and R. Edwards (1997) (eds) Single Mothers in an International Context: Mothers or Workers? London: UCL Press.

Duncan, S.S. and R. Edwards (1999) *Lone Mothers, Paid Work and Gendered Moral Rationalities.* Basingstoke: Macmillan.

Duncan, S.S. and D.P. Smith (2004) 'And then the lover: can we all now choose individual fulfilment?'. *In Seven Ages of Man and Woman: A Look at life in the Second Elizabethan Era* (eds) I. Stewart and R. Vaitilingam. Swindon: ESRC. 16–19.

Dunford, M. and A.J. Fielding (1997) 'Greater London, the South East Region and the wider Britain: metropolitan polarization, uneven development and inter-regional migration'. In *People, Jobs and Mobility in the New Europe* (eds) H.H. Blotevogel and A.J. Fielding. Chichester: John Wiley and Sons.

Dunne, G.A. (1997) *Lesbian Lifestyles: Women's Work and the Politics of Sexuality*. London: Macmillan.

Dunne, G.A. (1998) 'Pioneers behind our own front doors': Towards greater balance in the organisation of work in partnerships. *Work, Employment and Society* **12.2**, 273–297.

Durning, A.T. (1996) *The Car and the City: 24 Steps to Safe Streets and Healthy Communities*. Seattle: Northwest Environment Watch.

DWP (2004) *Households Below Average Income 1994/95–2002/3*. London: Department of Work and Pensions, Corporate Document Services.

Dyck, I. (1990) 'Space, time and renegotiating motherhood: an exploration of the domestic workplace'. *Environment and Planning D: Society and Space* **8**, 459–483.

Edinburgh City Council (1998) *North East Edinburgh Local Plan Written Statement*. Edinburgh: Edinburgh City Council.

Edinburgh Solicitors Property Service (ESPS) (2004) *Property Price Report*. Viewed on-line 8.07.2004 http://www.esps.co.uk/news_data/reports/

Ehrenreich, B. (2001) *Nickel and Dimed: On (Not) Getting By in America*. New York: Metropolitan.

Ehrenreich, B. and A. Hochschild (eds) (2003) *Global Woman: Nannies, Maids and Sex Workers in the New Economy*. London: Granta Books.

Ellegård, K. (1999) 'A time geographical approach to the study of everyday life of individuals – a challenge of complexity'. *GeoJournal* **48**, 167–175.

Ellis, C. (2002) 'The New Urbanism: critiques and rebuttals'. *Journal of Urban Design* **7.3**, 261–91.

England, K. (1993) 'Changing suburbs, changing women: geographic perspectives on suburban women and suburbanization'. *Frontiers: A Journal of Women's Studies* **14.1**, 24–43.

England, K. (2000) "It's really hitting home': The home as a site for long-term health care'. In the 'In the field' section of the special issue on "Healthy communities through women's eyes" in *International Women and Environment Magazine* **8/49**, 25.

England, P. (1992) *Comparable Worth: Theories and Evidence*. New York: Aldine De Gruyter.

England, P. (2000) 'Marriage, the costs of children and gender inequality'. In *The Ties That Bind: Perspectives on Marriage and Cohabitation* (ed.) L.J. Waite. New York: Aldine de Gruyter.

English-Lueck (2002) *Cultures@siliconvalley*. Stanford: Stanford University Press.

Esping-Andersen, G. (1990) *The Three Worlds of Welfare Capitalism*. Cambridge: Polity.

Esping-Andersen, G. (1996) *Welfare States in Transition*. London: Sage.

Esping-Andersen, G. (1999) *Social Foundations of Postindustrial Economies*. Oxford: Oxford University Press.

Etzioni, A. (1993) *The Parenting Deficit*. London: Demos.

Evans, L. (1992) 'The impact of demographic trends in the United Kingdom on women's employment prospects in the 1990s'. *In Issues in Contemporary Economics 4*. (eds) N. Folbre, B. Bergman, B. Agarwi and M. Floro. Athens, Greece: International Economics Association 101.

Fagnani, J. and J. Brun (1994) 'Lifestyles and locational choices – trade-offs and compromises: A case study of middle class couples living in the Ile-de-France region'. *Urban Studies* **31.6**, 921–934.

Fagnani, J. and M. Letablier (2004) 'Work and family life balance: the impact of the 35 hour law in France'. *Work, Employment and Society* **18.3**, 551–573.

Fainstein, S.S. and M. Harloe (1992) 'Introduction'. In *Divided cities: New York and London in the Contemporary World* (eds) S. Fanstein, I. Gordon and M. Harloe (eds). Oxford. Blackwell.

Ferber, M.A. and J.A. Nelson (eds) (1993) *Beyond Economic Man*. Chicago: University of Chicago Press.

Ferri, E. and K. Smith (1996) *Parenting in the 1990s*. London: Family Policy Studies Centre.

Fielding, A.J. (1991) 'Migration and social mobility: South East England as an escalator region'. *Regional Studies* **26.1**, 1–15.

Fischer, C.S. (2000) 'Ever-more rooted Americans'. Paper presented to the Center for Working Families Workshop. Berkeley: University of California at Berkeley.

Fishman, R. (1987) *Bourgeois Utopias. The Rise and Fall of Suburbia*. New York: Basic Books.

Flaherty, J. and P. Dornan (2004) *Poverty: The Facts*. London: CPAG.

Florida, R. (2002) *The Rise of the Creative Class – and How it's Transforming Work, Leisure, Community and Everyday Life*. New York: Basic Books.

Folbre, N. (1994) *Who Pays for the Kids? Gender and the Structures of Constraint*. London: Routledge.

Folbre, N. (2001) *The Invisible Heart: Economics and Family Values*. New York: The New Press.

Folbre, N. and J.A. Nelson (2000) 'For love or money: or both?' *The Journal of Economic Perspectives* **14.4**, 123–140.

Forrester, J.W. (1971) *World Dynamics*. Cambridge, Mass: Wright-Allen Press.

Foucault, M. (1977) *The Archaeology of Knowledge*. London: Tavistock.

Frankel, J. (1997) *Families of Employed Mothers: an International Perspective*. New York: Garland Press.

Franklin, B. and M. Tait (2002) 'Constructing an image: The urban village concept in the UK'. *Planning Theory* **1.3**, 250–272.

Fraser, E. and N. Lacey (1993) *The Politics of Community: A Feminist Critique of the Liberal Communitarian Debate*. Hemel Hempstead: Harvester Wheatsheaf.

Freeman, D. (2002) 'The impact of bonus payments on the Average Earnings Index'. *Labour Market Trends* **110.12**, 89–95.

Frey, W.H. (2003) *Metropolitan Magnets for International and Domestic Migrants*. Washington DC: Brookings Institution.

Friberg, T. (1993) *Everyday Life: Women's Adaptive Strategies in Time and Space* (translated by Madi Gray). Stockholm: Swedish Council for Building Research.

Fullerton, K. (2001) 'Despite the hard times ahead, Nickels keeps promising more goodies'. *Seattle Weekly* October 25 2001.

Fulton, W. (2000) 'Does slow growth have a chance in California?' Northern
  News, Northern Section, California Chapter, American Planning Association,
  April 2000.

Furedi, F. (2001) *Paranoid Parenting* . Harmondsworth: Penguin.

Gahan, C. and M. Hannibal (1998) *Doing Qualitative Research Using QSR
  NUD*IST*. London: Sage.

Galbraith, J.K. (1998) *Created Unequal: The Crisis in American Pay*. New York: Free
  Press.

Galbraith, J.K. and M. Berner (eds) (2001) *Inequality and Industrial Change: A
  Global View*. Cambridge: Cambridge University Press.

Galinsky, E. and D. Friedman (1995) *Women: The New Providers. Whirlpool
  Foundation Study, Part 1*. New York: Families and Work Institute. 36–38.

Gallie, D., M. White, Y. Cheng and M. Tomlinson (1998) *Restructuring the
  Employment Relationship*. Oxford: Clarendon Press.

Gans, H.J. (1962) 'Urbanism and suburbanism as ways of life'. In *Human
  Behaviour and Social Processes* (ed.) A.M. Rose. London: Routledge.

Gardiner, J. (1997) *Gender, Care and Economics*. Basingstoke: Macmillan.

Gardiner, J. (2000) 'Rethinking self-sufficiency: employment, families and
  welfare'. *Cambridge Journal of Economics* **24.6**, 671–689.

Garreau, J. (1991) *Edge City: Life on the New Frontier*. New York: Doubleday.

Germain, A. and D. Rose (2000) *Montréal: The Quest for a Metropolis*. Chichester,
  UK: John Wiley & Son.

Gershuny, J. and J.P. Robinson (1988) 'Historical changes in the household division of labour'. *Demography* **25.4**, 537–52.

Gershuny, J. and O. Sullivan (2001) 'Cross-national changes in time-use: some
  sociological (hi)stories re-examined'. *British Journal of Sociology* **52.2**, 331–347.

Giddens, A. (1984) *The Constitution of Society*. Oxford: Polity Press.

Giddens, A. (1987) *Social Theory and Modern Sociology*. Oxford: Polity Press.

Giddens, A. (1998) *The Third Way: The Social Renewal of Social Democracy*.
  Oxford: Polity Press.

Gilbert, M. (1997) 'Identity, space and politics: a critique of poverty debates'. In
  Thresholds in Feminist Geography (eds) J.P. Jones III, H.J. Nast and S.M. Roberts.
  Lanham, MD: Rowman and Littlefield. 29–45.

Gill, R.C. (2002) 'Cool, creative and egalitarian? Exploring gender in project
  based new media work'. *Information, Communication and Society* **5.1**, 70–89.

Gillespie, A. (1992) 'Communications technology and the future of the city'. In
  Sustainable Development and Urban Form (ed.) M. Breheny. London: Pion.

Giuliano, G. and D. Narayan (2003) 'Another look at travel patterns and urban
  form: the US and Great Britain'. *Urban Studies* **40.11**, 2295–2312.

Glaeser, E.L. and J.M. Shapiro (2001) *City Growth and the 2000 Census: Which
  Places Grew and Why*. Center on Urban and Metropolitan Policy. the
  Brookings Institute: Washington DC.

Glover, J. (2002) 'The 'balance' model: theorising women's employment behaviour'. In *Analysing Families: Morality and Rationality in Policy and Practice* (eds)
  A. Carling, S. Duncan and R. Edwards. London: Routledge.

Goelman, A. (2004) 'The co-workplace: teleworking in the neighbourhood'.
  Journal of the American Planning Association **70.1**, 108–9.

Goldthorpe, J.E. (1987) *Family Life in Western Societies: a Historical Sociology of
  Family Relationships in Britain and North America*. Cambridge: Cambridge
  University Press.

Goodin, R., B. Heady, R. Muffels, H-J. Dirven (1999) *The Real Worlds of Welfare Capitalism*. Cambridge: Cambridge University Press.

Goodman, A., P. Johnson and S. Webb (1997) *Inequality in the UK*. Oxford: Oxford University Press.

Googins, B. (2000) 'A 'third way' on the work-life issue'. In Family Business – a Demos Collection (ed.) Helen Wilkinson. London: Demos.

Gornick, J.C. and M.K. Meyers (2003) *Families That Work: Policies for Reconciling Parenthood and Employment*. New York: Russell Sage Foundation.

Gottlieb, B.H., E.K. Kelloway and E.J. Barham (1998) *Flexible Work Arrangements: Managing the Work-Family Boundary*. Chichester: John Wiley.

Graham, B. (2000) 'San Francisco's artistic heritage'. *San Francisco Chronicle*. 19 October 2000.

Graham, S. (1997) 'Telecommunications and the future of cities: debunking the myths'. *Cities* 14, 21–29.

Graham, S. (1998) 'The end of geography or the explosion of place? Conceptualising space, place and information technology'. *Progress in Human Technology* 22.2, 165–185.

Graham, S. and S. Guy (2002) 'Digital space meets urban place: sociotechnologies of urban restructuring in downtown San Francisco'. *City* 6.3, 369–382.

Graham, S. and S. Marvin (2001) *Splintering Urbanism: Networked Infrastructures, Technological Mobilities, and the Urban Condition*. London and New York: Routledge.

Granovetter, M. (1974) *Getting a Job: Study of Contacts and Careers*. Harvard, Mass.: Harvard University Press.

Greater London Authority (GLA) *Towards the London Plan*, accessed on-line http: www.london.gov.uk. London: Greater London Authority.

Green, A. (1995) 'The geography of dual-career households: a research agenda and selected evidence from secondary data sources for Britain'. *International Journal of Population Geography* 1, 29–50.

Gregory, D. and J. Urry (1985) *Social Relations and Spatial Structure*. Basingstoke: Palgrave Macmillan.

Gregson, N. and M. Lowe (1994) *Servicing the Middle Classes: Class, Gender and Waged Domestic Labour in Contemporary Britain*. London: Routledge.

Gross, H.E. (2001) 'Work, family and globalization: broadening the scope of policy analysis'. In *Working Families: the Transformation of the American Home* (eds) R. Hertz and N.L. Marshall. Berkeley: University of California Press.

Gullestad, M. (1984) *Kitchen-Table Society: Case Study of the Family Life and Friendships of Young Working-Class Mothers in Norway*. Oslo: Universitetsforlaget. US distribution, New York: Columbia University Press.

Haddon, L. and R. Silverstone (1993) *Teleworking in the 1990s: A View from the Home*. Sciency Policy Research Unit. Brighton: University of Sussex.

Hafner, K. and M. Lyon (1996) *Where Wizards Stay up Late: The Origins of the Internet*. New York: Touchstone.

Hägestrand, T. (1976) 'Geography and the study of interaction between society and nature'. *Geoforum* 7, 329–34.

Hägestrand, T. (1982) 'Diorama, path and project'. *Tijdschrift voor Economische en Sociale Geographie* 73, 323–39.

Hair Hunts, H.J. (1998) 'Relatives as child care givers: after hours support for non-traditional workers'. *Journal of Family and Economic Issues* 19.4, 315–341.

Hakim, C. (1991) 'Grateful slaves and self-made women: fact and fantasy in women's work orientation'. *European Sociological Review* **7.2**, 101–121.

Hakim, C. (1996) *Key Issues in Women's Work: Female Heterogeneity and the Polarization of Women's Employment*. London: Athlone.

Hakim, C. (2000) *Work-Lifestyle Choices in the 21st Century: Preference Theory*. Oxford: Oxford University Press.

Halfacree, K.H. and P.J. Boyle (1993) 'The challenge facing migration research: the case for a biographical approach'. *Progress in Human Geography* **17.3**, 333–48.

Hall, P. (1976) *London: Metropolis and Region*. Oxford: Oxford University Press.

Hall, P. (1990) The Bay Area in the 21st century: shall we survive? *Working Paper 501, Institute for Urban and Regional Development*. University of California at Berkeley. February 1990.

Hall, P. (1998) *Cities in Civilisation*. London: Widenfield and Nicholson.

Hall, P. (2000) 'Creative cities and economic development'. *Urban Studies* **37.4–6**, 639–649.

Hall, P. and U. Pfeiffer (2000) *Urban Future 21: A Global Agenda for Twenty-First Century Cities*. London: E & F Spon.

Hamilton, F.E. (1987) 'Silicon forest'. In *Portland's Changing Landscape* (eds) L.W. Price. Portland: University of Portland Press (for the American Association of Geographers).

Hamnett, C. (1994) 'Social polarisation in global cities: theory and evidence'. *Urban Studies* **31**, 401–424.

Hamnett, C. (1999) *Winners and Losers: Home Ownership in Modern Britain*. London: UCL Press.

Hamnett, C. (2003) *Unequal City: London in the Global Arena*. London: Routledge.

Handy, S. (1993) 'Regional versus local accessibility: neo-traditional development and its implications for non-work travel'. *Built Environment* **18**, 256–67.

Handy, S.L. and P.L. Mokhtarian (1995) 'Planning for telecommuting. Measurement and policy issues'. *Journal of American Planning Association* **61**, 99–111.

Hanson, S. and G. Pratt (1995) *Gender, Work and Space*. London: Routledge.

Hardill, I. (2002) *Gender, Migration and the Dual Career Household*. London and New York: Routledge.

Hardill, I., A.E. Green, A.C. Dudleston and D.W. Owen (1997) 'Who decides what? Decision making in dual-career households'. *Work, Employment and Society* **11.2**, 313–26.

Hardin, G. (1968) 'The tragedy of the commons: the population problem has no technical solution; it requires a fundamental extension of morality'. *Science* **16.2**, 1243–8.

Harkness, S. and J. Waldfogel (1999) 'The family gap in pay: evidence from seven industrialized countries'. *Working Paper 29, Centre for the Analysis of Social Exclusion CASE*. London: London School of Economics.

Hartman, C. (1984) *The Transformation of San Francisco*. Totowa, NJ: Rowman & Allanheld.

Harvey, D. (1982) *The Limits to Capital*. Chicago: University of Chicago Press.

Harvey, D. (1988) 'The geographical and geopolitical consequences of the transition from Fordist to Flexible Accumulation'. In *America's New Market Geography: Nation, Region and Metropolis* (eds) G. Sternlieb and J.W. Hughes. New Jersey: The State University of New Jersey Press.

Harvey, D. (1996) *Justice, Nature, and the Geography of Difference.* Cambridge, Mass: Blackwell.

Harvey, T. (1996) 'Portland, Oregon: regional city in a global economy'. *Urban Geography* **17.1**, 95–114.

Hattery, A. (2001) *Women, Work and Family.* London: Sage.

Haug, P. (1986) 'U.S. high technology multinationals and Silicon Glen'. *Regional Studies* **20.2**, 103–116.

Hayden, A. (1999) *Sharing the Work, Sparing the Planet: Work Time, Consumption and Ecology.* London and New York: Zed Books.

Hayes, D. (1989) *Behind the Silicon Curtain: the Seductions of Work in a Lonely Era.* London: Free Association Books.

Hebbert, M. (1998) *London: More by Fortune Than Design.* Chichester: John Wiley and Sons.

Henderson, H. (1990) Paradigms in Progress: Life Before Economics. Indianapolis: Knowledge Systems.

Henry, N. and D. Massey (1995) 'Competitive time-space in high-technology'. *Geoforum* **26.1**, 49–64.

Henton, D. and K. Walesh (1998) *Linking the New Economy to the Livable Community.* San Francisco: The James Irvine Foundation.

Hertz, R. (1986) *More Equal Than Others: Women and Men in Dual-Career Marriages.* Berkeley: University of California Press.

Hertz, R. (1991) 'Dual career couples and the American dream: self-sufficiency and achievement'. *Journal of Comparative Family Studies* **22.2**, 247–263.

Hetherington, P. (2003) 'Prescott may build on US satire to create homes'. *The Guardian* Saturday October 11 2003, 14.

Heymann, J. (2000) *The Widening Gap: Why America's Working Families are in Jeopardy and What Can be Done About it.* New York: Basic Books.

Hillman, M. (1983) *Energy and Personal Travel: Obstacles to Conservation.* London: Policy Studies Institute.

Hillman, M. (ed.) (1993) *Children, Transport and the Quality of Life.* London: Policy Studies Institute.

Hillman, M., J. Adams and J. Whitelegg (1990) *One False Move... A Study of Children's Independent Mobility.* London: Policy Studies Institute.

Himmelweit, S. (1995) 'The discovery of unpaid work: the social consequences of the expansion of work'. *Feminist Economics* **1.2**, 1–20.

Hinchliffe, S. (1996) 'Helping the earth begins at home: the social construction of socio-environmental responsibilities'. *Global Environmental Change* 6, 53–62.

Hine, J., T. Rye, and M. Hulse (2000) 'Using land-use planning to manage transport demand: a survey of Scottish experience'. *Local Environment* **5.1**, 33–53.

Hirsch, F. (1977) *The Social Limits to Growth.* London: Routledge.

Hirschman, A.O. (1970) *Exit, Voice and Loyalty: Responses to Decline in Firms, Organizations and States.* Harvard: Harvard University Press.

Hochschild, A.R. (1989) *The Second Shift.* New York: Avon Books.

Hochschild, A.R. (1997) *The Time Bind: When Work Becomes Home and Home Becomes Work.* New York: Metropolitan Books.

Hodgson, G.M. (1988) *Economics and Institutions: a Manifesto for Modern Institutional Economics.* Cambridge: Polity Press.

Hoffman, L. (1989) 'Effects of maternal employment in the two-parent family'. *American Psychologist* **448**, 283–292.

Holloway, S. (1998) 'Local childcare cultures: moral geographies of mothering and the social organization of pre-school children'. *Gender, Place and Culture* **5.1**, 29–53.

Hood, J.C. (1983) *Becoming a Two-Job Family.* New York: Praeger.

Horner, M.W. (2004) 'Spatial dimensions of urban commuting: a review of major issues and their implications for future geographic research'. *The Professional Geographer* **56.2**, 160–173.

Hutton, W. (1995) 'High-risk strategy is not paying off', *The Guardian Weekly,* 12 November 1995.

Hutton, W. (1996) *The State We're In.* London: Vintage.

Incomes Data Services (IDS) (2003) 'Working hours and holidays'. www.incomesdata.co.uk/infotime/eutable.pdf.

IPPC (2001) *Climate Change 2001: Synthesis Report, Summary for Policy-Makers.* Internet: http://www.grida.no/climate/ippc-tar/

Jacobs, B.D. (1992) *Fractured Cities: Capitalism, Community and Empowerment in Britain and America.* London and New York: Routledge.

Jacobs, J. (1961) *The Death and Life of Great American Cities.* Harmondsworth: Penguin.

Jarvis, H. (1997) 'Housing, labour markets and household structure: questioning the role of secondary data analysis in sustaining the polarizing debate'. *Regional Studies* **31.5**, 521–31.

Jarvis, H. (1999) 'Identifying the relative mobility prospects of a variety of household employment structures, 1981–1991'. *Environment and Planning A* **31**, 491–505.

Jarvis, H. (1999a) 'The tangled webs we weave: household strategies to coordinate home and work'. *Work, Employment and Society* **13.2**, 223–245.

Jarvis, H. (2001) 'Urban sustainability as a function of compromises households make deciding where and how to live: Portland and Seattle compared'. *Local Environment* **6**, 239–256.

Jarvis, H. (2002) ''Lunch is for wimps': what drives parents to work long hours in 'successful' British and US cities?' *Area* **34.4**, 340–53.

Jarvis, H. (2003) 'Dispelling the myth that preference makes practice in residential location and transport behaviour'. *Housing Studies* **18.4**, 587–606.

Jarvis, H. (2005) 'Moving to London time: household co-ordination and the infrastructure of everyday life'. *Time and Society* **14.1**, 133–154.

Jarvis, H.A.C. Pratt and P. Cheng-Chong Wu (2001) *The Secret Life of Cities: The Social Reproduction of Everyday Life.* Harlow: Pearson.

Jencks, C. (1996) 'The city that never sleeps'. *New Statesman,* June 28 1996, 1–3.

Jessop, B. (2002) *The Future of the Capitalist State.* Cambridge: Polity.

Jesuit, D. and T. Smeeding (2002) 'Poverty and Income Distribution'. *Luxembourg Income Study Working Paper* **293**. Maxwell School of Citizenship and Public Affairs, New York: Syracuse University.

Johnson, K.M. and C.L. Beale (1998) 'The rural rebound'. *Wilson Quarterly* **12** (Spring), 16–27.

Jordon, B., M. Redley and S. James (eds) (1994) *Putting the Family First: Identities, Decisions and Citizenship.* London: UCL Press.

Kabeer, N. (1994) *Reversed Realities: Gender Hierarchies in Development Thought.* London: Verso.

Kahn, A.E. (1966) 'The tyranny of small decisions: market failure, imperfections, and the limits of economics'. *Kylos* **19**, 23–47.

Kaplan, M. (1999) 'American neighbourhood policies: mixed results and uneven evaluations'. In *Neighbourhood Regeneration: an International Evaluation* (eds) R. Alterman and G. Cars. London/ New York: Mansell. 28–44.

Karsten, L. (2003) 'Family gentrifiers: challenging the city as a place simultaneously to build a career and to raise children'. *Urban Studies* **40.12**, 2573–2583.

Kasarda, J.D. and Kwok-Fai Ting (1993) *The Impact of Skill Mismatches, Spatial Mismatches and Welfare Disincentives on City Joblessness and Poverty*. Cambridge, MA: Lincoln Institute on Land Policy.

Katz, P. (1994) *The New Urbanism: Toward an Architecture of Community*. New York: McGraw Hill.

Katzev, R. (2003) 'Car sharing: a new approach to urban transportation problems'. *Analyses of Social Issues and Public Policy* **3.1**, 65–86.

Kay, J. (2003) *The Truth About Markets: Why Some Countries are Rich and Others Remain Poor*. London: Penguin Books.

Kelbaugh, D. (1997) *Common Place: Toward Neighbourhood and Regional Design*. Seattle: University of Washington Press.

Kitamura, R., N. Kazuo and K. Goulias (1990) 'Trip chaining behaviour by central city commuters: a causal analysis of time-space constraint'. In *Developments in Dynamic and Activity Based Approaches to Travel Analysis*. Brookview, VT.: Gower. 145–170.

Kramer, D. (2000) 'Tradition and change in domestic roles and food preparation'. *Sociology* **34.2**, 323–333.

Kristensen, G. (1997) 'Women's economic progress and the demand for housing: theory and empirical analysis based on Danish data'. *Urban Studies* **34.2**, 403–418.

Kudrle, R.T. and T.R. Marmor (1984) 'The development of welfare states in North America'. In *The Development of Welfare States in Europe and America* (eds) P. Flora and A.J. Heidenheimer. New Brunswick: Transaction Books.

Kuran, T. (1991) 'Cognitive limitations and preference evolution'. *Journal of Institutional and Theoretical Economics* **147.2**, 241–274.

Kvale, S. (1996) *InterViews: an Introduction to Qualitative Research Interviewing*. London: Sage.

Kwan, M. (1999) 'Gender, the home-work link, and space-time patterns of non-employment activities'. *Economic Geography* **75**, 370–94.

Kwan, M. and J. Weber (2003) 'Individual accessibility revisited: Implications for geographical analysis in the twenty-first century'. *Geographical Analysis* **35.4**, 341–53.

Land, H. (2002) 'Spheres of care in the UK: separate and unequal'. *Critical Social Policy* **22.1**, 13–32.

Land, H. (2002a) 'Building on sand? Facing the future'. *Daycare Trust Policy Paper* **4**. London: Daycare Trust.

Land Registry for England and Wales (2004) *Residential Property Price Reports (Quarterly)*. London. Internet: http://wwwlandreg.gov.uk/publications

Landers, R.M., J.B. Rebitzer and L.J. Taylor (1996) 'Rat race redux: adverse selection in the determination of work hours in law firms'. *American Economic Review* **86** .3, 329–348.

Landry, C. (2000) *The Creative City: a Toolkit for Urban Innovators*. London: Earthscan.

Lawler, S. (2000) Mothering the Self: Mothers, Daughters, Subjects. London: Routledge.

Lawson, T. (1997) *Economics and Reality*. London & New York: Routledge.

Layard, R. (2002) 'Rethinking public economics: the implications of rivalry and habit'. Centre for Economic Performance, LSE, Mimeo, 22 March 2002.

Layard, R. (2003) 'What would make a happier society?' Lecture 3 in the series 'happiness: has social science a clue?' Lionel Robbins Memorial Lecture, London: London School of Economics, March 5th 2003.

Lea, R. (2004) 'Personal view: Work-life campaigners are no more misguided than social engineers'. *The Daily Telegraph*, Monday January 12 2004.

Lear, L. (1998) *Rachel Carson: Witness for Nature*. New York: Owl Books.

Leech, D. and E. Campos (2003) 'Is comprehensive education really free?: a case-study of the effects of secondary school admissions policies on house prices in one local area'. *Journal of the Royal Statistical Society Series A* **166.1**, 135–154.

Lees, L. (1994) 'Re-thinking gentrification: beyond the positions of economics or culture'. *Progress in Human Geography* **18**, 137–50.

Lees, L. (2000) 'A reappraisal of gentrification: towards a 'geography of gentrification''. *Progress in Human Geography* 24.4, 389–408.

Leiss, W. (1988) *The Limits to Satisfaction: an Essay on the Problem of Needs and Commodities*. Kingston: McGill-Queens University Press.

Leith Lofts (2004) Internet: http://www.sust-concepts.co.uk/x709%20leithlofts.htm. Accessed August 20 2004.

Lever, W.F. (2002) 'The knowledge base and the competitive city'. In *Urban Competitiveness: Policies for Dynamic Cities* (ed.) I. Begg. Bristol: The Policy Press. 11–33.

Ley, D. (1996) *The New Middle Class and the Remaking of the Central City*. Oxford & New York: Oxford University Press.

Lewis, J. (1992) 'Gender and the development of welfare regimes'. *Journal of European Social Policy* **2.3**, 157–171.

Lewis, J. (2002) 'Individualisation, assumptions about the existence of an adult worker model and the shift towards contractualism'. In *Analysing Families: Morality and Rationality in Policy and Practice* (eds) A. Carling, S. Duncan and R. Edwards. London: Routledge.

Lewis, S., D.N. Israeli and H. Hootsmans (1992) *Dual-Career Families: International Perspectives*. London: Sage.

Levy, F.S. and R.C. Michel (1991) *The Economic Future of American Families: Income and Wealth Trends*. Washington D.C.: The Urban Institute Press.

Litman, T. (2003) *Evaluating Criticism of Smart Growth*. Victoria B.C: Victoria Transport Policy Institute.

Logan, J.R. (2003) *America's Newcomers*. Report for the Lewis Mumford Center for Comparative Urban and Regional Research. Albany: University of Albany.

Logan, J.R., D. Oakley, P. Smith, J. Stowell and B. Stultz (2001) *Separating the Children*. Washington DC: Lewis Mumford Center.

Logan, J.R. and R. Swanstrom (eds) (1990) *Beyond the City Limits: Urban Policy and Economic Restructuring in Comparative Perspective*. Philadelphia: Temple University Press.

Lothian Regional Council (1994) *Lothian Structure Plan. Secretary of State's Draft: Final Modifications – Annexe*. Edinburgh: Lothian Regional Council.

Low Pay Unit (LPU) (1994) 'No let-up in the growth of low pay'. *The New Review*. December 1993/January 1994, 8–10.

Lyman, I. (1998) 'What's behind the growth in homeschooling – public school problems prompt parents into homeschooling'. *USA Today magazine* (Society for the Advancement of Education). September 1998. New York: USA Today magazine.

Lynch, K. (1960) *The Image of the City*. Cambridge, Mass.: MIT Press.

Mason, J. (1999) 'Living away from relatives: kinship and geographic reasoning'. In *Changing Britain: Families and Households in the 1990s* (ed.) S. McRae. Oxford: Oxford University Press.

Matteucci, J. (1998) The New Housing Boom – Former Industrial Areas Draw Developers to San Francisco. *San Francisco Chronicle*. January 28 1998, accessed online: http://www.hollidaydevelopments.come?i/12-marq-chronicle.pdf.

McClements, D. (1977) 'Equivalence scales for children'. *Journal of Public Economics* **8**, 191–210.

McDowell, L. (1997) *Capital Culture: Gender at Work in the City*. Oxford: Blackwell.

McDowell, L. (1999) *Gender, Identity and Place: Understanding Feminist Geographies*. Cambridge: Polity Press.

McDowell, L. and G. Court (1994) 'Missing subjects: gender, power and sexuality in merchant banking'. *Economic Geography* **70**, 229–51.

McKendrick, J., S. Cunningham-Burley and K. Backett-Milburn (2003) *Life in Low Income Families in Scotland: Research Report for the Scottish Executive*. Edinburgh: Centre for Research on Families and Relationships.

McRae, S. (1986) *Cross-Class Families: a Study of Wives' Occupational Superiority*. Oxford: Clarendon Press.

McRae, S. (2003) 'Constraints and choices in mothers' employment careers: a consideration of Hakim's Preference Theory'. *British Journal of Sociology* **54.3**, 317–338.

Marshall, A. (2000) *How Cities Work: Suburbs, Sprawl, and the Roads Not Taken*. Austen: University of Texas Press.

Marshall, A. (2001) *Waterfronts in Post-Industrial Cities*. London: Spon Press.

Marston, P. (2005) 'Parents drive 5,000 miles every year for children'. *The Daily Telegraph*. Friday January 14 2005, 8.

Marvin, S. and S. Graham (1994) 'Privatisation of utilities: The implications for cities in the UK'. *Journal of Urban Technology* **2.1**, 47–66.

Massey, D. (1996) 'Masculinity, dualisms, and high technology'. *In BodySpace: Destabilizing Geographies of Gender and Sexuality* (ed.) N. Duncan. London: Routledge. 109–26.

Mayor of London (2001) *The Mayor's Transport Strategy*. London: Greater London Authority. Highlights available online: http://www.london.gov.uk/approot/mayor/strategies/transport/pdf/highlights2.pdf

Mazza, L. and Y. Rydin (1997) 'Urban sustainability: discourses, networks and policy tools'. *Progress in Planning* **47.1**, 1–74.

Mead, L. (1986) *Beyond Entitlement: The Social Obligations of Citizenship*. New York: Free Press.

Meadows, D.H., D.L. Meadows, J. Randers and W.W. Behrens (1972) *The Limits to Growth: A Report of the Club of Rome's Project on the Predicament of Mankind*. London: Earth Island Limited.

Meeker, B.F. (1971) 'Decisions and exchange'. *American Sociological Review* **36**, 485–495.

Metro (1995) *Regional Urban Growth Goals and Objectives*. Amended and Adopted 14 December 1995. Portland: Metro.

Metro (1997) *Framework 2040 Plan*. Portland: Metro.

Middleton, S., K. Ashworth and I. Braithwaite (1997) *Small Fortunes: Spending on Children, Children's Poverty and Parental Sacrifice*. York: Joseph Rowntree Foundation.

Miles, M.B. and A.M. Huberman (1984) *Qualitative Data Analysis: a Sourcebook of New Methods*. Beverly Hills, Ca.: Sage.

Mills, C. (1988) 'Life on the upslope: the postmodern landscape of gentrification'. *Environment and Planning D: Society and Space* 6, 169–89.

Mitchell, W. (1995) *City of Bits: Space, Place and the Infobahn*. Cambridge, MA: MIT Press.

Mittler, D. (1999) 'Enviromental space and barriers to local sustainability: evidence from Edinburgh, Scotland'. *Local Environment* 4.3, 353–365.

Mokhtarian, P.L., G.O. Collantes and C. Gertz (2004) 'Telecommuting, residential location, and commute-distance travelled: evidence from the State of California employees'. *Environment and Planning A* 36.10, 1877–97.

Momsen, J.H. et al. (1999) *Gender, Migration and Domestic Service*. New York: Routledge.

Monk, S. (2000) 'The 'key worker' problem: the link between employment and housing', In *Restructuring housing systems: from social to affordable housing?* (eds) S. Monk and C. Whitehead. York: Joseph Rowntree Foundation.

MORI (2004) *Homeowners: Sons and Daughters, a Survey of Parents who are Owner Occupiers*. Survey carried out for the Joseph Rowntree Foundation by the MORI Social Research Institute. York: Joseph Rowntree Foundation.

Morris, L. (1990) *The Workings of the Household: A US–UK comparison*. Cambridge: Polity Press.

Moss, L. (2005) 'Poor patient access to NHS dentists 'totally unacceptable'. *The Scotsman*, PA Health Correspondent, Sunday 13 February 2005.

Nabhan, G. and S. Trimble (1994) *The Geography of Childhood: Why Children Need Wild Places*. Boston: Beacon Press.

National Center for Bicycling and Walking (NCBW) (2004) '*Introduction*': http://www.bikewalk.org/safe_routes_to_scholls/SR25_introduction.htm (accessed 25 July 2004).

National Personal Transportation Survey (NPTS) (1995) *National Passenger Transport Survey*. On-line, http://www.bts.gov/tmip/Washington. Washington DC: US Department of Transport.

National Statistics Online (2001) *Census 2001, Key Statistics for Inner London and Outer London*. Internet: http://www.statistics.gov.uk/census2001/

National Statistics Online (2004) *Census 2001*. Internet: http://www.statistics.gov.uk/census2001/

National Travel Survey (2003) *Transport Statistics Bulletin SB (04) 31, National Travel Survey 2003 Results*. London: Transport Statistics, Department or Transport in association with National Statistics Online.

Neathey, F. (2001) 'Implementation of the working time regulations'. *DTI Employment Research Series* 11. London: Department of Trade and Industry.

Nelson, M.K. and Smith, J. (1999) *Working Hard and Making Do: Surviving in Small Town America*. Berkeley: University of California Press.

Newman, P. (1999) 'Transport: reducing automobile dependence'. In *The Earthscan Reader in Sustainable Cities (ed.)* D. Satterthwaite. London: Earthscan.

Newman, P. and J. Kenworthy (1999) *Sustainability and Cities: Overcoming Automobile Dependence*. Washington DC: Island press.

Nicholsan, L. (ed.) (1990) *Feminism/ Postmodernism*. London: Routledge.

Nickols, S.Y. and K.D. Fox (1983) 'Buying time and saving time: strategies for managing household production'. *Journal of Consumer Research* **10**, 197–208.

O'Brien, M. and D. Jones (1996) 'Family life in Barking and Dagenham'. In *Rising in the East: the regeneration of East London* (eds) T. Butler and M. Rustin. London: Lawrence & Wishart.

O'Connor, J.S., A. Shola Orloff and S. Shaver (1999) *States, Markets, Families: Gender, Liberalism and Social Policy in Australia, Canada, Great Britain and the United States*. Cambridge: Cambridge University Press.

O'Riordan, T. (1981) *Environmentalism*. London: Pion.

Office of the Deputy Prime Minister (ODPM) (1999) *Living Places: Urban Renaissance in the South East*: Background Report. London: ODPM.

Office of the Deputy Prime Minister (ODPM) (2002) *Planning: Delivering a Fundamental Change*. London: ODPM.

Office of the Deputy Prime Minister (ODPM) (2003) *Sustainable Communities: Building for the Future*. London: ODPM

OECD (1999) *Working Hours: Latest Trends and Policy Initiatives. Chapter 5*. Accessed on-line: www.oecd.org/dataoecd/8/51/2080270.pdf

OECD (2000a) *Economic Survey of the United States*. OECD Policy Brief. www.oecd.org/publications/Pol_brief/

OECD (2000b) *Health Data*. OECD Statistics on-line: www.oecd.org/dataoecd/

OECD (2001) *Taxation Data*. OECD Statistics on-line: www.oecd.org/dataoecd/

OECD (2002a) *Country Profiles*. http://www.oecd.org/

OECD (2002b) *ICT Database. August 2002*: www.oecd.org/

OECD (2003) *Gender Co-ordination at the OECD*. http://www.olis.oecd.org/olis/ 2003doc.nsf/LinkTo/C(2003)197 (accessed on-line July 25 2004).

Oldenburg, R. (1999) *The Great Good Place: Cafés, Coffee Shops, Bookstores, Bars, Hair Salons and Other Hangouts at the Heart of a Community*. (first published in 1989.) New York: Marlowe and Company.

ONS/LRC (2001) *Focus on London 2000*. London: The Stationary Office/ Government Office for London.

ONS (1991a) *Census Report for Scotland – Travel to Work. Local Base Statistics for the City of Edinburgh*. London: HMSO.

ONS (2000) New Earnings Survey (Revised December 2001) Analysis by Region, Table A21. London: HMSO.

Orfeuil, J-P. & I. Salomon (1993) 'Travel patterns of the Europeans in everyday life'. In *A Billion trips a day: tradition and transition in European travel patterns*. Dordrecht, Netherlands: Boston MA: Kluwer Academic Publishers, 33–50.

Orloff, A.S. (1993) 'Gender and the social rights of citizenship: the comparative analysis of gender relations and welfare states'. *American Sociological Review* **58.3**, 303–8.

Ostler, M. (2000) 'My Night in a 'Stepover' Hotel'. *San Francisco Chronicle*, 23.10.2000.

Oswald, A. (2000) 'A non-technical paper on the case for road pricing'. *Transport Review* Winter 1999/2000, 28–29.

Pacione, M. (1997) *Britain's Cities: Geographies of Division in Urban Britain*. London: Routledge.

Pacione, M. (2001) *Urban Geography: A Global Perspective*. London: Routledge.

PA News (2004) 'Ministers 'confused' over school run and parents' choice' *Times Higher Educational Supplement*, July 7 2004, http://www.tes.co.uk/breaking_news/story.asp?id=23630

Palm, R. and A. Pred (1974) 'A Time-Geographic Perspective on Problems of Inequality for Women'. Institute of Urban & Regional Development, *University of California Working Paper no. 236*. Berkeley, Ca.: University of California at Berkeley.

Parent Watch (2004) 'Parental peekaboo: working parents now can ease their guilt and angst by watching their kids at day care, all over the Net'. Internet: http://www.parentwatch.com/contact/press/display.asp?p=p_0008. Accessed August 8 2004.

Parkes, D. and N. Thrift (1980) *Times, Spaces and Places*. Chichester: Wiley.

Parkinson, M. (2001) 'Key challenges for European cities: achieving competitiveness, cohesion and sustainability'. *Area* **33.1**, 78–80.

Pateman, C. (1989) 'The patriarchal welfare state', In *The Disorder of Women: Democracy, Feminism and Political Theory (ed.)* C. Pateman. Cambridge: Polity Press.

The Peabody Trust (2004) Peabody's live/work scheme in Westferry Road. Docklands, London: The Peabody Trust, online: http://www.peabody.org.uk/main.index.htm

Peck, J. and A. Tickell (2002) 'Neoliberalizing space', *Antipode* **34.3**, 380–404.

Pennington, M. (2000) *Planning and the Political Market: Public Choice and the Politics of Government Failure*. London: Athlone.

Pennington, M. (2002) *Liberating the Land. The Case for Private Land-Use Planning*. London: Institute of Economic Affairs.

Pepper, D. (1996) *The Roots of Modern Environmentalism*. London: Routledge.

Perrons, D. (1999) 'Flexible working patterns and equal opportunities in the European Union: conflict or compatibility'. *European Journal of Women's Studies* **6.4**, 391–418.

Perrons, D. (2001) 'The new economy and the work-life balance: opportunities and constraints for women and men'. Paper presented at the *Conference on Gross Domestic Product vs Quality of Life*, Ballagio, January.

Perrons, D. (2003) 'The new economy and work-life balance: conceptual explorations and a case study of new media'. *Gender, Work and Organization* **10.1**, 65–93.

Perrons, D. (2004) *Globalization and Social Change: People and Places in a Divided World*. London: Routledge.

Peters, P., K.G. Tijdens and C. Wetzel (2004) 'Employees' opportunities, preferences, and practices in telecommute adoption'. *Information & Management* **41.4**, 469–482.

Petherick, A. (1999) 'Living over the shop'. *Urban Design Quarterly* **70**, 18–19.

Pfau-Effinger, B. (1993) 'Modernisation, culture and part-time work'. *Work, Employment and Society* **7.3**, 383–410.

Pfau-Effinger, B. (1998) 'Gender cultures and the gender arrangement – a theoretical framework for cross-national gender research'. *Innovation* **11.2**, 147–166.

PG&E (1995) *The San Francisco Bay Area – Emergence of a New Economy*. San Francisco. PG&E.

Pilcher, J. (2000) 'Domestic divisions of labour in the twentieth century: change slow-a-coming'. *Work, Employment and Society* **14.4**, 771–80.

Pillinger, J. (2001) 'Work/life balance: finding new ways to work'. Paper commissioned by PCS, Inland Revenue and TUC as part of the Our Time project for Inland Revenue staff seminars, Brighton and Worthing 15 October 2001. Available on-line: http://www.tuc.org.uk/work_life/tuc-4022-f0.cfm

Pimental, D. and M. Giampieto (1995) *Food, Land, Population and the U.S. Economy*. Washington DC: Carrying Capacity Network.

Piore, M. and C. Sabel (1984) *The Second Industrial Divide*. New York: Basic Books.

Pipes, R.J. (1998) *The colonies of Stockbridge, 2nd edn*. Edinburgh: Lomond Books.

Platman, K. (2004) "Portfolio careers' and the search for flexibility in later life'. *Work, Employment and Society* **18.3**, 573–601.

Pliskin, N. (1998) 'Explaining the paradox of telecommuting'. *Business Horizons*, March–April, 73–77.

Potts, G. (2002) 'Competitiveness and the social fabric: links and tensions in cities'. In *Urban Competitiveness: Policies for Dynamic Cities* (ed.) Begg, I. Bristol: The Policy Press.

Prasad, R. (2000) 'Poll reveals crucial role of grandparents in childcare: 'linchpins' of family spend three days a week with grandchildren'. *The Guardian – Society*, December 14 2000.

Prasad, R. (2003) 'Spotlight on sofa surfers'. *The Guardian – Society*, November 5 2003, http://society.guardian.co.uk/print/0,3858,4789302-111919,00.html

Pratt, A.C. (1996) 'Coordinating employment, housing and transport in cities: an institutional perspective'. *Urban Studies* **33**, 1357–1375.

Pratt, A.C. (2000) 'New Media, the New Economy and New Spaces'. *Geoforum* **31**, 425–436.

Pratt, A.C. (2002) 'Hot jobs in cool places. The material cultures of new media product spaces: the case of South of the Market, San Francisco'. *Information, Communication & Society* **5.1**, 27–50.

Pratt, A.C. and R. Ball (eds) (1994) *Industrial Property: Policy and Economic Development*. London: Routledge.

Pratt, G. (1998) 'Grids of difference: place and identity formation'. In *Cities of Difference* (eds) R. Fincher and J.M. Jacobs. London: Guilford Press.

Pratt, G. (2004) *Working Feminism*. Edinburgh: Edinburgh University Press.

Pred, A. (1981) 'Social reproduction and the time-geography of everyday life'. *Geografisker Annaler* **63B**, 5–22.

Preston, V., D. Rose, G. Norcliffe and J. Holmes (2000) 'Shift work, childcare and domestic work: divisions of labour in Canadian paper mill communities'. *Gender, Place and Culture* **7**, 5–29.

Pryne, E. (2004) 'Oregon to test mileage tax as replacement for gas tax'. *Seattle Times*, Monday July 05 2004, also available online: http://seattletimes.nwsource.com/html/localnews/2001972174_mileagetax05m.html

Pucher, J. (1997) 'Bicycling boom in Germany: a revival engineered by public policy', *Transportation Quarterly* **51.4**, 31–46.

Putnam, R.D. (2000) *Bowling Alone: The Collapse and Revival of American Community*. New York: Simon and Schuster.

Puttick, H. (2001) 'Small class size is private school trump: parents want individual attention'. *Edinburgh Evening News*, Thursday May 24 2001: 11.

Pryke, M.D. (1991) 'An international city going global: spatial change in the City of London'. *Environment and Planning D: Society and Space* **9.2**, 197–222.

Reay, D. (2000) 'A useful extension of Bourdieu's conceptual framework?: emotional capital as a way of understanding mothers' involvement in their children's education'. *The Sociological Review* **48.4**, 568–85.

Redmond, T. (2000) 'The Soul of the City'. *San Francisco Bay Guardian*. October 18 2000: 12.

Rees, W.E. (1992) 'Ecological footprints and appropriated carrying capacity: what urban economics leaves out'. *Environment and Urbanization* **4**, 121–130.

Reeves, R. (2001) *Happy Mondays: Putting the Pleasure Back into Work*. Harlow: Momentum.

Reich, R. (2001) *The Future of Success: Work and Life in the New Economy*. London: Heinemann.

Rhodes, E. (2000) 'Tech millionaires rewriting rules'. *The Seattle Times, Home Values*. Wednesday March 8, 2000.

RICS (2003a) 'RICS blames homes crisis on lack of social housing, as underclass grows'. RICS Press Release, 18 August 2003. http://www.rics.org/ricscms/bin/show?class=PressRelease&template=/includes/showpr.html&id=984 (accessed 6th July 2004).

RICS (2003b) 'Housing underclass grows'. RICS press release, 10 December 2003. http://www.rics.org/ricscms/bin/show?class=PressRelease&template=/includes/showpr.html&id=1084 (accessed 6th July 2004).

Richardson, D. (1993) *Women, Motherhood and Childrearing*. London: Macmillan.

Roberts, I. (2003) 'Car Wars'. *The Guardian*, Saturday 18 January 2003: 20.

Robinson, J. and Godbey, G. (1999) *Time for Life: The Surprising Ways Americans Use Their Time, 2nd edn*. University Park, PA: The Pennsylvania State University Press.

Rootes, C., Adams, D. and Saunders, C. (2001) 'Local environmental politics in England: environmental activism in South East London and East Kent compared', *Centre for the Study of Social and Political Movements Working Paper 1/2001*. Kent: University of Kent.

Roschelle, A.R. and T. Wright (2003) 'Gentrification and social exclusion: spatial policing and homeless activist responses in the San Francisco Bay Area. In *Urban Futures: Critical Commentaries on Shaping the City* (eds) M. Miles and T. Hall. London: Routledge.

Rose, D. (1989) 'A feminist perspective of employment restructuring and gentrification: the case of Montreal'. In *The Power of Geography* (eds) J. Wolch and M. Dear. London: Macmillan.

Rose, N. (1996) 'Governing 'advanced' liberal democracies'. In *Foucault and Political Reason: Liberalism, Neoliberalism and Rationalities of Government* (eds) A. Barry, T. Osborne and N. Rose. London and New York: Routledge.

Rose, N. (1999) *Governing the Soul: The Shaping of the Private Self. 2nd edn*. London: Free Association Press.

Rose, K. and J. Silas (2001) *Achieving Equity through Smart Growth: Perspectives from Philanthropy*. Oakland Ca.: Policy Link and Funders' Network for Smart Growth and Livable Communities.

Ross, A. (1997) 'Jobs in cyberspace', posted to Nettime 27.6.97 (copy available at Nettime archive, http://www.nettime.org/nettime.w3archive/).

Rowan, A. (1990) The essential Edinburgh, in Harrison, P. (ed.) *Civilising the city: quality or chaos in historic towns*, The Proceedings of an International Conference held in Edinburgh, 29th March–1st April 1990, Edinburgh: Nic Allen (31–41).

Rowbotham, S. (1997) *A Century of Women: the History of Women in Britain and the United States*. London: Penguin.

Rubery, J., C. Smith, C. Fagan and D. Grimshaw (1998) *Women and European Employment*. London and New York: Routledge (194–256).

Rubin, R.M. and Riney, B.J. (1994) *Working Wives and Dual-Earner Families*. Westport, CT: Praeger.

Rudlin, D. and Falk, N. (1999) *Building the 21st Century Home: the Sustainable Urban Neighbourhood*. Oxford: The Architectural Press.

Rydin, Y. (2003) *Urban and Environmental Planning in the UK, 2nd edn*. Basingstoke: Palgrave.

Sainsbury, D. (1994) *Gendering Welfare States*. London: Sage.

Saracevic, A.T. (2001) 'Dot-job toll snowballs to 12,828 in January'. *San Francisco Chronicle B-2*. Tuesday January 30 2001.

Sassen, S. (1991) *The Global City: New York, London, Tokyo*. Princeton, N.J.: Princeton University Press.

Saunders, P. (1990) *A Nation of Home Owners*. London: Unwin Hyman.

Sayer, A. (1992) *Method in Social Science: A Realist Approach. 2nd edn*. (first published in 1984). London: Routledge.

Sayer, A. (2000) *Realism and Social Science*. London: Sage.

Sayer, A. and R. Walker (1992) *The New Social Economy*. Oxford: Blackwell.

Schoon, N. (2001) *The Chosen City*. London and New York: Spon Press.

Schor, J. (1992) *The Overworked American: The Unexpected Decline of Leisure*. New York: Basic Books.

Schor, J.B. (1995) 'Can the North stop consumption growth? Escaping the cycle of work and spend'. In *The North, the South and the Environment: Ecological Constraints and the Global Economy* (ed.) V. Bhaskar and A. Glyn. London: Earthscan.

Schumacher, E.F. (1974) *Small is Beautiful: Economics as if People Matter*. London: Penguin.

Schwartz, D.B. (1994) *An Examination of the Impact of Family-Friendly Policies on the Glass Ceiling*. New York: Families and Work Institute.

Scott, A. (2000) *The Cultural Economy of Cities*. London: Sage.

Scott, J. and J. Duncombe (1992) 'Gender role attitudes in Britain and the USA'. In *Women and Working Lives: Divisions and Change* (eds) S. Arber and N. Gilbert. London: Macmillan.

Scottish Executive (1999) *The Electronics Industry in Scotland*. Edinburgh: Scottish Office.

Scottish Executive (2001) *Designing Places: A Policy Statement for Scotland – Confident, Competitive and Compassionate Scotland*. Edinburgh: Scottish Executive.

Scottish Executive (2001a) *Scottish Transport Statistics* Chapter 12: personal and cross-modal travel, on-line http://www.scotland.gov.uk/stats/bulletins. Edinburgh: Scottish Executive.

Seattle City Council (2003) 'Seattle council priorities in '03: transportation, economic development, social programs'. *Seattle Council Press On-line*. Mar 3rd 2003. Seattle: Seattle City Council. Internet: http://www.seattlepresonline.com/article-10094.html

Seattle Press (2004) The Changing face of Ballard, accessed on-line 26/01/2004: http://www.seattlepress.com/article-8670.html

Sen, A. (1981) *Poverty and Famine: An Essay on Entitlement and Deprivation*. Oxford: Clarendon Press.

Sen, A. (1990) 'Gender and co-operative conflict'. In *Persistent Inequalities: Women and World Development* (ed.) I. Tinker. New York: Oxford University Press.

Sen, A. (1993) 'Internal consistency of choice'. *Econometrica* **61.3**, 495–521.

Sennett, R. (1998) *The Fall of Public Man*. London: Faber and Faber.

Sennett, R. (1998a) *The Corrosion of Character: the Personal Consequences of Work in the New Capitalism*. New York and London: W.W. Norton.

Sennett, R. (2000) 'Street and office: two sources of identity'. In *On the Edge: Living with Global Capitalism* (eds) W. Hutton and A. Giddens. London: Random House.

Silverstone, R. (1993) 'Time, information and communication technologies and the household'. *Time and Society* **2**, 283–311.

Singell, L.D. and J.H. Lillydahl (1986) 'An empirical analysis of the commute to work patterns of males and females in two-career households'. *Urban Studies* **2.1**, 119–129.

Skinner, C. (2003) *Running Around in Circles: Coordinating Childcare, Education and Work*. York: Joseph Rowntree Foundation/Policy Press.

Slow Cities (2004) http://www.matogmer.no/slow_cities_citta_slow.htm (accessed July 23 2004).

Smart, C. and B. Neale (1998) *Family Fragments?* Cambridge: Polity Press.

Smith, D.E. (1987) *The Everyday World as Problematic: a Feminist Sociology*. Boston: Northeastern University Press.

Smith, J. and I. Wallerstein (1992) *Creating and Transforming Households: the Constraints of the World Economy*. Cambridge: Cambridge University Press.

Smith, N. (1996) *The New Urban Frontier: Gentrification and the Revanchist City*. London: Routledge.

Smith, N. (2002) 'New globalism, new urbanism: gentrification as global urban strategy'. *Antipode* **34.3**, 427–450.

Smithers, R. (1998) 'Finding a nanny for the nineties'. *The Guardian*, November 7 1998.

Smithers, R. (2004) "Dad time' in 12-months maternity leave plan'. *The Guardian*. Friday May 28 2004.

Smits, J., C.H. Mulder and P. Hooimeijer (2003) 'Changing gender roles, shifting power balance and long-distance migration'. *Urban Studies* **40.3**, 603–613.

Snaith, J. (1990) 'Migration and dual-career households'. In *Labour Migration* (eds) J.H. Johnson and J. Salt. London: David Fulton.

Social Exclusion Unit (SEU) (2003) *Making the Connections: Final Report on Transport and Social Exclusion*. London: Social Exclusion Unit.

Sohmer, R.R. and Lang, R.E. (2003) 'Downtown rebound'. In *Redefining Urban and Suburban America, Evidence From Census 2000* (eds) B. Katz and R.E. Lang (eds). Washington DC: Brookings Institution Press. 63–75.

Soja, E. (2000) *Postmetropolis: Critical Studies of Cities and Regions*. Malder, MA.: Blackwell.

Solnit, R. and Schwartzenberg, S. (2000) *Hollow City: the Siege of San Francisco and the Crisis of American Urbanism*. New York and London: Verso.

Solomon, B.D. and Heiman, M.K. (2001) 'The California electric power crisis: lessons for other states'. *The Professional Geographer* **53.4**, 463–468.

Somerville, J. (2000) *Feminism and the Family: Politics and Society in the UK and USA*. Basingstoke: Macmillan.

Sommers, P. and D. Carlson with M. Stanger, S. Xue and M. Miyasaka (2000) *Ten Steps to a High Tech Future: the New Economy in Metropolitan Seattle*. University of Seattle, prepared for the Brookings Institute. Washington DC: Centre on Urban and Metropolitan Affairs.

Southerton, D. (2003) "Squeezing time': allocating practices, co-ordinating networks and scheduling society'. *Time and Society* **12.1**, 5–25.

Standing, K. (1999) 'Negotiating the home and the school: low income, lone mothering and unpaid schoolwork'. In *Gender, Power and the Household* (eds) L. McKie, S. Bowlby and S. Gregory. Basingstoke: Macmillan.

Stanworth, C. (2000) 'Women and work in the information age'. *Gender, Work and Organization* **7.1**, 20–32.

Starkey, P. (2004) 'Manifesto: first time buyers need help – a £50,000 loan from the government'. *Fabien Review* **116.2** Summer 2004.

Stephens, J. (1999) 'A fight for her time: challenges facing professional mothers'. In *Gender, Power and the Household* (eds) L. McKie, S. Bowlby and S. Gregory. Basingstoke: Macmillan.

Stichter, S. and J. Parpart (1988) *Women, Employment and the Family in the International Division of Labour*. London: Macmillan.

Strassmann, W.P. (2001) 'Residential mobility: contrasting approaches in Europe and the United States'. *Housing Studies* **16.1**, 7–20.

Strauss, A. and J. Corbin (1998) *Basics of Qualitative Research*. London: Sage.

Suarez, R. (1999) *The Old Neighbourhood: What We Lost in the Great Suburban Migration. 1966–1999*. New York: The Free Press.

Sullivan, O. (2000) 'The division of domestic labour: twenty years of change?' *Sociology* **34.3**, 437–456.

Summerskill, B. and S. Ryle (2001) 'Mothers put careers at risk with second child'. *The Observer*. 18 March 2001.

Swyngedouw, E. and M. Kaika (2000) 'The environment of the city... or the urbanization of nature'. In *A Companion to the City* (eds) G. Bridge and S. Watson. Oxford: Blackwell.

Talen, E. (1999) 'Sense of community and neighbourhood form: an assessment of the social doctrine of new urbanism'. *Urban Studies* **36.8**, 1361–1379.

Taylor-Gooby, P. (2001) 'Sustaining state welfare in hard times: who will foot the bill'. *Journal of European Social Policy* **11.2**, 133–147.

Taylor-Gooby, P. (ed.) (2001a) *Welfare States Under Pressure*. London: Sage.

Taylor-Gooby, P. (ed.) (2004) *New Risks, New Welfare: The Transformation of the European Welfare State*. Oxford: Oxford University Press.

Teitz, M.B. (1990) 'California Growth: hard questions, few answers'. *California Policy Choices* **6**, 8–10.

Teitz, M.B. (1996) 'American Planning in the 1990s: evolution, debate and challenge'. *Urban Studies* **33**, 649–671.

Tewdwr-Jones, M. (ed.) (1996) *British Planning Policy in Transition: Planning in the 1990s*. London: UCL Press.

Thompson-Fawcett, M. (2003) "Urbanist' lived experience: resident observations on life in Poundbury'. *Urban Design International* **8**, 67–84.

Thorns, D.C. (2002) *The Transformation of Cities: Urban Theory and Urban Life*. Basingstoke: Palgrave.

Thornley, A. and Y. Rydin (2002) *Planning in a Global Era*. Aldershot: Ashgate.

Thrift, N. (1995) 'A hyperactive world', in *Geographies of Global Change: Remapping the World in the Late Twentieth Century* (eds) R.J. Johnston, P.J. Taylor and M.J. Watts. Oxford: Blackwell.

Timmermans, H., T. Aventze and Chang-Hyeon Joh (2002) 'Analyzing space-time behaviour: new approaches to old problems'. *Progress in Human Geography* **26.2**, 175–190.

Tönnies, F. (1887) *Community and Association (Gemeinschaft und Gesellschaft)*. Translated by C.P. Lomis in 1955. London: Routledge and Kegan Paul.

Toynbee, P. (2003) *Hard Work: Life in Low-Pay Britain*. London: Bloomsbury.

Trades Union Congress (TUC) (2002) *About Time: A New Agenda for Shaping Working Hours*. London: TUC.

Trades Union Congress (TUC) (2003) TUC Briefing http://www.aasa.org.uk/wtd.html viewed on-line August 6 2003.

Treviston, C. (1999) 'Grocers scan online strategies'. *The Oregonian*. 27 July 1999.

Tronto, J. (2004) 'Vicious circles of privatised care'. Paper presented in the 'Rethinking Care' session of the CAVA *Rethinking Care Relations, Family Lives and Policies Symposium*, 3–4 December 2004, University of Leeds.

Tunstall, R. (2004) 'Using the US and UK Censuses for Comparative Research'. *Report for the Brookings Institute*. Washington DC.: Brookings Institute.

Turner, A. (2001) *Just Capital: The Liberal Economy*. Basingstoke: Macmillan.

Turner, J. and M. Grieco (1998) 'Gender, transport and the New Deal: the social policy implications of gendered time, transport and travel'. *Paper presented at the Social Policy Association conference*, Lincoln. Available on-line: http://www.art.man.ac.uk/transres/spconf2.htm

Turok, I. (1993) 'Inward investment and local linkages: how deeply embedded is Silicon Glen?' *Regional Studies* **27**, 401–17.

Ullman, E. (1997) *Close to the Machine*. San Francisco: City Lights.

Urban Task Force (UTF) (1999) *Towards an Urban Renaissance (Chair R. Rogers)*. London: DETR – now ODPM.

Urban Villages Forum (1998) Briefing paper viewed on-line at http://www.urban-villages-forum.org.uk December 10th 2003.

Urban Village Forum (2003) http://www.urban-villages-forum.org.uk

U.S. Bureau of Labor Statistics (BLS) (1997) *Monthly Labour Review*. Accessed on-line: http://stats.bls.gov/opub/

U.S. Census Bureau (1990) *USA Counties Census of Population*. Accessed on-line at http://govinfo.library. Washington DC: Bureau of Census.

U.S. Census Bureau (1999) Building Permit Activity. Data accessed via the internet: http://tier2.census/cgi-win/bldgprmt/prmtplac/

US Census Bureau (2000) Census 2000 Gateway, http://www.census.gov/main/www/Cen2000.html

US Department of Commerce (1999) *Vehicle Inventory and Use Survey. Bureau of Census 1999*. Washington DC: U.S. Department of Commerce. Internet: http://www.commerce.gov/

U.S. Department of Housing and Urban Development (HUD) (1996) *New American Neighbourhoods: Building Homeownership Zones to Revitalize Our Nation's Communities*. Washington D.C.: Government Printing Office.

U.S. Department of Housing and Urban Development (1999) *The State of the Cities, Third Annual Report*. June 1999. viewed on-line http://www.huduser.org/publications/polleg/tsoc99/ 13.01.03

U.S. Department of Housing and Urban Development (2000) *The State of the Cities Data System (SOCDS)*. Washington DC. HUD. Accessed on-line: http://socds.huduser.org/index.html

U.S. Department of Housing and Urban Development (2004) *U.S. Housing Market Conditions, 1ˢᵗ Quarter 2004*. U.S. Department of Housing and Urban Development Office of Policy Development and Research, http://www.huduser.org/periodicals (accessed 14 June 2004).

U.S. Department of Housing and Urban Development (2004) *An Analysis of Mortgage Refinancing, 2001–2003*. Washington DC: U.S. Department of Housing and Urban Development Office of Policy Development and Research.

Valentine, G. (1998) 'Doing household research: interviewing couples together and apart'. *Area* **31**, 67–74.

Vilhelmson, B. (1999) 'Daily mobility and the use of time for different activities. The case of Sweden'. *GeoJournal* **48**: 177–185.

Villaraigosa, A. (2000) 'America's Urban Agenda: a View From California'. *The Brooking Review* **18.3**, 48–51.

Vincent, C., S.J. Ball and S. Pietikainen (2004) 'Metropolitan mothers: mothers, mothering and paid work'. *Women's Studies International Forum* **27.5–6**, 571–587.

Vuchic, V.R. (1999) *Transportation for Livable Cities*. Rutgers: Centre for Urban Policy Research.

Wallman, S. (1984) *Eight London Households*. London: Tavistock.

Walker, R. (1995) 'Landscape and city: four ecologies of residence in the San Francisco Bay Area'. *Ecumene* **2.1**, 33–56.

Walker, R. (1996) 'Another round of globalization in San Francisco'. *Urban Geography* **17.1**, 60–94.

Walker, R. (1998) 'The Americanization of British welfare: a case study of policy transfer'. *Focus* **19**, 32–40.

Walker, R. (1998a) 'An appetite for the city'. In *Reclaiming San Francisco: History, Politics, Culture* (eds) J. Brook, C. Carlsson and N.J. Peters. San Francisco. City Lights.

Walking Bus (2004) www.walkingbus.com, accessed August 4ᵗʰ 2004.

Wallace, I. (1990) *The Global Economic System*. London: Unwin Hyman.

Walsh, J. (1999) 'Myths and counter-myths: an analysis of part-time female employees and their orientation to work and working hours'. *Work, Employment and Society* **13.2**, 179–203.

Warde, A. (1991) 'Gentrification as consumption: issues of class and gender'. *Environment and Planning D: Society and Space* **9**, 223–32.

Watts, J. (2002) 'Workaholic parents bless the guardian angel mummy'. *The Guardian*. Capital Letters in Tokyo, 18. Saturday August 10.

Weiss, M.A. (2000) 'Within neighbourhoods'. In *Charter of the New Urbanism* (eds) Congress of the New Urbanism. New York: McGraw-Hill.

Whitting, S. (2000) 'Groups that keep the heat on'. *San Francisco Chronicle*, C1. 16 October 2000.

Wheelock, J. and K. Jones (2002) 'Grandparents are the next best thing: informal childcare for working parents'. *Journal of Social Policy* **31.3**, 441–464.

White, M. and P. Allmendinger (2003) 'Land-use planning and the housing market: a comparative review of the UK and USA'. *Urban Studies* **40. 5–6**, 953–972.

Wilcox, S. (2003) *Can Work, Can't Buy: Local Measures of the Ability of Working Households to Become Home Owners*. York: Joseph Rowntree Foundation.

Wilkinson, H. (1994) *No Turning Back: Generations and the Genderquake*. London: Demos.

Willmott, P. and Young, M. (1957) *Family and Kinship in East London*. London: Routledge and Kegan Paul.

Wilson, W.J. (1987) *The Truly Disadvantaged: the Inner City, the Underclass, and Public Policy*. Chicago: Chicago University Press.

Wilson, W.J. (1996) *When Work Disappears: the World of the New Urban Poor*. New York: Knopf.

Wildavsky, A. (1987) 'Choosing preferences by constructing institutions: a cultural theory of preference formation'. *American Political Science Review* **81.1**, 3–21.

Williams, C. and Windebank, J. (1995) 'Social polarization of households in contemporary Britain: a 'whole economy' perspective'. *Regional Studies* **29**, 723–28.

Windebank, J. (2001) 'Dual-earner couples in Britain and France: gender divisions of domestic labour and parenting work in different welfare states'. *Work, Employment and Society* **15**, 269–290.

Winterbottam (1990) Introduction. In Harrison, P. (ed.) *Civilising The City: Quality or Chaos in Historic Towns*. The Proceedings of an International Conference held in Edinburgh, 29th March–1st April 1990, Edinburgh: Nic Allen.

Wollman, H. (1992) Understanding cross national policy transfers: the case of Britain and the USA. *Governance* **5.1**, 105–112.

World Bank (2002) *World Development Indicators for OECD Developed Countries*. Washington: World Bank.

World Wildlife Fund (WWF) (2000) *Living Planet Report*. London: World Wildlife Fund. Accessed on-line: www.wwf-uk.org/

www.allwomencount.net

www.princess –foundation.org

www.transport2000.org.uk

Young, M. and P. Willmott (1973) *The Symmetrical Family: a Study of Work and Leisure in the London Region*. London: Routledge and Kegan Paul.

Zukin, S. (1988) *Loft Living: Culture and Capital in Urban Change*. London: Radius.

Zukin, S. (1991) *Landscapes of Power: From Detroit to Disneyland*. Berkeley: University of California Press.

Zukin, S. (1995) *The Cultures of Cities*. London: Blackwell.

Index

Note: Page numbers followed by *tab* indicate information in a table, those followed by *n* in a note (*tab* followed by n indicates information in the note of a table).